Progressive Sexuality Education

This book engages contemporary debates about the notion of secularism outside of the field of education to consider how secularism shapes the formation of progressive sexuality education. Focusing on the US, Canada, Ireland, Aotearoa-New Zealand, and Australia, this text considers the affinities, prejudices, and attachments of scholars who advocate secular worldviews in the context of sexuality education and some of the consequences that ensue from these ways of seeing.

This study identifies and interrogates how secularism infuses progressive sexuality education. It asks readers to consider their own investments in particular ways of thinking and researching in the field of sexuality education and to think about how these investments have developed and how they shape existing discourses within the field. It hones in on how progressive sexuality education has come to develop in the way that it has and how this relates to conceits of secularism. This book prompts a consideration of how progressive scholarship and practice might get in the way of meaningful conversations with students, teachers, and peers who think differently about the field of sexuality education.

Mary Lou Rasmussen is associate professor of education at Monash University, Australia.

Routledge Research in Education

For a full list of titles in this series, please visit www.routledge.com

128 Organizational Citizenship Behavior in Schools
Examining the impact and opportunities within educational systems
Anit Somech and Izhar Oplatka

129 The Age of STEM
Educational policy and practice across the world in Science, Technology, Engineering and Mathematics
Edited by Brigid Freeman, Simon Marginson and Russell Tytler

130 Mainstreams, Margins and the Spaces In-between
New possibilities for education research
Edited by Karen Trimmer, Ali Black and Stewart Riddle

131 Arts-based and Contemplative Practices in Research and Teaching
Honoring Presence
Edited by Susan Walsh, Barbara Bickel, and Carl Leggo

132 Interrogating Critical Pedagogy
The Voices of Educators of Color in the Movement
Edited by Pierre Wilbert Orelus and Rochelle Brock

133 My School
Listening to parents, teachers and students from a disadvantaged educational setting
Lesley Scanlon

134 Education, Nature, and Society
Stephen Gough

135 Learning Technologies and the Body
Integration and Implementation In Formal and Informal Learning Environments
Edited by Victor Lee

136 Landscapes of Specific Literacies in Contemporary Society
Exploring a social model of literacy
Edited by Vicky Duckworth and Gordon Ade-Ojo

137 The Education of Radical Democracy
Sarah S. Amsler

138 Aristotelian Character Education
Kristján Kristjánsson

139 Performing Kamishibai
Tara McGowan

140 **Educating Adolescent Girls Around the Globe**
Edited by Sandra L. Stacki and Supriya Baily

141 **Quality Teaching and the Capability Approach**
Evaluating the work and governance of women teachers in rurual Sub-Saharan Africa
Alison Buckler

142 **Using Narrative Inquiry for Educational Research in the Asia Pacific**
Edited by Sheila Trahar and Wai Ming Yu

143 **The Hidden Role of Software in Educational Research**
Policy to Practice
By Tom Liam Lynch

144 **Education, Leadership and Islam**
Theories, discourses and practices from an Islamic perspective
Saeeda Shah

145 **English Language Teacher Education in Chile**
A cultural historical activity theory perspective
Malba Barahona

146 **Navigating Model Minority Stereotypes**
Asian Indian Youth in South Asian Diaspora
Rupam Saran

147 **Evidence-based Practice in Education**
Functions of evidence and causal presuppositions
Tone Kvernbekk

148 **A New Vision of Liberal Education**
The good of the unexamined life
Alistair Miller

149 **Transatlantic Reflections on the Practice-Based PhD in Fine Art**
Jessica B. Schwarzenbach and Paul M.W. Hackett

150 **Drama and Social Justice**
Theory, research and practice in international contexts
Edited by Kelly Freebody and Michael Finneran

151 **Education, Identity and Women Religious, 1800–1950**
Convents, classrooms and colleges
Edited by Deirdre Raftery and Elizabeth Smyth

152 **School Health Education in Changing Times**
Curriculum, pedagogies and partnerships
Deana Leahy, Lisette Burrows, Louise McCuaig, Jan Wright and Dawn Penney

153 **Progressive Sexuality Education**
The Conceits of Secularism
Mary Lou Rasmussen

154 **Collaboration and the Future of Education**
Preserving the Right to Think and Teach Historically
Gordon Andrews, Warren J. Wilson, and James Cousins

Progressive Sexuality Education
The Conceits of Secularism

Mary Lou Rasmussen

NEW YORK AND LONDON

First published 2016
by Routledge
711 Third Avenue, New York, NY 10017

and by Routledge
2 Park Square, Milton Park, Abingdon, Oxon OX14 4RN

Routledge is an imprint of the Taylor & Francis Group, an informa business

© 2016 Taylor & Francis

The right of Mary Lou Rasmussen to be identified as author of this work has been asserted by her in accordance with sections 77 and 78 of the Copyright, Designs and Patents Act 1988.

All rights reserved. No part of this book may be reprinted or reproduced or utilised in any form or by any electronic, mechanical, or other means, now known or hereafter invented, including photocopying and recording, or in any information storage or retrieval system, without permission in writing from the publishers.

Trademark notice: Product or corporate names may be trademarks or registered trademarks, and are used only for identification and explanation without intent to infringe.

Library of Congress Cataloging-in-Publication Data
CIP data has been applied for.

ISBN: 978-0-415-84272-3 (hbk)
ISBN: 978-0-203-75846-5 (ebk)

Typeset in Sabon
by Apex CoVantage, LLC

For my parents, Marie and Jack Rasmussen and Lou Preston

Contents

Acknowledgements xi

1 Introduction 1

2 Faith, Progressive Sexuality Education, and Queer Secularism: Unsettling Associations 28

3 Sexuality Education in Public Schools in Australia and Aotearoa-New Zealand 48
MARY LOU RASMUSSEN AND FIDA SANJAKDAR, MONASH UNIVERSITY; KATHLEEN QUINLIVAN, UNIVERSITY OF CANTERBURY, CHRISTCHURCH, NEW ZEALAND; LOUISA ALLEN, UNIVERSITY OF AUCKLAND, NEW ZEALAND; ANNETTE BROMDAL, UNIVERSITY OF SOUTHERN QUEENSLAND; CLIVE ASPIN, INDEPENDENT RESEARCHER, SYDNEY, AUSTRALIA.

4 Sex Panics, Sexuality Education, and Secular Explanations 71

5 Pleasure/Desire, Secularism, and Sexuality Education 87

6 On Not Feeling Homophobic 104

7 Progressive Public Pedagogies of Pregnancy and Choice 125

8 Ireland, Canada, and Australia: Tracing Progressive Sexuality Education Across Borders 144

Conclusion: The Conceits of Secularism in Sexuality Education 177

Index 191

Acknowledgements

Writing this book has taken longer than anticipated. I want to thank the publishers for sticking with this project through challenging times. Given the length of time it has taken to pull this book together, I have also had the benefit of many conversations with peers that have helped in the production of this manuscript, including William Pinar at University of British Columbia, who was a generous host in the early stages of research for this book, as well as Mary Bryson and Janice Stewart at UBC's Institute for Gender, Race, Sexuality, and Social Justice. I also want to thank Jen Gilbert, who hosted a paper presentation at York University in Toronto, and Wayne Martino, who also invited me to speak at the University of Western Ontario. Nancy Lesko gave me the opportunity to discuss ideas associated with this text in a class with graduate students at Teachers College, Columbia University, and Susan Talburt also hosted a lecture relating to the book at the Institute for Women's, Gender, and Sexuality Studies at Georgia State University. I also want to thank Irina Schmitt, for an invitation to present my work on *Juno* at the Centre for Gender Studies at Lund University, and Daniel Marshall for joining me on the Rainbow Tour, where we have engaged in many conversations about this manuscript.

In England, Ireland, and Wales I was also given opportunities to present on research related to this project. At University of Limerick, at the invitation of Aoife Neary, I was able to discuss ideas on secularism and sexuality education in the Irish context at a seminar "New Foundations: School 'Ethos' and LGBT Sexualities." I was also able to present ideas relating to homophobia and religious and cultural difference at an Economic and Social Research Council (ESRC)-sponsored seminar, "The Invaded Body," organized by Emma Renold at Cardiff University. A keynote address related to this book was also organized by Pam Alldred at Brunel University, at an event titled "Knowing Young People: The Politics of Researching Sexuality With Young People." I also want to thank Pam for helping me think more about the Irish context in relation the preparation of this manuscript.

I also want to thank Fida Sanjakdar, Clive Aspin, Annette Bromdal, Louisa Allen, and Kathleen Quinlivan, researchers with whom I worked on the Australian Research Council-funded Discovery Grant, *Sexuality Education* in Australia and New Zealand: Responding to Cultural and Religious Difference. This grant overlapped with the writing of this book in innumerable ways, and the conversations I had with these peers were incredibly generative in imagining this book project. I also want to publically acknowledge the intellectual generosity of this team in supporting me in the preparation of this monograph. I want especially to thank Louisa and Kathleen for their encouragement, stimulating conversations, and ongoing friendship.

In addition to the above, I also want to thank many peers who have been generous in talking through the ideas related to this book, especially Deana Leahy and Emily Gray in Melbourne for much gastronomic and intellectual stimulation. Anna Hickey-Moody, Jen Gilbert, Jessica Fields, Jane Kenway, Valerie Harwood, Jessica Ringrose, Mark Davis, Rob Cover, Peter Aggleton, and Amy Dobson have all been supportive friends and colleagues. The Faculty of Education at Monash University provided funding for two sabbaticals related to the preparation of this manuscript as well as hosting me in presenting a dean's lecture related to the project. Emma Rowe has been a fabulous interlocutor and editor in the final stages of the preparation of this manuscript.

My parents, Marie and Jack, continue to be proud supporters of my academic work, wherever it takes me. And, finally, to my partner Lou—with whom another adventure begins upon the completion of this book—your encouragement and patience during the preparation of this manuscript are incredible gifts.

Earlier versions of work that appear in this text have been published elsewhere. I thank the following publishers for permissions to revise and reprint this work. An earlier version of Chapter 3 appeared as "Revisiting Moral Panics in Sexuality Education" in *Media International Australia*, 135, 2010: 118–130. Earlier versions of Chapter 4 appeared as "Pleasure/Desire, Sexualism and Sexuality Education," 2013: 153–168, in Allen, L., Rasmussen, M., and Quinlivan, K. (eds.), *The Politics of Pleasure in Sexuality Education: Pleasure Bound*, New York. Routledge; and as "Pleasure/Desire, Sexualism and Sexuality Education" in *Sex Education*, 12, 2012: 469–481. Earlier versions of Chapter 5 appeared as "Taking Homophobia's Measure," *Confero: Essays on Education, Philosophy and Politics*, 1, no. 2, 2013: 1–27; and as "Taking Homophobia's Measure," 2014: 52–62 in Carlson, D. and Meyer, E. (eds.), *Gender and Sexualities Education: A Reader*, New York, Peter Lang.

1 Introduction

Gayle Rubin, in concluding her article "Thinking Sex" writes,

> Those who consider themselves progressive need to examine their preconceptions, update their sexual educations . . .
> (Rubin, 1992: 35)

Some progressive preconceptions about sexuality education in public schools that I examine in this text include the following:

- Sexuality education is optimal when it is underpinned by rigorous scientific research and rational debate.
- Sexuality education needs to promote sexual autonomy to ensure that young people are able to act as autonomous sexual subjects.
- Sexuality education is responsible for the cultivation of tolerance of sexual and gender diversity.
- Sexuality education in public education precludes discussion of the intersections among faith, religion, and morality (such conversations should happen in private settings, e.g., family, church, mosque, or temple).

I will demonstrate how these ideas have come, over time, to be associated with a transnational progressive project within sexuality education. These preconceptions are at once familiar and contradictory within the context of progressive sexuality education.

Joan Scott (2009) deploys the term *sexularism* to identify the synchronicities that adhere to the relationship between secularism and particular understandings of sexuality. Scott calls for a critique of the "idealized secular"—"[t]he most frequent assumption that secularism encourages the free expression of sexuality . . . removes transcendence as the foundation for social norms and treats people as autonomous individuals, agents capable of crafting their own destiny" (2009: 1). Inspired by Scott, I have been prompted to consider how "the idealized secular" structures knowledge and feelings within and about sexuality education. These structures are often difficult to distinguish from long-standing debates about the place of religion within secular states and about the privatization of religion and belief. They impact perceptions about the role of religion in sexuality education and shape debates about the place of reason and science in sexuality education. Secularisms are also interwoven with traditions of thought that draw on Christianity, neoliberalism, and democracy.

Secularisms in sexuality education are also informed by beliefs about processes of secularization. Jose Casanova argues,

> ... a general theory of secularization was developed that conceptualized these at first modern European, later increasingly globalized historical transformations, as part and parcel of a general teleological and progressive human and societal development from the primitive "sacred" to the modern "secular." The thesis of "the decline" and "the privatization" of religion in the modern world became central components of the theory of secularization.
>
> (Casanova, 2007)

To apply this understanding of secularization to sexuality education, it is necessary to think about what types of thinking about sexuality have been come to be seen as progressive and how this also shapes what is constituted as conservative. How have ideas about the decline and privatization of religion influenced imaginings of sexuality education? This book is, to my knowledge, the first attempt to grapple with the relationships among secularisms, processes of secularization, and sexuality education across diverse country contexts. I try to capture the ways in which secularisms impact research, advocacy, and pedagogical interventions related to sexuality education. I consider the ways in which religion is privatized in debates about sexuality education through recourse to discourses of science, reason, tolerance, democracy, autonomy, health, and salvation of "at-risk" youth.

The relationships among secularism, sexuality education, and different national contexts are also objects of inquiry in this text. How does secularism manifest in the US, a country where sexuality education has been at the heart of the culture wars? How is secularism manifest in a country like Australia, where comprehensive sexuality education is much less controversial, comparatively speaking? What shape does secularism take in Canada, a country that has strong secular traditions and where the state has intervened to mandate the provision of state-sanctioned sexuality education in evangelical schools in Quebec and Catholic schools in Toronto? How does secularism and sexuality education play out in a country like Ireland, where the Catholic Church continues to dominate public education provision? I consider how secularism in sexuality education is mediated by national context and what this might tell us about different varieties of secularism.

In the contemporary US context, where religious battles have and continue to play such a significant role in debates about sexuality education, there may be some skepticism about the value of an inquiry into the relationship between secularisms and sexuality education. Similarly, in a place like Ireland, where sexuality education is conditioned by the Catholic ethos, there may be concern that such critique might misfire, and that any critique of secularism in sexuality education will necessarily affirm the arguments of the religious right or the Catholic Church.

In her book *Terrorist Assemblages: Homonationalism in Queer Times*, Jasbir Puar (2007) states that she critiques *queer secularity* (a term I unpack further in Chapter 3) not to "provide ammunition to chastise, but rather generate greater room for self-reflection, autocritique, and making mistakes" (24). In writing this book, I am hoping to create space for different sorts of conversations about sexuality education with my colleagues, teacher education students, and people who work in the field of sexuality and schooling. This project has also made me less tolerant of discourses that equate being religious with being backward—and discourses seeking to preclude religion from the public sphere, including classroom conversations about sexuality education. This study has also led me to be much more critical of the politics of claiming the moniker of *progressive* in the field of sexuality education. I suspect that this has been disturbing because I feel that this is a space where critique of what constitutes progressivism can easily come to feel like, and be read as, accommodation of conservatism. Creating such a space is made more difficult by the characterization of sexuality education as a field of battle or a war (Irvine, 2002; Luker, 2006). I believe that researchers, educators, and advocates working in the field of sexuality education need to think more carefully about how secular preconceptions structure funding, research, education, advocacy, and activism.

The descriptor *progressive* is currently utilized both as a badge of pride and a term of abuse in the field of sexuality education. In conversation with Mendieta, Judith Butler argues that

> ... moving forward has to be distinguished from progress.... What cannot be brought forward? What is left behind? There's always something left behind, especially in aggressive notions of progress that hold out the promise of final redemption.
>
> (Butler, Habermas, Taylor, and West, 2011: 104)

I am not arguing that notions of progressivism in sexuality education are aggressive in the way constituted by Butler. However, I do think that labeling something as progressive suggests that certain understandings of sexuality are left behind and that what is being jettisoned is not always clear.

Heather Boonstra, a senior public policy associate of the Guttmacher Institute,[1] wrote a piece titled "Progressive and Pragmatic: The National

Sexuality Education Standards for U.S. Public Schools" (2012). This title denotes these standards as aligned with a progressive agenda, but the word *progressive* does not appear anywhere else in the document. At first glance this might seem unremarkable. Boonstra, an influential lobbyist in debates about sexuality education in the US, does not see the need to define what progressive means in this context. The standards, organized by grade and area, include the following:

- Anatomy and physiology
- Puberty and adolescent development
- Identity: fundamental aspects of people's understanding of who they are
- Pregnancy and reproduction: how pregnancy happens and decision making to avoid a pregnancy
- Sexually transmitted infections (STIs) and human immunodeficiency virus (HIV): understanding and avoiding HIV and other STIs, including how they are transmitted, their signs and symptoms, and the importance of testing and treatment
- Healthy relationships: successfully navigating changing relationships among family, peers, and partners
- Personal safety: identifying and preventing harassment, bullying, violence, and abuse (Boonstra, 2012: 3).

The absence of a definition or elaboration of progressive suggests Boonstra is speaking to the converted. Readers don't need a definition of progressive because anybody who knows the authors of the standards (such as nonprofit organizations Advocates for Youth[2], Answer,[3] and Sexuality Information and Education Council of the United States [SIECUS[4]]) will be aware of their stance on sexuality education. Boonstra collectively understands these organizations as responsible for the production of standards that underpin a progressive sexuality education.

It appears that there is some agreement about what constitutes a progressive sexuality education. But how did this consensus come about? I argue that the development of this consensus about what constitutes progressive in this context requires much more excavation and interrogation. There also needs to be some clarity about what is left behind in the elaboration of standards associated with a progressive sexuality education.

The Reverend Debra Haffner, a former CEO of SIECUS, and the director of the Religious Institute on Sexual Morality, Justice, and Healing is cited by Boonstra in the aforementioned article *Progressive and Pragmatic* (2012). In this piece Haffner objects to the standards outlined by Boonstra because she believes that they "will not fulfill young people's needs for information and education about sexuality issues, nor do they adequately provide a values-based framework for young people's decision making" (Haffner, 2012 in Boonstra 2012: 2). Boonstra deems Haffner's critique as worthy of inclusion in her discussion of the national standards for sexuality education, but the implications of this critique for the production of a progressive and pragmatic sexuality education is not spelled out by Boonstra. Haffner's objection suggests that there is a question of how values and religion influence sexuality education and religion. Haffner suggests that such questions may be left behind in Boonstra's conceptualization of progressive sexuality education.

Elsewhere Boonstra has been explicitly supportive of the role of faith-based organizations (FBOs) in advocacy for comprehensive sexuality education, arguing, "[t]he fact that people of faith support comprehensive sex education for religious reasons has a way of moving the political debate over sex education—and ultimately affecting policies that impact young people now and in their future" (Boonstra, 2008: 22). But this earlier advocacy of the involvement of FBOs in comprehensive sexuality education does not permeate the production of the national standards.

For Haffner, sexuality education is intrinsically related to religion and is the inspiration for her work in the promotion of sexuality education that would be constituted by many as progressive. In a piece in *The Huffington Post* titled "Yes, Sex Education in Kindergarten!," Haffner asserts her "theological commitment to truth telling," and therefore she

> support[s] sexuality education programs that are age appropriate, medically accurate, and acknowledge parents as the primary educators of their children. I wish political campaigns would make the same commitment. (2008: para. 7)

Haffner's theological commitment to comprehensive sexuality education is accompanied by an expressed desire for a values-based framework for sexuality education. Unlike Haffner, I have no theological commitments in relation to sexuality education provision. However, I have come to question progressive sexuality education standards that do not explicitly engage with questions of faith, belief, and their relationship to values. What are the grounds for this separation? Are there ways in which religion and values can be usefully incorporated in progressive sexuality education? Should such topics be left behind in the production of a progressive sexuality education?

In an opinion piece in *The Washington Times* titled "Parental Outrage Can Protect Our Kids From 'Progressive' Sex-ed", Marybeth Hicks constitutes progressive sexuality education as synonymous with comprehensive sexuality education and constructs this approach to sexuality education as deliberately exploiting children (Hicks, 2010).[5] Hicks is certainly not alone in this view. In 2011 Pope Benedict XVI, in an address to foreign diplomats at the Vatican, stated that countries that mandated obligatory participation in sexuality education courses attack religious freedom because they "convey a neutral concept of the person and of life, yet in fact reflect an anthropology opposed to faith and to right reason" (AFP, 2011: para. 3).

Comprehensive sexuality education standards, such as those elaborated by Boonstra and the Guttmacher Institute, are seen by those who produce them as progressive and pragmatic. They are also highly political and informed first and foremost by health priorities, concurrently relegating religion as outside the bounds of a progressive vision of sexuality education.

I am not so naïve to believe that adding religion to the standards will mollify critics such as Hicks, nor is that my aim. I do think that Haffner's (2008) critique is one that should be attended to by researchers and advocates of progressive sexuality education. Why does Haffner see the sexuality education standards espoused by Boonstra as lacking? Is this is a fair critique? If so, what are the implications? Should it alter the way that progressive sexuality education is envisaged? My aim is not to convince Hicks or the Catholic Church to embrace comprehensive sexuality education.

Rather, the readers I have in mind here are other researchers, educators, and workers in health and health promotion who might "convey a neutral concept of the person and of life" in the way that they engage in sexuality education. I agree with Pope Benedict; I don't think that sexuality education is neutral. Moreover, the constitution of comprehensive sexuality education as progressive effectively plays into the hands of religious conservatives such as Hicks who seek to label this approach using the term *progressive* as a pejorative. How might losing the progressive tag, and thinking differently about the relationship between faith and comprehensive sexuality education (CSE), help in reimagining sexuality education?

A specific focus of this text is debates about sexuality education located in public schools, though the arguments expressed here clearly have implications for sexuality education more broadly. Wherever and whenever sexuality education is funded by government or nongovernment organizations as part of health promotion projects, the question of how publicly funded or secular organizations engage with people of diverse sexualities, ethnicities, and religious affiliations needs to be considered. In the Australian context, Marion Maddox in her text *Taking God to School* (2014) argues the importance of having conversations about the place of religion in public schools. In this text I want to argue the importance of having conversations about the place of religion in sexuality education in public schools. Another motivation for this study is a belief that discussions of religion, spirituality, morals, ethics, and belief all have a place in sexuality education. To my mind these things are as central to sexuality education as information about how to have safer sex and negotiate consent. In writing this book I also have a strategic aim, which is not to cede debates about the place of religion in sexuality education to those on the left and the right, who would seek to align religion with sexual conservatism. I also think that people like myself, who are not religious but are concerned with the production of a sexuality education that has wide reach and relevance, need to be articulate in their response to religious objections and advocacy for comprehensive sexuality education.

This study will afford insights into how secularism shapes sexuality education in different national contexts (US—see Chapter 2 through Chapter 7), (Canada and Ireland—see especially Chapter 8), (Aotearoa-New Zealand—see Chapter 3), (Australia—see Chapters 3, 5, 6, and 8). It is hoped that this transnational focus will afford insights into how progressive ideas travel, shape sexuality education in different national contexts, and assist in the reproduction of progressive tropes in the field of sexuality education.

While I consider how secularism and sexuality education are shaped across several sites, US popular culture and scholarship on sexuality education are a principal focus of study in this text. Debates about progressivism in sexuality education in the US permeate international understandings of the field and its visions for the future. For people living outside the US, it can be difficult to grasp why sexuality education has been, and continues to be, so contentious in this context. Janice Irvine (2002), Kristen Luker (2006), Jessica Fields (2008), and Nancy Kendall (2013) provide valuable discussions about how battles over sexuality education have developed and played out for individuals and within school districts, based on extensive ethnographic research. All these studies complicate the relationship between sexuality education and religion. *However, the question of how progressivism and secularism intersect in these debates has not been the subject of significant inquiry in this previous research.*

In the US, the place of religion in public education has been, and continues to be, the basis of much lobbying and controversy, with sex a common battleground for such disputes. In 1981 the US Congress passed the Adolescent Family Life Act (AFLA) to provide seed money for sex education initiatives that promote sexual abstinence until marriage (Christopher and Roosa, 1990). Subsequent legislation under the Clinton and Bush administrations strengthened the relationship between sex education and abstinence in the US, a relationship that has been somewhat diluted but by no means expunged during the Obama administration (see Guttmacher Institute, 2010). Bleakley, Hennessey and Fishbein (2006), in their cross-sectional survey of US adults' perceptions of different types of sex education programs, found respondents did not share the political will of their representatives for abstinence-only approaches.

This research needs to be considered alongside other surveys such as one conducted by The Pew Research *Religion and Public Life Project* (2005). This survey suggests respondents, including young people, are supportive of elements of abstinence and comprehensive approaches:

> The youngest Americans—those aged 18–24—are highly supportive of schools both promoting abstinence and providing information about birth control. Roughly eight-in-ten (83%) favor schools providing birth control information, while 75% think schools should teach teenagers to abstain from sex until marriage. (2005: 9)

Such surveys illuminate discrepancies between political and individual attitudes toward sexuality education while at the same time suggesting that respondents don't draw clear lines between comprehensive (progressive) approaches and abstinence approaches.

Between and within religious communities in the US, there are also debates about sexuality education provision. Janice Irvine (2002: 104) has highlighted tensions for the Christian right and conservative Catholics in their attempts to sell sexuality education programs that communicate the belief that sexuality is divine and pleasurable (but only when practiced according to their doctrine). The worry is that if it appears too divine, then the abstinence message might be a harder sell.

Relative to Canada, Australia, Aotearoa-New Zealand, and Ireland, debates about sexuality education have probably been most contentious in the US. Partially, this might be attributable to the fact that religious schools do not receive public funding in the US. Consequently the vast majority of students are educated in public schools. The comingling of students with families of diverse religious and secular affiliations within the US context ensures that sexuality education is a heightened source of contestation, research, and advocacy (Fine, 1988; Irvine, 2002; Luker, 2006; Moran, 2000).

ASSUMING THE PROGRESSIVE POSITION: TRACING FORMATIONS OF PROGRESSIVE SEXUALITY EDUCATION

Ann Pellegrini (2009), writing in the US context post 1979—the year, she points out, of the Iranian Revolution and the emergence of Jerry Falwell's moral majority—draws on the work of Janet Jakobsen (2002) to highlight the ideological divide and Anglo-American academic "alignment of the queer with the secular and of sexual conservatism with the religious" (207, 208). While Pellegrini provides explanations for these alignments in the Anglo-American context, such alignments have also taken route in places like Australia. In contemplating these alignments Pellegrini turns her attention to "the political and epistemological stakes of the secular academy's disidentification not just with religion, but with feelings coded as religious" (2009: 205). This is of concern to her because she believes that this queer secularism "may actually reinforce the claims of the right to a monopoly on religion" (Pellegrini, 2009: 208). Throughout this text I endeavor to illustrate that Pellegrini's observations about queer theory are also instructive for analyzing the production of what I am terming *progressive sexuality education*. I illustrate a tendency among supporters of sexuality education to construct religion as dangerous, irrelevant, or outside the bounds of a public sexuality education. This is problematic because it produces a conception of progressive sexuality education as somehow distinct from religion and belief.

The emergence of alliances between secular organizations and groups promoting sexuality education (a phenomenon that occurs across all five countries) is one manifestation of queer secularism in the field of sexuality education. Such alliances are forged (between secularism and progressivism sexuality education) based on the perception that these groups have mutual interests. One example of this is the Canadian Secular Alliance, a group that lobbies for defunding Ontario's Catholic Schools, which I expand upon further in Chapter 8. Toronto, Ontario, is a particularly interesting site for this study of progressivism in sexuality education because of the level of political and legal commentary about how Catholic schools in the Toronto school district need to accommodate curriculum reform in sexuality education as well as the provision of support for lesbian, gay, bisexual, and transgender (LGBTI)-identified students.

Association between notions of secular progressivism and comprehensive sexuality education are not confined to the Canadian context. For instance, Anna Miller, in a piece written for *The Nation* (2011) "Sex, Lies, and Michael Bloomberg," lauds New Jersey's decision to adopt CSE, noting that "every public high school is required to provide unbiased information on sexual health and disease prevention, *making New Jersey a model for progressive sexuality education*" (my emphasis).

In the logic of this report, being unbiased about the provision of sexual information, is equated with being progressive. Following this argument further, sexuality education that is explicitly associated with a faith-based perspective is constituted as biased and therefore no longer progressive. Such a position also suggests that progressive sexuality education has no agenda; it is simply about providing factual information. This portrayal of CSE as somehow apolitical has been critiqued by sexuality education researchers and conservative commentators alike. My concern is not only that such portrayals constitute progressivism as apolitical but also that they covertly locate religion as anathema to progressivism. While the previous passage is not an explicit rejection of religion, I perceive these types of discourses as producing progressive sexuality education as a field where religion is unwelcome because it is conceptualized as biased.

Another example of queer secularism's associations with progressivism and CSE is demonstrated by Lyba Spring. Writing for the Canadian Women's Health Network, Spring argues:

> Sexual health curricula. Who writes them, and for whom? Is a curriculum written for the benefit of students; or is their language carefully edited to assuage dissenting organizations and reassure jittery bureaucrats? When new curricula are published, opponents of sexual health education will inevitably be poised to cherry pick material to discredit the contents. Provincial governments worry about political backlash to progressive sex education that teaches about pleasure, choice, inclusion

and current sexual realities. And yet, that is the job of a sex educator. Comprehensive sexuality education is critical to society.

(Spring, 2013)[6]

In this portrayal, sexuality education is progressive when it is associated with pleasure (young people are conceptualized as autonomous beings who are already having sex), choice (and they might get pregnant and want an abortion), and inclusion (and they are not all straight). In this passage, religious perspectives are not explicitly mentioned. Spring only refers to unnamed dissenting organizations who oppose pleasure, choice, and inclusion, leaving the reader to conjure the associations in their own minds.

In the Australian context, and covering slightly different terrain, Lodwick (2012) draws on Jones's (2012) research on gay, lesbian, bisexual, trans, intersex, queer, and questioning students to suggest that "progressive sexuality education messages in classrooms [need to] address homophobia, sexual autonomy, sexual experimentation and even 'heterosexual' information" (Lodwick, 2012).

Such arguments closely mirror Spring's discussion of Canadian progressivism in sexuality education. Progressive sexuality education has come to be associated with the provision of unbiased information, sexual health, pleasure, choice, inclusion, reality, addressing homophobia, sexual autonomy, sexual experimentation, and somewhat curiously, the provision of heterosexual information. Progressive sexuality education is also constituted as something that any reasonable person who is interested in the sexual health of young people should get behind. For Spring, progressive sexuality education "is critical to society" (2013). The tone of such expressions is significant because of the certainty they convey: progressive sexuality may be contentious, but it is also indispensable to society because it is portrayed as unbiased and therefore critical.

In her book, *Politics of Piety: The Islamic Revival and the Feminist Subject*, Saba Mahmood (2005) attempts to diagnose the dis-ease of progressive leftists, like herself, in grappling with Islamic revival movements. In part she attributes this dis-ease to progressives associating these movements

> . . . with the appearance of religion outside of the private space of individualized belief. For those with well-honed secular-liberal and progressive sensibilities, the slightest eruption of religion into the public domain is frequently experienced as a dangerous affront, one that threatens to subject us to normative morality dictated by mullahs and priests. This fear is accompanied by a deep self-assurance about the truth of the progressive-secular imaginary, one that assumes that the life forms it offers are the best way out for these unenlightened souls, mired as they are in spectral hopes that gods and prophets hold out to them. (2005: xi)

This dis-ease with the shift of religion into the public sphere, as well as the self-assurance associated with the embrace of the progressive-secular imaginary, is also present in the production of progressive sexuality education. *This isn't to say that there are not good reasons for critiquing some religious influences in sexuality education.* But in making such critiques, it is also important to be mindful of the normative moralities that underpin progressive-secular imaginaries of sexuality education.

PROGRESSIVE SEXUALITY EDUCATION: A TRANSNATIONAL PROJECT

The transnationalization of sexuality education and anti-homophobia education through organizations such as United Nations Educational, Scientific, and Cultural Organization (UNESCO) highlights the importance of thinking about secular understandings of sexuality. UNESCO's 2009 Guidelines on Sexuality Education recognize that sexuality is influenced by diverse factors, including religion, biology, history, ethics, politics, and psychology, but at the same time the guidelines

> ... emphasise the importance of addressing the *reality* of young people's sexual lives: this includes those aspects of which policy-makers and others may personally disapprove. Decision-makers with a duty of care have to recognize that good scientific evidence and public health imperatives should take priority over personal opinion. (2009: 7, italics in original)

In the guidelines there is recognition of the complexities of sexuality and an insistence upon the dominance of science and public health imperatives. In these guidelines public health and science are seen to be in the public interest, and opposition to such initiatives is framed as personal opinion. Religion is something that needs to be considered, just not at the expense of "good scientific evidence and public health imperatives" (UNESCO, 2009: 7). While UNESCO marks the significance of diverse factors influencing sexuality, it clearly prioritizes evidence-based research.

Focusing on the US context, in their book *Love the Sin: Sexual Regulation and the Limits of Religious Tolerance* (2004), Janet Jakobsen and Ann Pellegrini argue:

> The predominant understanding of religious freedom in the United States depends on the privatization of religion. Religious difference is acceptable—is tolerated—if it is contained in the private sphere. This practice is problematic not only for many members of religious "minorities," but also for many Christians, who argue that the idea that religion is or should be only a private concern does damage to religious

practice and underestimates the many benefits religion might contribute to American civic life. (2004: 117)

This understanding of the privatization of religion is also apparent in the UNESCO guidelines on sexuality education. Religion, in the UNESCO document, is constituted as something personal—it is not seen as something that could be in the public interest. Arguing against this progressive tendency that seeks to privatize religion, Jakobsen and Pellegrini argue for the "free exercise of sex . . . based in a robust pluralism that makes room for competing and even contradictory visions of the good life, both those that are religious and those that are not" (2004: 123). Such an approach goes against the grain of some who argue for a progressive sexuality education because they perceive religion, specifically conservative Christianity or Catholicism, as deleterious to young people's sexual autonomy.

Evaluations of sexuality education in terms of progressivism often evaluate the extent to which a sexuality program might be characterized as having proceeded along the path of secularization and away from moralizing discourse associated with religiosity. These types of evaluations of sexuality education programs are occurring in Australia, Europe, Asia, and North America. Next I consider a few examples of such research and the ways in which they are framed by secular views of sexuality education.

Turning first to the European context, Nataša Bijelić, in an article titled, "Sex Education in Croatia: Tensions Between Secular and Religious Discourses," argues:

> Secular and religious discourses are characterized by different social values and political positions. Representatives of the religious discourse hold more traditional values, which include patriarchal, authoritarian, ethnocentric and national features, while representatives of the secular discourse hold more modern, liberal values and support gender equality and nondiscrimination (Labus, 2005). (Bijelić, 2008: 337)

Throughout the article Bijelić sets up a clear dichotomy between secular and religious discourses. Bijelić also goes on to complicate this, arguing later in the article that young people who are religious often have

> . . . opposing attitudes on sexuality to those propounded by their religion and church (Marinovic´ Jerolimov, 2002: 123). . . . This discrepancy may suggest that religiously based sex education that targets religious youth will not be effective. (Bijelić, 2008: 340, 341)

According to Bijelić's analysis there is some propensity for young people to assimilate both religious and secular discourses. But in the framing of Bijelić's argument, secular and religious perspectives do not overlap, and religiously informed sexuality education is seen as unlikely to be effective for young people, regardless of their religious affiliations. Yet young people who are religious in Croatia undoubtedly hold various perspectives on the religiously based sex education they receive.

Writing about sexuality education in the Indonesian context, Brigitte Holzner and Dede Oetomo (2004) critique sexuality education provisions that are informed by religious perspectives because they reinforce messages portraying sex outside of marriage as unhealthy and dangerous. Drawing on the United Nations' Convention of the Rights of the Child as well as the Cairo declaration about reproductive and sexual rights (41), they advocate instead for the implementation of a rights-based approach:

> Central to this discourse is the idea of competence of adolescents: to be able to make decisions about sex in a mature way. The notion of competent citizenship includes participation, access, equal and just treatment. . . . Differently from the prohibitive, regulatory framework, this discourse is permissive and builds on the enlightenment principle of rationality, in contrast to the idea of an irrational sexual drive in search of satisfaction. A citizenship discourse supports a belief in self-control through rational choice, not requiring outside controls. (2004: 41)

They argue this alternative "discourse of competence and citizenship would more adequately reflect the actual sexual behavior of youth" (2004: 40). For Holzner and Oetemo religious sexuality education needs to be replaced by sexuality education that is more realistic—because it reflects what young people do, not what adults hope they might do. In the framing of Holzner and Oetomo's argument, religious teaching is situated as distinct from discourses of competence and citizenship, and the emphasis is therefore on working toward keeping these discourses separate, at least within the sphere of sexuality education. Holzner and Oetemo's argument is strongly embedded in a progressive approach. They clearly emphasize decision making, autonomy, rights discourses, equality and citizenship, and rationality as a necessary counter to a more prohibitive sexuality education.

In her study of sex education in the *bustees* (urban slums) of Kolkata, Kabita Chakraborty, also working in a Muslim-majority context, takes a different approach.

> In the bustees, for safe-sex education to be a well-received part of learning about sex, it must be contextualized to reflect the lived experience of romantic and sexual relationships that young people participate in. Finally, a sex education programme for the bustees must draw on the Qur'an's extensive teachings regarding respect for one's partner, sexual hygiene and personal health, and recognize this text as an important resource in developing a sex education curriculum.
> (Chakraborty, 2010: 277)

Chakraborty's vision for a contextualized approach to sexuality approach highlights the importance of sexuality education that reflects young people's sexual and religious cultures. Arguably, approaches to sexuality education that construct secular and religious approaches as necessarily in tension or at odds may render both approaches less effective.

In some international evaluations the US is seen as more conservative than comparable nations on the subject of sexuality education because the line between the sacred and the secular is hotly contested in the US context. In an international comparative analysis of sexuality education provision, Heather Weaver, Gary Smith, and Susan Kippax (2005) characterize sexuality education in Australia, the Netherlands, and France as "pragmatic and sex positive," while the United States is characterized by its abstinence-based sexual education policy (171). In making this comparison one of the things they consider is "the general framing of sex and sexuality (e.g. whether religious or pragmatic acknowledgement of young people's sexuality)" (2005: 174). In the way this analysis is constructed, it is possible to see how religion is conceptualized in relation to sexuality education in countries that constitute themselves as comparable. This particular international comparison places religion and pragmatism as distinct; one is religious, or one is pragmatic (progressive). Such comparisons reflect how secularization shapes sexuality education debates, reproducing characterizations of sexuality education as abstinence only (AO)—or—progressive (Fine and McClelland, 2006; Lesko, 2010).

It appears that one purpose of international comparative research on sexuality education is to provide an empirical basis for the superiority of a pragmatic approach in terms of sexual health outcomes. Weaver, Smith, and Kippax argue that the analysis they have undertaken

> . . . indicates that those countries with pragmatic and sex positive government policies (France, Australia and especially the Netherlands) have better sexual health-related statistics than the one country with a primarily sexual abstinence-based policy (the United States). (2005: 171)

The takeaway message from this study is that abstinence-based policies in the US are associated with religiosity, and together these associations are correlated nationally with higher rates of unplanned pregnancy and abortion among women age 15 to 19 as well as lower contraceptive use and higher rates of HIV and STIs. Such data are consequently used as a reason to advocate for a more secular sexuality education program—such as those in Australia, the Netherlands, and France (the comparative countries in this study).

Effat Merghati-Khoei, Naria Abolghasemi, and Thomas Smith's article " 'Children Are Sexually Innocent': Iranian Parents' Understanding of Children's Sexuality" (2014) looks at comprehensive sexuality education in the Iranian context. The authors argue the comprehensive approach could be utilized within this context, with the exception of teaching about "homosexuality, bisexuality, these are highly restricted topics and cannot be applied legally in Iranian contexts" (593). The authors explicitly grapple with the question of how religion might influence the provision of such an approach and note:

> Evidently, Islamic morals may be read to be compatible with the natural growth of sexuality as part of being human (Merghati-Khoei, Whelan, and Cohen, 2008). Even so, a culture of silence is the predominant view of sexuality in Iran, and this view is often justified by a religious frame. (Merghati-Khoei, Whelan, and Cohen, 2014: 588)

Here specific elements of a progressive approach are seen as compatible with Islamic morals in Iran. US researchers who argue for alignment between CSE and FBOs are seen by Merghati-Khoei, Abolghasemi, and Smith as potential role models for the implementation of CSE in the Iranian context (Boonstra, 2008). CSE is an approach that has increasingly broad international consensus, even in countries with strong traditions of admitting religion into the public sphere. The adoption of a comprehensive approach by UNESCO underscores the importance of continuing to interrogate the foundations of this approach and how it grapples with its stated commitments to recognition of religious and cultural diversity.

SUBTRACTION STORIES IN SEXUALITY EDUCATION

A key figure in recent scholarly discussions of secularism is Charles Taylor. Drawing on Taylor enables me to explicate how ideological divisions between secularism and religion establish certain intellectual mandates. In writing about Taylor's *A Secular Age*, Michael Warner, Jonathan Van Antwerpen, and Craig Calhoun state that this text "displaces the commonsense opposition between the religious and the secular with a new understanding in which this opposition appears only as a late and retrospective misrecognition" (2010: 17). In applying this argument to sexuality education, it prompts the question of whether battles over sexuality education are a form of misrecognition in which progressives and conservatives appear to be only in opposition.

Taylor's suggestion that opposition between religion and secularism is misrecognized is based on his critique of the view that modernity inevitably marginalizes religion. He focuses on "how conditions of secularity have come to shape both contemporary belief and unbelief alike" (2010: 5). Inspired by Taylor, this text focuses on what such claims might mean for sexuality education—what are the conditions of secularity in sexuality education and how have they come to shape oppositional thinking between the religious and the secular? For Taylor, this type of oppositional thinking is a misrecognition that is based in what he terms "subtraction stories" that identify

> [a] certain essential tendency or character which holds everywhere and always of human beings . . . [A]n example of this . . . is the picture of human agents as essentially individuals operating by instrumental reason . . . [I]n the subtraction story . . . we have just shucked off some false beliefs, some fears of imagined objects.
> (Taylor, 301, 303, in Warner, Van Antwerpen and Calhoun, 2010).

Taylor explicitly rejects "subtraction theories" that associate religiosity with transcendence and irrationality and secularism with naturalism and rationality. Taylor does not see secularity as the absence of religion from public spaces or the separation of church and state because within this logic, people tend to see secularism and religion as somehow distinct. For Taylor, the very idea of secularity is predicated on particular understandings about belief. In undertaking his study of secularism, Taylor states that his aim is to provoke conversations "between a host of different positions, religious, nonreligious, antireligious, humanistic, antihumanistic, and so on, in which we eschew mutual caricature and try to understand what 'fullness' means for the other" (Taylor, 318, in Warner, Van Antwerpen and Calhoun, 2010). An aim of this text is to provoke conversations about different positions related to sexuality education from a perspective that doesn't seek to privilege a particular ideology at the outset.

Such provocations demand a move away from the misrecognition already described above. A misrecognition is evident in Alesha Doan and Jean Calterone Williams's book *The Politics of Virginity: Abstinence in Sex Education* (2008). Doan and Calterone Williams frame debates about sexuality education in the US as part of a broader range of morality policies where there is a juxtaposition of "culturally progressive and secularist beliefs against culturally traditional and religiously fundamentalist beliefs" (2008: 8). The basis of arguments on both sides is also outlined:

> Opponents of abstinence-only education primarily base their arguments on public health issues and draw on scientific studies from a variety of disciplines that link comprehensive sexuality education to positive health indicators. The pro-abstinence only coalition uses morality as the foundation for its support; however advocates also rely on research to gain credibility for their side. (2008: 12)

In this characterization of the debate over abstinence in sexuality education in the US context, Doan and Calterone-William do not seek to unsettle this binary; they place themselves firmly on the side of those they would situate as culturally progressive and secular. This is a position that I have also occupied and one I strategically continue to adopt, though increasingly hesitantly.

To have a legible position in debates about sexuality education, it is sometimes necessary to align oneself with one set of beliefs or the other. People will also assume a queer academic that utilizes queer theory is, ipso facto, culturally progressive. In writing this text one aim is to unsettle this framing of debates about sexuality education because of the way it aligns religion, fundamentalism, and traditionalism as well as progressivism with secularism. In seeking to question and destabilize these alignments, my hope is that different sorts of questions and investigations might take place—for instance, thinking about how secularism can be morally conservative and religion culturally progressive.

In this text I move beyond the idea of admitting religion's progressivism, which is by no means a revelatory claim. Rather, I consider how it might be possible to enrich conceptualizations of sexuality education, in research and practice, via an engagement with ways of thinking about sexuality, agency, pleasure, and homophobia that are overtly political, moral, religious, and sometimes antagonistic.

A specific focus is identifying and analyzing the types of thinking commonly associated with progressivist points of view in sexuality education. This undertaking will enable a better appreciation of how progressivism is constituted as well as taking seriously critiques of sexuality education that bristle at the alleged neutrality of progressivism. I want to create a space in which the field of sexuality education might think more about diversity in terms of religiosity and secularity, alongside its current preoccupations with sexual and gender minorities, race, and class.

The subtitle for this book borrows from William Connolly's text *Why I Am Not a Secularist* (1999). In this text Connolly draws attention to the ways in which distinctions are frequently drawn between the public and the private, and the sacred and the secular, using particular secular conceits (1999: 4).[7] Two of these conceits include the ideas that secularism equals progressivism and modernity and tat religion equals conservativism and tradition.

These binaries can operate to foreclose differing points of views and perspectives. As Judith Butler (2008) points out in her article *Sexual Politics, Torture, and Secular Time*: "struggles for sexual expression depend upon the restriction and foreclosure of rights of religious expression (if we are to stay within the liberal framework), and so we can see something of an antinomy within the discourse of liberal rights itself" (6). The notion that religious and sexual expressions are conflictual or exclusive is, as I demonstrate throughout this text, one of the conceits of secularism in sexuality education. Framing sexuality education in terms of rights discourses is also problematic, as Butler points out, because such a path sees religious and sexual freedoms set at odds with one another in sexuality education discourse, a path that reinforces the misrecognition described by Taylor above.

WHAT'S A QUEER THEORIST LIKE YOU DOING IN A PLACE LIKE THIS? A BRIEF BIOGRAPHY OF THE RESEARCH QUESTION

I am writing this book from the perspective of somebody who is now non-religious but who grew up in a Catholic family. We went to mass most Sundays, but attendance dropped off for all the children while we were in our teens. Both my parents still attend, Dad on a daily basis.

While I have been working on this text, several people have inquired about my motivation in undertaking such a project. Maybe wrongly I sometimes assume a subtext behind this inquiry (though I also admit this is likely my own paranoid reading)—something along the lines of—what's a queer theorist like you doing in a place like this?

Professor Bill Pinar was, I think, the first colleague to put this question to me, while I was a visiting scholar in his Centre for the Study of the Internationalization of Curriculum Studies at the University of British Columbia in Vancouver, Canada. In short, I think Pinar wanted to know the biography of my research question, what baggage I brought along to this investigation. While my own experiences of religion and sexuality education cannot be neatly mapped to this project, I think that some parts of my biography are relevant insofar as they have shaped my desire to create a space for more variety in conversations about the place of sexuality education in public schools.

Like many Australians, my own schooling took place exclusively in Catholic schools—though these Catholic schools were by no means exclusive in terms of the religiosity of teachers and students. My primary school was coeducational, but my secondary school was single sex. As my mother put it, when I recently inquired as to how I ended up at my secondary school (Siena Ladies College), Catholic parents put their children in Catholic schools. Her decision to do this was as unremarkable as our neighbors' decision to send their children to the local public school. My three oldest brothers were ejected from or rejected Catholic schooling and were moved to the local public high school, while Damian, the brother closest in age to me, took the opposite path—transferring from the local high school to a Catholic boys' school. My parents were not averse to crossing religious boundaries in terms of school choice. Like other Australian parents who are in a position to choose where their children will be educated, my parents' consumption of education was guided by what they thought was best for their children, by their own experiences of religious education, and by their affinities with the local Catholic community. This notion of choice in education provision has proliferated in Australia since the 1970s. Successive Australian federal governments have widened provision of public funding to private and religious schools.

Dominican nuns oversaw my secondary education. Some were, in my memory, feminists who were strong on liberation theology. Social justice was big on their religious education agenda, and this was manifest in the service element of our curriculum, though on reflection, the types of service in which we engaged was principally of the variety that engaged those seen to be less fortunate. I also remember that these same nuns hired ex-priests (now married) and gay men (I knew they were gay as at least one of them frequented the same gay bar as my older brother).

My experience of Catholic schooling was also characterized by homophobia (though I am sure public school students have also hurled homophobic taunts) and a sexuality education that highlighted marriage and the rhythm method and gave no hint of other forms of sexual relationships. While lesbianism was officially absent in the curriculum, it was a constant presence in the taunts of peers on the playground and in the locker room—taunts that I readily produced, safe in the knowledge of my own straight credentials (at least at the time) while also knowing that my own brother was gay. To him, and to me, lesbians seemed worthy of contempt.

In presenting on this research in preparation for this book, I have received comments from peers suggesting that it gives solace to the continuation of religious involvement in public education. I do believe that public schools and public funding of education should be able to create space for discussions of religion. In countries such as Australia, where public funding of religious schools has been a significant part of the history of education, I also believe that sexuality education curriculum can and should reflect the religious tenets espoused by religious schools. This isn't to say that I agree with all the sexuality education undertaken in religious schools in Australia. It is recognition that parents, as well as young people, are integral to the process of imagining what constitutes appropriate sexuality education and that not all parents or young people will concur with my embrace of the comprehensive approach. This research has therefore been constituted as complicit in the sustenance of a religious education system that has condoned the sexual abuse of countless children through covering up the sexual crimes of clergy. I don't see my role here as defender of the Catholic Church. But one of my aims is not to replace muscular Christianity with an even more muscular formation of secularity.

The desire to undertake this book project may in some way relate to my own experience of having a secular and fundamentalist feelings touch. At the age of 15 my older brother Damian (the next in line to me) was killed in a car accident on New Year's Eve. Inevitably this event shook things up at home. I remember it (misremember it?) as a catalyst for my father's evangelical turn—to which I was briefly hailed—but I promptly rejected these overtures. The laying on of hands at the youth group was not for me. Dad continues to be a daily churchgoer, still believing in the infallibility of the Lord. My mother always rejected this route and is quick to critique the Catholic Church, though she continues her alliance. Nor are my siblings churchgoers.

For me, coming out post-university, both parents have been incredibly supportive. Dad is accepting of my partner, my friends, and me—while likely continuing to pray I might be liberated from what he perceives as my sexual transgressions. Maybe in part because of this quietly agonistic relationship with Dad, I do believe that sexuality education in public schools needs to attend more thoughtfully to religious and cultural differences. I believe that sexuality education practice and research that circulates within the public square will be strengthened if it can better incorporate differences related to sexuality, culture, race, and religion. This book is an attempt to grasp and critically interrogate contemporary habits of thought that are conditioned by particular understandings of secularism in sexuality education.

STRUCTURE OF THE BOOK

Throughout this book I think about progressive sexuality education as sometimes aligned with CSE. But CSE and progressive sexuality education are not identical in my mind, and there are many variations of each. In trying to elaborate my understanding of progressive sexuality education and its various relationships to secularism, I look in numerous places: the enactment of sexuality education curriculum in the classroom; curriculum frameworks; curriculum designed to combat homophobia and cultivate pleasure in sexuality education; media panics related to sexuality education; a comedy show; and popular films about choice. This approach is informed by research and by conversations with peers—especially people from the US, Canada, Aotearoa-New Zealand, and Ireland.

In some ways this approach might dilute the power of the analysis because the sites appear geographically and contextually distinct. One of the things that has struck me as I have worked on this project is how progressive sexuality education travels across borders, within and beyond schools and classrooms. Understandings of progressivism in relation to sexuality are clearly not confined to education; these notions of progressivism are part of public conversations that are being staged, in different iterations, across numerous sites. Discourses within education inform how diverse publics understand and feel what it means to be progressive in relation to sexuality (and what it means to be seen as not progressive). These discourses and structures of feeling within sexuality education are, in turn, shaped by popular and broader scholarly conversations about sexuality, modernity, enlightenment, and tolerance. This is part of the rationale behind my decision not to focus this analysis solely on what is happening within schools, official curricula, and classrooms. Such an analysis would run the risk of painting progressive sexuality education as something which is somehow distinct from broader cultural fabrics, when I hope to demonstrate that habits of thought and feeling associated with progressivism are fundamentally difficult to unpack—precisely because they are a part of what Saba Mahmood (2005) terms a *progressive-secular imaginary*—and what Connolly (1999) constructs as the conceits of secularism.

In Chapter 2, I examine diverse relationships among religion, secularism, and progressive sexuality education—predominantly focusing on the US context. I consider how these relationships work to both disrupt and affirm particular understandings about sexuality education and its relationship to religion. Turning to a performance by a gay comic at an Australian comedy festival, I consider how this event might be read as a form of progressive sexuality education. In analyzing this event I am keenly aware of the tropes that are associated with the public performance of the progressive position. My participation in the event also speaks to the attractions of progressivism—and the public pedagogical pleasures that can align with collective celebrations of sexual exceptionalism and queer secularism (ideas borrowed from Jasbir Puar's *Terrorist Assemblages*). Following on from this I consider how notions of sexual autonomy, decision making, and freedom from religion—themes apparent at the comedy night—also shape scholarly discourses within sexuality education.

Key elements in the "process known as secularization," identified by Janet Jakobsen and Ann Pellgrini, including ideas about reason, Enlightenment ideals, modernity and progress, the privatization of religion, and the concomitant separation of church and state are the subjects of inquiry in this coauthored chapter. Chapter 3 is the sole coauthored chapter because it draws directly on research funded by the Australian Research Council in an investigation of cultural and religious difference in sexuality education in public schools in Australia and Aotearoa-New Zealand. The participants all attended culturally and religiously diverse public schools. In interviews conducted with participants (students in secondary school), we considered the place of religion and culture in our participants' perceptions of sexuality education. In analyzing our data we have been struck by the ways in which ideas about secularization, including notions of a democratic sexuality education, shape the space of sexuality education. While Chapter 3 focuses on how understandings of secularization frame participants' understandings of sexuality education, the focus in Chapter 4 is on how researchers identified with the comprehensive approach account for religious objections to this approach.

Within academic research on sexuality education, there is a tendency to draw on the notion of moral panic to better understand opposition to comprehensive sexuality education. I briefly consider the formation of moral panic discourse and some contemporary scholarly debates about the limitations of moral and sex panic. I then move to a focus on the work of US researcher Janice Irvine, a significant figure in framing the relationship between moral panics and debates within sexuality education in the US. I also consider Australian research on moral panics in sexuality education that engages with Irvine to consider how notions of moral panic travel across scholarly borders. While Irvine's work has focused on the role of the religious right in the production of moral and sex panics, my focus is on the role of researchers, who might see themselves as progressive, in the production of moral panic discourses.

Discourses related to pleasure, desire, autonomy, and sexual freedom in sexuality education are explored in Chapter 5. These discourses have been important components of researchers' visions for a more progressive sexuality education for more than 20 years, a trend inspired by Michelle Fine's (1988) seminal article, *Sexuality, Schooling, and Adolescent Females: The Missing Discourse of Desire*. I consider how discourses related to these concepts have been taken up in the US and internationally by researchers who have been sympathetic to Fine's lament regarding the missing discourse of desire in sexuality education. Drawing on Joan Scott and Talal Asad's writings on secularism, I consider how such scholarship may work to reinforce distinctions between religious freedom and sexual freedom, and health and morality—distinctions that rest on particular understandings of secularization and sexual liberation that conceptualize agency and autonomy as located within the individual.

The concept of homophobia and its relationship to anti-homophobia initiatives in education is my focus in Chapter 6. Akin to Daniel Monk's (2011) study of homophobic bullying in schools in England, my goal here is to understand anti-homophobia education as part of a broader political project that has received little critical attention within the field of sexuality education. I perceive anti-homophobia education as part of the ways in which young people, teachers, and teacher educators are being trained to think about what it means to be tolerant of people who claim diverse forms of embodiment, gender, and sexual identity. How do attempts to educate against homophobia grapple with cultural and religious differences in the ways people think about gender, sexuality, and sexual difference? Monk illustrates how imaginings of "a post-homophobic time" (2011: 191) shape the solutions posed to the problem of homophobia. I consider how this notion of "post-homophobic time" simultaneously reinforces the vulnerability of gay youth while affirming understandings about those responsible for their victimization.

Public pedagogies of choice, as depicted in contemporary films about abortion and related commentaries (*Juno; Knocked Up; Precious; Waitress; Obvious Child; 4 months, 3 Weeks, and 2 Days*) are the subject of Chapter 7. The messages that viewers might learn about abortion and choice through these films are the substance of much debate. In the scope of this book, such debates interest me because of what they can reveal about contradictory readings of what it means to be progressive. So while Chapter 6 focuses on the politics of progressive approaches to anti-homophobia education (where there appears to be more consensus about what lessons must be learned), Chapter 7 attends to the politics of choice and to the contestations that adhere to different understandings of choice, autonomy, and states of exception. In particular, I consider Penelope Deutscher's discussion of how abortion has come to be perceived as only permissible in specific exceptional

Introduction   23

cases. Tracing thinking about states of exception in these public pedagogies of choice helps me explore the politics that inform diverse perspectives that may be known as progressive. This analysis illustrates that progressivism, like conservatism, is by no means univocal on issues related to sexuality. Here I also explicitly explore some of my own attachments to progressivism in sexuality education in relation to debates about choice.

Moving on from public pedagogies of choice, I explore the relationship between secularism and sexuality education in three national contexts: Ireland, Australia, and Canada. These countries all continue to publicly fund religious schools—with Canada and Australia also having large numbers of schools that are constituted as public and nonreligious. How is secularism understood in Irish secondary schools that have a long Catholic history and continuing association with Catholicism? How do researchers and educators distinguish between religious, national, and secular influences in the ways curricula are crafted and enacted in these quite distinct country contexts? How does secularism manifest in a country like Australia, where state and federal governments are crafting quite distinct curricula related to sexuality education? And, what type of sexuality education is appropriate in a country like Australia, where young people are increasingly attending government-funded religious schools while declaring themselves as having no religious affiliations in the national census in ever-greater numbers? How do debates about sexuality education, public funding of religious schools, and support groups for LGBTI youth intersect in Toronto, Ontario? And how do gay politics and what Barbara Baird (2008) terms "child fundamentalism" (where saving the children takes on particular types of moral force) intersect in debates about sexual freedom and the rights of LGBTI youth? How is democratic sexuality imagined in Edmonton, Alberta, and what can this tell us about the place of reason, religion, and science in contemporary imaginings of sexuality education?

I conclude this book by bringing together the theoretical contributions that have been made throughout the text as well as making suggestions for how these might impact on future research on sexuality education. I also make suggestions for how sexuality education curriculum and pedagogy in public school contexts might take account of varieties of secularism and the religious and cultural differences that permeate public schools.

NOTES

1. The Guttmacher Institute's mission is to "advance sexual and reproductive health and rights through an interrelated program of research, policy analysis and public education designed to generate new ideas, encourage enlightened public debate and promote sound policy and program development. The Institute's overarching goal is to ensure the highest standard of sexual and reproductive health for all people worldwide." See Guttmacher Institute (1996–2014).

2. Advocates for Youth is a nonprofit organization that works both in the US and in developing countries with a sole focus on adolescent reproductive and sexual health.
3. Answer is a national organization that provides and promotes unfettered access to comprehensive sexuality education for young people and the adults who teach them.
4. SIECUS affirms that sexuality is a fundamental part of being human, one that is worthy of dignity and respect. We advocate for the right of all people to accurate information, comprehensive education about sexuality, and sexual health services. SIECUS works to create a world that ensures social justice and sexual rights.
5. Alesha Doan and Jean Calterone-Williams in *The Politics of Virginity* identify three primary types of sexuality in the US context: "comprehensive sexuality education, abstinence-based (sometimes called abstinence-plus) education, and abstinence-only education. All teach abstinence from sexual activity as a healthy choice for teens. Comprehensive sexuality education addresses wide-ranging information on sexual health, contraceptives and sexual activity, and relationships . . . [A]bstinence based programs contain some information on contraceptives, abstinence-only education does not provide contraceptive information, except in terms of failure rates and dangerous side effects. Abstinence-only instruction teaches teens that all premarital sexual activity, for both teens and adults and including most premarital sexual acts in addition to intercourse, are unhealthy physically and psychologically" (2008: 18–19).
6. See http://www.cwhn.ca/en/node/46087.
7. In the last 20 years the concept of secularism has been the subject of much scholarship. Probably the most influential text in this regard is Charles Taylor's *A Secular Age* (2007). Taylor and Connelly aside, other influential scholars in this field include Michael Warner, Jonathan Van Antwerpen, Craig Calhoun (*Varieties of Secularism in a Sexual Age*), Saba Mahmood (*The Politics of Piety: The Islamic Revival and the Feminist Subject*), and Talal Asad (*Formations of the Secular: Christianity, Islam, Modernity*). The relationship between secularism and sexuality is a particular focus of the work of Janet Jakobsen and Ann Pellegrini (*Love the Sin: Sexual Regulation and the Limits of Religious Tolerance*) and their edited collection (*Secularisms*); these texts have been pivotal in helping me think through the relations between sexuality and secularism in education.

REFERENCES

AFP (Agence France-Presse). (2011). *Pope says sex education an 'attack on religious freedom'*, published on ABC News website. Available from: http://www.abc.net.au/news/2011-01-11/pope-says-sex-education-an-attack-on-religious/1900696 (Last accessed July 17, 2014).

Baird, B. (2008). Child Politics, Feminist Analyses. *Australian Feminist Studies*, 23(57): 291–305.

Bijelić, N. (2008). Sex Education in Croatia: Tensions between Secular and Religious Discourses. *European Journal of Women's Studies*, 15(4): 329–343.

Bleakley, A., Hennessy, M., & Fishbein, M. (2006). Public Opinion on Sex Education in US Schools. *Archives of Pediatrics and Adolescent Medicine*, 160(11): 1151–1156.

Boonstra, H.D. (2008). Matter of faith: Support for comprehensive sex education among faith-based organizations. *Guttmacher Policy Review*, 11(1), 17–22.
———. (2012). Progressive and Pragmatic: The National Sexuality Education Standards for U.S. Public Schools. *Guttmacher Policy Review*, 15(2): 2–7.
Butler, J. (2008). Sexual Politics, Torture, and Secular Time. *The British Journal of Sociology*, 59(1): 1–23.
Butler, J., Habermas, J., Taylor, C., & West, C. (2011). *The Power of Religion in the Public Sphere*. Edited and introduced by Mendieta, E., & VanAntwerpen, J. New York: Columbia University Press.
Casanova, José. (2007). Secular, secularizations, secularisms. The Immanent Frame website. Available from http://blogs.ssrc.org/tif/2007/10/25/secular-secularizations-secularisms/ (Last accessed April 13, 2015).
Chakraborty, K. (2010). Unmarried Muslim Youth and Sex Education in the Bustees of Kolkata. *South Asian History and Culture*, 1(2): 268–281.
Christopher, F.S., & Roosa, M. W. (1990). An Evaluation of an Adolescent Pregnancy Prevention Program: Is "Just Say No" Enough? *Family Relations*, 39(1): 68–72.
Connolly, W.E. (1999). *Why I Am Not a Secularist*. Minneapolis: University of Minnesota Press.
Doan, Alesha, E., & Calterone-Williams, J. (2008). *The Politics of Virginity: Abstinence in Sex Education*. Westport, Connecticut: Praeger.
Fields, J. (2008). *Risky Lessons: Sex Education and Social Inequality*. New Brunswick: Rutgers University Press.
Fine, M. (1988). Sexuality, Schooling, and Adolescent Females: The Missing Discourse of Desire. *Harvard Educational Review*, 58(1): 29–53.
Fine, M., & McClelland, D. (2006). Sexuality Education and Desire: Still Missing After All These Years. *Harvard Educational Review*, 76(3): 297–338.
Guttmacher Institute. (1996–2014). *About the Guttmacher Institute*. Available from https://www.guttmacher.org/about/index.html (Last accessed on July 19, 2014).
———. (2010). *Lemonade from Lemons: The Obama Administration's Plan for Implementing the Title V Abstinence Education Program*. Guttmacher Policy Review, 13(3). Available from https://agi-usa.org/pubs/gpr/13/3/gpr130324.pdf (Last accessed July 19, 2014).
Haffner, D., Rev. (2008). Yes, Sex Education in Kindergarten! *Huffington Post*. Available from http://www.huffingtonpost.com/rev-debra-haffner/yes-sex-education-in-kind_b_126899.html (Last accessed on July 17, 2014).
———. (2012). New minimum standards for sex education: progress or retreat? RH Reality Check, January 15, 2012. Available from http://rhrealitycheck.org/article/2012/01/15/new-minimum-standards-sex-education-progress-or-retreat/ (Last accessed on November 12, 2014).
Hicks, M. (2010). Parental Outrage Can Protect Our Kids from 'Progressive' Sex-ed. *Washington Times*. Available from http://www.washingtontimes.com/news/2010/sep/14/parental-outrage-protect-kids-progressive-sex-ed/?page=all (Last accessed on July 17, 2014).
Holzner, B.M., & Oetomo, D. (2004). Youth, Sexuality and Sex Education Messages in Indonesia: Issues of Desire and Control. *Reproductive Health Matters*, 12(23): 40–49.
Irvine, J. (2002). *Talk about Sex: The Battles Over Sex Education in the United States*. California: University of California Press.
Jakobsen, J. R. (2002). Can Homosexuals End Western Civilization As We Know It? Family Values in a Global Economy. In Arnaldo Cruz-Malave and Martin F. Manalansan (Eds.), *Queer globalizations: Citizenship and the Afterlife of Colonialism*, 49–70. New York: New York University Press.

Jakobsen, J. R., & Pellegrini, A. (2004). *Love the Sin: Sexual Regulation and the Limits of Religious Tolerance*. Boston, Mass.: Beacon Press.

Jones, T. (2012). Sexual subjects: GLBTIQ student subjectivities in Australian education policy. Unpublished doctoral dissertation, La Trobe University. Available from: http://arrow.latrobe.edu.au:8080/vital/access/manager/Repository/latrobe:34108

Kendall, N. (2013). *The Sex Education Debates*. Chicago: University of Chicago Press.

Lesko, N. (2010). Feeling Abstinent? Feeling Comprehensive? Touching the Affects of Sexuality Curricula. *Sex Education*, 10(3): 281–297.

Lodwick, M. (2012). Bullying in Schools. *La Trobe University*. Available from: http://www.latrobe.edu.au/news/articles/2012/article/bullying-in-schools (Last accessed 13 November, 2014).

Luker, K. (2006). *When Sex Goes to School: Warring Views on Sex—and Sex Education—Since the Sixties*. New York: Norton.

Maddox, M. (2014). *Taking God to School: The End of Australia's Egalitarian Education?* Crows Nest, N.S.W: Allen & Unwin.

Mahmood, S. (2005). *Politics of Piety: The Islamic Revival and the Feminist Subject*. Princeton, New Jersey: Princeton University.

Merghati-Khoei, E., Abolghasemi, N., & Smith, T. (2014). "Children Are Sexually Innocent": Iranian Parents' Understanding of Children's Sexuality. *Archives of Sexual Behavior*, 43(3): 587–595.

Miller, A. L. (2011). Sex, Lies and Michael Bloomberg. *The Nation*. Available from http://www.thenation.com/blog/162708/sex-lies-and-michael-bloomberg# (Last accessed July 17, 2014).

Monk, D. (2011). Challenging Homophobic Bullying in Schools: The Politics of Progress. *International Journal of Law in Context*, 7(2): 181–207.

Moran, J. P. (2000). *Teaching Sex: The Shaping of Adolescence in the 20th Century*. Cambridge, Mass.: Harvard University Press.

Pellegrini, A. (2009). Feeling Secular. *Women & Performance: A Journal of Feminist Theory*, 19(2): 205–218.

The Pew Forum on Religion and Public Life. (2005). *No conflict between abstinence, birth control*. Available from http://www.pewforum.org/2005/08/03/abortion-and-rights-of-terror-suspects-top-court-issues/ (Last accessed July 17, 2014).

Puar, J. K. (2007). *Terrorist Assemblages: Homonationalism in Queer Times*. Durham: Duke University Press.

Rubin, G. (1992). Thinking Sex: Notes for a Radical Theory of the Politics of Sexuality. In C. S. Vance (Ed.), *Pleasure and Danger: Exploring Female Sexuality* (pp. 267–319) ["Scholar and Feminist IX Conference: Towards a Politics of Sexuality", Held at Barnard College in New York in 1982]. Sydney, Australia: Pandora. Available from https://www.ipce.info/library_3/pdf/rubin_thinking_sex.pdf (Last accessed April 13, 2015).

Scott, J. W. (2009, April 23). *Sexularism*. Ursula Hirschman Annual Lecture on Gender and Europe, Florence, Italy.

Spring, L. (2013). Spring Talks Sex—Sex ed: Let's get real. *Canadian Women's Health Network*. Available from www.cwhn.ca/en/node/46087 (Last accessed November 5, 2014).

Taylor, C. (2007). *A Secular Age*. Cambridge, Mass.: Belknap Press of Harvard University Press.

UNESCO. (2009). *International Guidelines on Sexuality Education: An Evidence Informed Approach to Effective Sex, Relationships and HIV/STI Education*. Paris,

France: UNESCO. Available from http://www.refworld.org/docid/4a69b8902.html (Last accessed November 5, 2014).

Warner, M., VanAntwerpen, J., & Calhoun, C. J. (Eds.). (2010). *Varieties of Secularism in a Secular Age*. Cambridge, Mass.: Harvard University Press.

Weaver, H., Smith, G., & Kippax, S. (2005). School-based Sex Education Policies and Indicators of Sexual Health Among Young People: A Comparison of the Netherlands, France, Australia and the United States. *Sex Education: Sexuality, Society and Learning*, 5(2): 171–188.

2 Faith, Progressive Sexuality Education, and Queer Secularism
Unsettling Associations

I am an advocate of sexuality education programs that are influenced by comprehensive approaches. I strongly believe that advocacy for comprehensive sexuality education is important, especially given the politics of sexuality education in the US context and internationally (Rose, 2005). In writing this text I don't want to set up a binary that suggests that the world is neatly divided between those who support CSE and those who would support abstinence-based approaches[1]. Jessica Fields, in her book *Risky Lessons*, questions the perception that there are clear distinctions between the approaches, based on extensive observation of sexuality education lessons in North Carolina schools. She notes:

> . . . the idea that sex is normal and natural prevailed in teachers' everyday classroom practice. The sharp distinction between abstinence-only and comprehensive policies did not correspond to a sharp divide between the classroom instruction about bodies that the two curricula provided. (2008: 104)

Fields' observations are an important reminder that sexuality education, *in practice*, may not appear as divided as it does in sexuality education debates. At the same time, Fields acknowledges that liberal visions for sexuality education (in which young people have conversations about sexuality, responsible decision making, and the mechanics of reproduction) are "so taken-for-granted in today's secular public education that it is easy to forget that science supports an ideological system . . ." (2008: 102). This naturalization of different versions of secular sexuality education interests me in this book. How did this set of positions become naturalized? And what are some of the consequences of this imagining of secular versions of sexuality education as simply reflecting modern reality? I consider how comprehensive approaches have been creatively adapted to engage young people in the US who are religiously affiliated and also how they have been implicated in the production of religious and secular binaries.

The progressive sexuality education that I explore in this chapter happens within schools, in out-of-school programs, and at public events (specifically I focus on a comedy festival act). I recognize that these places are incredibly distinct, with different audiences and purposes. But looking across these sites, it is possible to see how particular sets of ideas, which I associate with secularism, produce and reference the "taken-for-granted" understandings that are apparent to Fields. The focus in this chapter is predominantly the US context, because this is where distinctions between abstinence and comprehensive approaches have been most pronounced and most contested. While these ideas have their roots in the US, they also have resonance beyond the US, including Australia, where I live (see also Chapter 3). I consider how comprehensive approaches interact with and sometimes frame relations among religiosity, sexuality education, and secularism, and I consider FBOs' relationships with comprehensive approaches. I also draw on Nancy Lesko's *Feeling Abstinent? Feeling comprehensive?* (2010); her examination of the role of affect in structuring feelings toward these different approaches is placed alongside two ideas of Jasbir Puar's "sexual exceptionalism" and "queer secularism." I identify and trace some of the relations among queer secularism, abstinence-versus-comprehensive binaries, and their associated affects; I think about how these affective binaries are sustained via sexual exceptionalism and queer secularism.

TEEN BIRTHRATES, RELIGIOSITY, AND SEXUALITY EDUCATION PROVISION IN THE US

The research that I analyze below looks at how sexuality education in the US influences adolescent birthrates. There is recognition within this research that sexuality education cannot be isolated from the broader social context, including issues such as religiosity, race and ethnicity, social class, and state policies on abortion. Whether one is for or against teaching about religion in public school contexts, religion is always going to be a significant part of many young people's cultural contexts. The research below suggests the salience of religion as a contextual factor that needs to be addressed in the provision of sexuality education, whether it is framed within a comprehensive or abstinence-based approach.

The relationship between religiosity and teenage pregnancy in the US context is explored in a recent longitudinal study, which considers 24 states in the US. Cavazos-Rehg et al. (2012) in their article "Associations Between Sexuality Education in Schools and Adolescent Birthrates," found a strong link between *religiosity and increased levels of teenage birth rates* (my emphasis). The authors maintain that the findings of the study "underscore the strong influence of religiosity and abortion policies on adolescent birthrates." They also make the caveat that this association is "above and beyond sexuality education":

> *Teaching more sexuality education* did not lower adolescent birthrates when accounting for state characteristics (ie, higher religiosity, stricter

abortion policies, and sociodemographic characteristics). (2012: 139, my emphasis)

Despite their research finding that there is no relationship between more sexuality education and a decline in adolescent birthrates, Cavazos-Rehg et al. (2012) argue that all US states need to "embrace comprehensive sexuality education" (139). I would argue that these findings are not an endorsement of any style of sexuality education. It is most likely an argument for more research that can consider how sexuality education can specifically target young people who have higher levels of religiosity and live in states with restricted access to sexual and reproductive health services, including abortion.

In their study of demography and teen birth rates in the US between 2000 and 2008, Zhou Yang and Laura Gaydos (2010) also note "the significant positive influence of religiosity on birth rates across age and race" and they state *"this effect could be independent of policy"* (521, my emphasis). Akin to Cavazos-Rehg et al., Yang and Gaydos found a strong correlation between religiosity and birth rates. The variables that Yang and Gaydos took into account include Medicaid waivers, abstinence funding, parental consent, religiosity, demography, and socioeconomic status. The dependent variable was teen birthrate (518). They found that "religiosity had a significant influence on teen birth rates across age and race . . . [C]onservative religious beliefs strongly predict [an increase in] teen birth rates" (520). So, Yang and Gaydos suggest, provisionally, that regardless of how conservative or progressive a state's policies might be regarding sexuality education, that conservative religiosity may counter this influence, and therefore teen birth rates will not diminish.

Both these quantitative studies suggest that religion strongly influences teen birthrates *regardless of the type and amount of sexuality education provision experienced by young people*. If one accepts that religion is an important factor in each of these studies, and sexuality education as currently taught (comprehensive or abstinence based) does not necessarily impact adolescent birthrates, then what is an appropriate response? Indeed, Yang and Gaydos' (2010) conclusion is that "religiosity had a significant influence on teen birth rates . . . [C]onservative religious beliefs strongly predict [an increase in] teen birth rates" (520). Somewhat contrary to these reported findings reported, Kathrin Stranger Hall and David Hall (2011), in recent quantitative research on abstinence-only education and teen pregnancy trace a relationship between abstinence-only sexuality education and increases in teen pregnancy.

Following on from establishing this link, Stranger-Hall and Hall argue:

> An important first step towards lowering the high teen pregnancy rates would be states requiring that comprehensive sex education (with abstinence as a desired behavior) is taught in all public schools. Another

important step would involve specialized teacher training . . . As a further modification, "sex education" could be split into a coordinated social studies component (ethics, behavior and decision-making, including planning for the future) and a science component (human reproductive biology and biology of STDs, including pregnancy and STD prevention), each taught by trained teachers in their respective field. (2011: 9)

Stranger-Hall and Hall's suggestions for future directions accord with my own past understandings of how sexuality education can be enhanced—many might continue to concur with their recommendations. I see such suggestions as potentially limited in what they can achieve because of their failure to substantially engage issues related to religiosity and sexuality education. There is one mention in this article on the relationship between religiosity and teen pregnancy, which suggests that these are positively correlated, but the suggestions for future directions don't sufficiently address this issue. To my mind, ethics, sexual citizenship, and references to decision making (all cited as integral to the reduction of teen pregnancy rates) have become secular codes that theoretically may make space for discussions of religiosity but generally tend not to be explicit about these connections.

How does progressive sexuality education address these links between religiosity and teen birthrates? How does sexuality education that is avowedly secular engage with religious communities? How do progressive approaches, which are predicated on science, reason, and an explicit absence of discourses related to morality, engage young people who are religious, committed to abstinence, and clearly sexually active? Is developing a pedagogical form of address to engage with these young people to use birth control even a possibility, given the social contexts in which they negotiate sexuality?

It is incumbent upon researchers in sexuality education to understand how religion and progressivism are mutually entangled—a progressive approach cannot nullify the influence of religion, and presumably the reverse is also true. Young people are engaging in abstinence-based sexuality education, declaring a strong religious affiliation, and having sexual relations. Both religious and progressive commentators who continue to argue the superiority of religious *or* secular approaches in terms of young people's sexual decision making, freedom, and liberation may miss important opportunities to engage young people in conversations about sexuality. What would sexuality education provision look like if researchers and practitioners assumed that secular *and* religious perspectives are intrinsic to the production of sexuality education?

I don't want to appear naïve about the politics that shape sexuality education provision in the US. I recognize sexuality education provision in the US is highly contextual. I also understand that religion may be left out of suggestions for future directions in sexuality education for myriad reasons:

it may be seen as too controversial; as potentially running afoul of federal, state, and local statutes that preclude schools from offering religious instruction; as anathema to education about ethics and decision making; and as contrary to public health imperatives and to scientific education about sexuality.

Regardless of the location in which they are enacted—within and outside the US, sexuality education research and programs (religious and secular) are often bound by a religious–secular binary at the outset, and this shapes the politics, philosophy, aims, and aspirations of researchers, practitioners, parents, and young people. To try and demonstrate just how this binary can shape practice, I consider an article by Jesse Mills, titled "I Should Get Married Early: Culturally Appropriate Comprehensive Sex Education and the Racialization of Somali Masculinity" (2014). I also explore these connections further in Chapter 3, based on observations in research conducted in sexuality education classrooms in Australia and Aotearoa-New Zealand.

COMPREHENSIVE SEXUALITY EDUCATION AND THE SOMALI COMMUNITY IN SAN DIEGO

Jesse Mills's study of a CSE program aimed at recently arrived Somali young men living in San Diego illustrates some of the misfires and misrecognitions that can occur when progressive ideas are enacted or perceived as regulatory. This is one example of how a progressive approach to sexuality education can produce a set of alignments that have the potential to reinforce religious conservatism, therefore minimizing the efficacy of a comprehensive approach.

Mills observes the day-to-day operations of Project Brotherhood, Responsibility, and Outreach (Project B.R.O.): a CSE program aimed largely at young Somali men recently arrived in San Diego, California. The education program takes a comprehensive approach, aiming

> (1) to provide young men with the knowledge about sexuality they need for good decision-making; (2) to encourage respect for themselves and others; (3) to help young men understand the importance of self-responsibility, especially in the area of sexual behavior; (4) to help young men increase their level of meaningful communication with their parents; and (5) to prevent partner violence by encouraging healthy relationships. (2012: 11)

Mills sees this attempt by sexuality educators to reach out to the Somali community as informed by US racial stereotypes. He also observes the imperatives placed on health educators to stick to particular "scientific" scripts in the provision of sexual health education because they feel the need to rationalize funding and perpetuate their own employment as credible sexual health researchers and educators (9, 10).

Educators in this program embraced a message of abstinence (while seemingly, according to Mills, not engaging these same young men's strong cultural and religious commitment to abstinence). Explicit within the program was a focus on health experts depicted as the most authoritative figures that young men should consult in discussions of sexuality. This was apparent in Project B.R.O.'s investment "in replacing African authorities with the ideologies and institutions of abstinence and personal responsibility. This tension was clear in Project B.R.O.'s failed attempt to engage parents" (2012: 18). For Mills, this pedagogical assemblage may have had the unintended consequence of reinforcing a particularly patriarchal version of Somali Muslim masculinity.

This manifested in conversations between participants about staff attitudes that were seen as too liberal on the subject of homosexuality, hooking up, and having multiple partners (as long as you practiced safe sex) but critical of the practice of men taking more than one wife. Mills argues that such logic did not shift the perspectives of the young men he spoke to. Rather, in response they were inclined to adopt homophobic beliefs, effectively enabling them to "claim Islam and mainstream normalcy within their own culture. That same homophobia, however, also substitutes individualistic heteronormativity for the collective community-formation characterized by homosocial intimacy" (2012: 28). In this study, young men recognized the power associated with the straight marriage bond, but at the same time they had to reckon with accompanying prohibitions associated with homosocial intimacy, also a part of this same individualistic heteronormativity.

Mills attributes educators' failures in the implementation of this comprehensive sexuality education program to its underpinnings in

> ... the broader structures of humanitarianism [that] rely on racist and sexist stereotypes that conform to prevailing social values as stakeholders may not have enough knowledge or critical perspective, or, more likely, may not feel in a position to disrupt the mainstream from which vital good will flows.
>
> The distorted threat of Somali sexuality allowed Project B.R.O. to come into being, yet the program's misplaced reliance on the culture of poverty ideology and easy shift to a more diffused multiculturalist framework secured its role of surveiling and disciplining abjected youth of color. (2012: 30)

The desirability and availability of funding for the implementation of CSE programs targeting minority youth (even if they happened to practice relatively low levels of unsafe sex) resulted in the implementation of a program that understood these young men through the lens of poverty and racialization. It also, reportedly, failed to engage with the role of religion and community and the changing attitudes of these young men's female peers. The secular underpinning, implicit within many instantiations of the comprehensive approach, contributed to Project B.R.O.'s failure to apprehend the significance of religion in shaping young people's understandings of sexuality. It is evident that the program's architecture was embedded in secular understandings of sexual decision making, abstinence, and sexual freedom that ensured that these young men and the workers in the program had agendas that were mutually unintelligible, if not antagonistic. It is also noteworthy that workers in this program didn't, *at least according to Mills*, conduct this critical appraisal themselves. Rather, Mills characterizes the workers as clinging to narratives that reinforce progressive ideas about sexuality as well as reinforcing racial and class stereotypes about the young men they were paid to "help."

This analysis of Project B.R.O should not be read in isolation. In many ways the approach being adopted by the workers in this program is entirely unremarkable; it reflects some taken-for-granted understandings about the intrinsic value of a comprehensive approach. My discussion of Mills suggests something of a gap between progressive approaches and faith-based communities in the US. In the next section, distinctions between comprehensive and faith-based approaches are not straightforward.

FAITH IN PROGRESSIVISM

In a review of comprehensive and abstinence-based approaches to sexuality education being utilized within FBOs and community-based organizations (CBOs) in the US, David Landry, Laura Linberg, Alison Gemmell, Heather Boonstra, and Lawrence Finer demonstrate that faith is no predictor of the approach people might take toward sexuality education. These researchers are from the Guttmacher Institute, a progressive think tank on sexuality education. My decision to point out these researchers' institutional location is in part informed by a desire to construct them as credible in their assessment of FBOs. To this end I am privileging evidence-based analyses of FBOs—a secular maneuver?

In analyzing the barriers to provision of a comprehensive sexuality organization, Landry et al. (2011) note that CBOs are often funded under the auspices of public health initiatives and that this limits what they are able to achieve because they are locked into prevention programs and may not provide broader youth development or recreational activities. This is particularly significant in relation to the ideas I am exploring in this text because it speaks to the ways in which funding of sexuality education reinforces secular–religious binaries. If sexuality education garners support principally on the basis of its prophylactic effects, then funding programs that go beyond this logic may be difficult to justify.

In their analysis, Landry et al. (2011) suggest potential benefits associated in not being confined within a progressive approach, arguing that "faith based-organizations are usually not solely driven by public health outcomes and may be better able to incorporate a variety of lesson plans and topics in a comprehensive sexuality education program" (93). So FBOs may be more likely to vary progressive scripts and go beyond a focus on health imperatives (96).

The notion that CBOs are limited by a focus on health and risk prevention is an argument that has been made by numerous commentators (Allen, 2004; Lottes, 2013). Allen (2004) emphasizes the importance of thinking about pleasure and desire in sexuality education, going beyond a focus on the mechanics of sexuality education, a position she critically revisits in "Pleasure's Perils" (2012). Lottes argues for operationalizing connections between discussions of sexual health and sexual rights, discussions that she recognizes have to engage values and beliefs. While Lottes and Allen have been critical of the narrow focus of CSE, the critiques already cited have not engaged questions of how religion might play a role in complicating discussion of rights, pleasure, and desire in sexuality education.

Advocates of an abstinence-based approach do draw on progressive discourses to capture the imagination of Christian young people. For instance, *sex positive* sexuality education, a term often harnessed by supporters of the comprehensive approach (see Landry et al., 2011), has also been mobilized by Christian sex counselors. In *Teaching Sex: The Shaping of Adolescence in the 20th Century*, Jeffrey Moran argues:

> In the long run, perhaps sexual "liberals" in SIECUS [Sexuality Education and Information Council of the US] and elsewhere should not worry too much. Abstinence education and the modern conservative movement have deep roots in American culture and are by no means immune to the cultural changes they claim to despise. For example, the LeHayes have tried to approach sexual expression more positively than the conservative tradition dictates, and Irvine cites evidence that other Christian sex counselors have angered some of their allies by attempting to make their presentations more explicit, more sensational. What happens when the first generation of abstinence educators looks into the blank faces of its students and realizes that what Christian conservatives had believed for so long to be the unspoiled innocence of youth is, in fact, nothing more than the crying ignorance of the American teenager? (Moran, 2003: 288, 289)

Moran's *Teaching Sex* draws our attention to processes of secularization within progressive and conservative approaches, but somewhat confusingly, at least for this reader, he also affirms progressive approaches. While Moran doesn't perceive CSE as the antidote for the ignorant American teenager, he does want to ease the concerns of liberals who worry about the proliferation of abstinence discourses in the US. Maybe echoing Fields, Moran does this by suggesting that progressive and conservative sexuality education provision is not always as far apart as one might think.

Moran perceives something of a blending of Christian conservatism and the liberalism of SIECUS.

Moran also softly mocks Christian conservatives for their misrecognition of ignorance as innocence. The assumption here from Moran is that young people who are the subject of abstinence-based approaches are essentially indistinguishable from their peers—essentially he proposes that adults should perceive young Americans as ignorant on the subject of sexuality, not innocent. This analysis doesn't appear to entertain the notion that young people might be innocent and ignorant, devout and promiscuous.

In thinking through debates about abstinence, innocence, and ignorance, I have found the work of Charles Taylor quite instructive. He comes at debates about celibacy and abstinence from a slightly different angle. He suggests that such debates bring forth the ignorance of Christians and secularists alike, "what Vatican rule-makers and secularist ideologies unite in not being able to see, is that there are more ways of being a Catholic Christian that either have yet imagined. And yet this shouldn't be so hard to grasp" (Taylor, 2007: 504). The importance of this insight (which is surely not new) is that attempts to see secularism and Christianity as separate flies in the face of the blending of these ideologies, historically and in the present, and the ways this impacts people's beliefs and practices.

Nancy Lesko also sees similarities between comprehensive and abstinence approaches to sexuality education. But for Lesko this similarity is apparent in their affective structures; both approaches are marked by feelings of certainty about their own truths, and by a belief that freedom can be achieved if people would only adhere to their particular version of truth, secular or religious. She argues that

> ... both CSE and AO supporters are nostalgic, viewing the current state of sex education as a loss, or compromise, and a far distance from a preferred education about sex, gender, marriage, and authority. (2010: 285)

In responding to this nostalgia, Lesko thinks about how sexual knowledge might be imagined otherwise:

> Memories and longings are not to be split off from science or psychology, but rather linked in liberal studies that resist final conclusions and wholeness and emphasize open inquiry (Weis and Carbondale-Medina 2000). These are possible orientations in doing sexuality education differently—moving away from instrumentalist messages to locate sexual knowledge within history, society, and individuals' lives and meanings.
> (Lesko, 2010: 293, my emphasis)

I share Lesko's desire to see sexuality education as moving away from instrumentalist messages. The open inquiry she suggests needs to apprehend not only politics, history, and society but also the place of religion, spirituality, ethics, and belief in the production of individuals' lives and meanings.

Open inquiry is another idea associated with a progressive approach to sexuality education. This is because open inquiry is predicated on the assumption that young people (and their families) see the value in the contestation of ideas related to sexuality. In their Pew Research report, "Religion in the Public Schools," the authors suggest open inquiry may be untenable for religious groups who insist upon the teaching of biblical truths about religion (and I would argue sexuality) to young people, within and outside schools (The Pew Forum on Religion and Public Life, 2007). While some opponents of comprehensive approaches might baulk at the idea of open inquiry, supporters of comprehensive approaches might resist any introduction of religion and belief in public instruction on sexuality education—including the open inquiry proposed by Lesko. This objection may be inspired by a strong belief that the space of public education is ideally defined by the absence of religion. I make this point to illustrate how the advocacy of open inquiry in sexuality education is a political position—just as arguing that religion has no place in public schools is a political position. Both positions can be justified and opposed via different interpretations of secularism in the US context.

SEXUAL EXCEPTIONALISM, QUEER SECULARISM, AND SEXUALITY EDUCATION, WITHIN AND OUTSIDE THE ACADEMY

I have found Puar's notions of sexual exceptionalism and queer secularism instructive in thinking about the underpinnings of progressive sexuality education. Puar sees queer sexual exceptionalism as "wedded to individualism and that rational liberal humanist subject" (2007: 22). She also associates this sexual exceptionalism with the idea that being queer is transgressive, but also aligned to

> liberal humanism's authorization of the fully self possessed speaking subject, untethered by hegemony or false consciousness . . . rationally choosing modern individualism over the ensnaring bonds of family. (2007: 22–23)

Notions of sexual freedom, rationality, modern individualism, and autonomy are, to my mind, intrinsic to the project of progressive sexuality education. This isn't to say that those outside this progressive project are somehow beyond reproach. It is recognition of how sexual exceptionalism is sustained by circuits of power and privilege infused by race, class, and citizenship (Puar, 2007: 13).

These ideas prompted my analysis of pedagogical approaches to anti-homophobia education (see Chapters 6 and 8), where I consider how progressive sexuality educators reinforce the importance of performing particular types of tolerance toward sexual and gender diversity; performances in which religious affiliations that are marked by racial, citizenship, and class differences are in tension with, and/or obfuscated by, the necessity of public performances of support for sexual freedom. Utilizing Puar's ideas, I have also been prompted to consider how progressive sexuality education normalizes particular ideas around transgression, sexual pleasure, and agency (see later sections and Chapter 5). My aim is not to undo these norms but to direct attention to the ways in which these ideas are sustained and to attend to the norms on which they depend for sustenance (Puar, 2014: 209).

In later writing, Puar interweaves sexual exceptionalism with her notion of queer secularism, describing the latter as structures of feeling or thought that "inhabits a space of refusal in relation to religiosity and the opportunities religious affiliations and attachments might allow" (2014: 207). These relations also obscure "the Christian basis upon which such a queer secular position relies, and which it foments" (2014: 207). This is particularly significant for Mills's analysis of how comprehensive sexuality education engages with young Somali men, newly arrived in the US, who identify as Muslim. Relations between secularism and Islam are quite differently inflected to relations between secularism and Christianity. Approaches to sexuality education that fail to register this difference are complicit in submerging these differences and potentially refusing to acknowledge and discuss what this might mean for pedagogies related to sexuality education.

Utilizing these ideas, I focus on how different formations of secularism are interwoven with imaginings of progressive sexuality education. These relations may be consciously held and explicitly elaborated. They may also shape thought and affects in such ways that particular ideas come to be taken for granted and perceived as part of the normal structure of modern sexuality education.

Nancy Lesko, a researcher with whom I identify because she is strongly associated with progressive ideas in sexuality education, explicitly attends to the ways in which certain feelings associated with AO and CSE have become taken for granted. Lesko notes:

> From my location in the academy, abstinence approaches are generally associated with tradition, backwardness, and conservative religion-infused public policy, while comprehensive sex education is linked with modernity, scientific accuracy, and freedom to talk about and enact sexuality
>
> (Lesko, 2010: 281; Pigg, 2005)

This analysis by Lesko focuses on how feelings toward AO and CSE direct us in specific ways while also attending to the ways in which feelings about AO and CSE might touch. In her analysis of AO and CSE, Lesko worries about "ceding space to conservative religious advocates and undermining the tenuous support for CSE" (2010: 294). This anxiety, which have I shared throughout the drafting of this text, speaks to the power of secular discourses of sexuality education.

My focus takes a different slant; I am interested in tracing how secularisms continuously affirm CSE as modern, scientific, and associated with freedom. This tracing is intended to develop understanding about how the secular academy has arrived at a place where it construes abstinence approaches as traditional and backward. It is recognition that approaching AO as associated with tradition, backwardness, and conservative religiosity is insufficient as a means of understanding the appeal of AO.

The production of specific types of sexuality education as backward, and others as modern, has a range of effects beyond affirming the normative value of progressive approaches. One of these side effects is the production of a set of relations in which the "queer agential subject can only ever be fathomed outside the norming constriction of religion, conflating agency and resistance" (Puar, 2007: 13). Religion is constructed as particularly egregious within this set of relations—with Islam potentially constructed as especially problematic (Puar, 2014).

Puar's discussion of queer secularism focuses on the production of Muslims and Islam as backward (out of time), fundamentalist, non-White, and homophobic. She argues that these relations are "debatably avoidable to an extent for queers from other [religious] traditions such as Judeo-Christian" while also acknowledging that this formation of queer secularity is partially founded on "the denial of Christian fundamentalism as a state practice in the United States" (2007: 13). Ann Pellegrini, writing about the history of queer studies, which surely informs queer secularism, in the "Anglo-American mode," argues it "proceeds through a secular imaginary within which, religion, if it is to appear at all, must be made to appear as arch-conservative enemy of progress" (Pellegrini, 2009: 208). In debates relating to progressive sexuality education, predominantly White, Christian, fundamentalist groups are constructed as simultaneously backward/highly organized, fringe/mainstream, lacking in power/at the center of power, and authentic/disingenuous. Those associated with progressive and conservative camps might also jockey to be positioned on either side of these binaries, depending on the context in which they are located.

Being a queer agential subject within these sets of relations often means being seen as resistant to religion. In making this point, Puar reverses Jakobsen and Pellegrini's formulation that

> Of course "they" (those who are religious) hate "us," "we" are "queer."
> (Jakobsen and Pellegrini, 2003, in Puar, 2014: 205).

And, Puar proposes her own formulation:

> Of course "they" (those who are queer) hate "us," "we" are "religious."
> (Puar, 2014: 205)

Puar suggests it is important to keep both these formulations in mind, drawing our attention to the ways in which perceived antinomies between the "we" who are queer are the "we" who are religious give force to one another through their repetition. This formulation of Puar's also helps explain why when associating oneself with religion, or coming out as religious, it can sometimes be difficult to make oneself understood as sexually agentic, progressive, or modern.

Puar's comments about queer secularity in *Terrorist Assemblages* are written in relation to a photo of Poulumi Desai, an English multimedia artist who is holding a sign titled "I Am a Homosexual Also" while dressed as a Muslim cleric. This image sutures together queer, Arab, and fundamentalist Muslim by "interrupting both conventional epistemological and ontological renderings of this body" (2007: 13). The normalization and sometimes violent racialization and secularization of queerness are apparent for Puar in Desai's production of the queer Arab cleric. This image evokes fundamentalist religion and homosexual identity claims, a very queer juxtaposition. This pairing might be troubling for the Muslim cleric and for the liberal queer. It draws our attention to the garb of fundamentalism and, potentially, to the limits of progressive sexuality.

This performance of the Muslim cleric could also be imagined as a form of sexuality education that at once complicates and refuses secular religious binaries. Puar's discussion of queer secularity is part of a broader discussion in which she thinks about "the mechanics of queerness as a regulatory frame of biopolitics" (2007: 24). She sees queerness, in this regulatory frame, as automatically associating itself with transgression while simultaneously "erecting celebratory queer liberal subjects" complicit with "all sorts of other identity norms, such as nation, race, class, and gender, unwittingly lured onto the ascent toward whiteness" (2007: 24). Both CSE and AO are born from and reproduce White histories and archaeologies of sexuality (Moran, 2000)—histories that are implicated in the ways in which sexualities are racialized and how they can be racialized differently (Barnard, 2004). Expert knowledge within the field of sexuality education is also racialized because of the ways in which it is crafted out of secular understandings of sexuality that are inflected by liberalism (McKay, 1999), rights discourses (Lottes, 2013), and a focus on adolescent sexuality as normative (Tolman & McClelland, 2011).

Such histories have also resulted in popular formations of progressive sexuality education that embrace ideas of the autonomous liberal subject who is a rational decision maker, pleasure seeker, and knowledgeable risk taker. The character of Juno (see Chapter 7) in the eponymous movie is one example of this conflation—she is, in many ways, a celebratory queer subject (White, working class, smart, beautiful, transgressive, and pregnant but not maternal). Juno complicates secular norms because she is a sexually agential teen who can access abortion but chooses instead to go ahead with her pregnancy after seemingly little thought. Juno is queer, secular, and irrational. Somewhat akin to Desai, this is a juxtaposition that troubles familiar associations—there is an expectation that Juno, as a young sexually progressive woman with ready access to abortion will do the rational thing and exercise her right to choose—an abortion.

These configurations of queer secularism resonate for me in conversations I have with peers that may involve religion and pedagogies of sexuality education. The pertinence of these concepts in thinking about progressive norms in sexuality education was brought home while I was at a comedy gig, *Taxis, Rainbows and Hatred*. In the show Tom Ballard (a young, White, gay, Australian comic) ruminates on everyday acts of homophobia that he experiences, focusing especially on the numerous small incidents of homophobia he has experienced in taxis. Ballard also berates homophobic Ugandans, Russians, and Irish Catholics. One lesson conveyed in the show is that being gay is normal in contemporary Australia (Ballard also makes the point that Australia is generally exceptional in its tolerance of gays and lesbians—when compared to places like Uganda and Russia). The audience at the show appeared to connect with this representation of the celebratory queer liberal subject—this type of humor is familiar. Ballard and his representation of Australia and Australian's like him (the audience—this author) are hailed as fellow liberal subjects; we are a part of the fabric of the comedy festival's cultural program.

Ballard relates two stories during the show involving taxi drivers characterized as religious and homophobic. In the first encounter Ballard hails a taxi and the driver, recognizing him (by name) as a gay comic, suggests he pray and refuses to let him in the taxi, leaving him standing in the rain in the middle of the night in a regional town in New South Wales.[2] In the second encounter the driver, pointing to a drag queen outside the taxi, suggests to Ballard that all queers should be placed together, on an island, far away, so they can rot together.

Such incidences of everyday homophobia, while not equivalent, bear some resemblance to many incidences of everyday racism, sexism, and classism—affective responses to these different incidences are always inflected by the actors involved in these encounters and by the formulations that contextualize these actions. The possibility to forge affiliations across difference via some recognition that everyday acts of discrimination have multiple configurations—and that these encounters have different histories, affects and, effects—is not explored in this lesson.

A general lesson of the show appeared to be that those backward religious types can be pretty homophobic, but such intolerance shouldn't stop you from choosing to be yourself in the face of everyday acts of homophobia.

It is likely that this lesson is superfluous. The audience at the show of a well-known *gay* comedian is already on message. Going to the show might mimic many students' and teachers' encounters with progressive sexuality education. For many, an encounter with this style of sexuality education is unremarkable as they are already on message.

For those who do not agree with the message, speaking back to this style of pedagogy can be a difficult task. This performance of sexual exceptionalism left me wondering about the shared pleasures to be found in characterizing certain types of people as backward—which isn't to say that homophobia is unproblematic. Progressive sexuality education, *when it is underpinned by sexual exceptionalism and/or queer secularism*, is not that far removed from Ballard's gig. It inadvertently, teaches young people lessons about who is like *us*—and by virtue of curricular absences—who is not like *us*, the *us* being sexual progressives.

PROGRESSIVE SEXUALITY EDUCATION AND FREEDOM FROM RELIGION

Complex entanglements of sexuality, secularism, and Christianity in the US are examined by Jakobsen and Pellegrini in *Love the Sin: Sexual Regulation and the Limits of Religious Tolerance* (2004). Arguing against calls "for a stricter enforcement of the separation of church and state" (12) Jakobsen and Pellegrini point out that American secularism is not really that secular (13). Divisions between church and state are blurred by the public expressions of religiosity by political figures (every president must affirm his or her religiosity), by the celebration of religious holidays, and by the affirmation afforded religious rituals—marriage being a prime example. Given this reading of the US context, Jakobsen and Pellegrini argue for

> ... more public space for secularism ... We want the freedom not to be religious and the freedom to be religious differently. And we want both these positions to count as the possible basis for moral claims and public policy. (2004: 12–13)

This take on secularism and religion is integral to thinking sexuality education otherwise. Such a style of thought might perceive marriage equality as not distinct from religious discourse but something deeply infused with religious overtones, thereby refusing the characterization of queer and religion as necessarily separate.

Sexuality educators might engage young people in conversations about the value of marriage from diverse religious and secular perspectives—recognizing that both formations are interwoven with moral claims. Such an approach does not discount the important work of identifying and interrogating legal, economic, physical, and political violence experienced by "sexual others" (Puar, 2007: 10) and by "religious others" within and outside the US. This approach may not be perceived as distinct from Lesko's call for open inquiry. To my mind, what distinguishes this approach is its explicit engagement of religion, race, and culture as pertinent to public discussions of sexuality education—but not with a view to demonstrating, once again, how backward religious people are (see Ballard).

Apprehending the ways in which debates about "the political and the religious, the public and the private" (1–3) structure sexuality education also requires an examination of how specific notions of sexual freedom are conditioned by liberalism and poststructural feminism (Scott, 2009). Freedom in sexuality education has been associated with the production of autonomous and agentic sexual subjects (Corngold, 2013). To this end, Josh Corngold has endeavored to articulate a vision of sexuality education that promotes young people's minimalist autonomy, explicitly including cultural, religious, and ethnic attachments as part of his conception of autonomy. He writes:

> ... the conception of minimalist autonomy that I have begun to outline here is not so strong that it requires persons to foreswear close and enduring connections to faith, family, community, and tradition, neither is it so weak that it condones habitual deference or servility. To assert that someone could still count as an autonomous agent whose life decisions and aspirations are largely dictated or controlled by others is to depart grossly from the ordinary usage of the concept. An individual certainly need not abnegate all loyalties, allegiances, and interpersonal ties that bind in order to be considered autonomous. This person must, however, be willing and able, after duly considering various alternatives, to make key judgments and life decisions for him- or herself. (2013: 473)

At the heart of Corngold's approach is the autonomous individual, who can, ideally with the help of schools, parents, and peers "sift through and critically examine discrepant messages to which they are exposed" (465). It is possible to see here a characterization of the sexuality educator's role as to encourage young people "to enact self-determined goals and interests" (Mahmood, 2005: 10). Saba Mahmood perceives such ideas of autonomy and self-determination as central to liberal and progressive feminist thought.

Mahmood doesn't seek to diminish the transformative power of liberal and feminist discourses of autonomy (13), but she is critical of the imaginings of freedom that underpins such discourses. Drawing on liberal theorists distinctions between positive and negative freedom to illustrate the shape of freedom within this imaginary, she writes:

> In short, positive freedom may be best described as the capacity for self-mastery and self-government, and negative freedom as the absence

of restraints of various kinds on one's ability to act as one wants ... *Liberalism's unique contribution is to link the notion of self-realization with individual autonomy.*

(Mahmood, 2005: 10–11, my emphasis)

Feminism and liberalism, in this formulation, prioritize "the ability to autonomously 'choose' one's desires no matter how illiberal they may be" (Mahmood, 2005: 12). Similarly, within the context of sexuality education, there is a prioritization of the right of young people to make their own choices (Corngold, 2013), even if those choices sometimes might not be perceived as wise or healthy choices (Whitehead, 2005). In this imagining of sexual freedom, religion and belief can play a part in sexual decision making, but they are only admissible when they are seen as compatible with the cultivation of autonomous decision making, within the progressive-secular imaginary. This is because custom and tradition, and one might add religion and belief, are seen to impinge on sexual freedom, insofar as they may counter self-sovereignty. Within Corngold's vision for sexuality education, custom and tradition, religion and belief are acceptable as long as they are not perceived as contrary to self-sovereignty or autonomy.

Such conceptualizations of self-sovereignty are, Mahmood argues, apparent in the work of poststructural feminist critiques that have "highlighted the illusory character of the rationalist, self-authorizing, transcendental subject," which secures its authority by "performing a necessary exclusion of all that is bodily, feminine, emotional, and intersubjective (Butler, 1999; Gatens, 1996; Grosz, 1994)" (2005: 13, 14). In the following passage, Mahmood teases out some of the concerns she has with how notions of autonomy and poststructural feminism have produced their own norms:

> ... the normative political subject of poststructuralist feminist theory often remains a liberatory one, whose agency is conceptualized on the binary model of subordination and subversion. In doing so this scholarship elides dimensions of human action whose ethical and political status does not map onto the logic of repression and resistance ... I will suggest that it is crucial to detach the notion of agency from the goals of progressive politics. (2005: 14)

The detachment of notions of agency from progressivism is crucial for Mahmood in her study of devout women in Egypt who are associated with the mosque movement. This maneuver enables her to differently conceptualize practices that might be otherwise read as submissive within a frame informed by feminist poststructuralism.

What would it mean to conceptualize sexuality education without recourse to the binary of subordination and subversion? How might Mahmood's work invite different understandings of sexual agency—that may not be predicated on notions of self-sovereignty? Circumventing the subordination–subversion binary, Mahmood argues that

> the meaning and sense of agency cannot be fixed in advance ... [W]hat may appear to a be a case of deplorable passivity and docility from a progressivist point of view, may actually be a form of agency–but one that can be understood only from within the discourses and structure of subordination that create the conditions of its enactment. In this sense, agentival capacity is entailed not only in those acts that resist norms [queer secularism] but also in the multiple ways in which one *inhabits* norms. (2005: 15)

This detachment of agency from progressivism, articulated by Mahmood, can be instructive for how the sexually agentic subject is understood in the field of sexuality education. If one accepts Mahmood's insistence upon the detachment of progressivism from agency, what matters is not the resistance of norms. Such analysis involves attending to the multiple ways in which norms can be enacted.

Annamarie Jagose (2012) has provided an interesting illustration of this point in her rethinking of women who fake orgasm. Rather than conceptualizing these women as submissive, Jagose seeks to understand the conditions in which the fake orgasm is produced, recognizing that faking it is about much more than submission. Similarly, other sexual practices that may, at first glance appear to the sexuality educator or researcher as passivity or the refusal of self-sovereignty, might on closer inspection, be instructive in reworking familiar understanding of sexual agency. In the field of sexuality education, such a move would require familiar conceptions equating progressivism with agency to come under scrutiny.

CONCLUSION

Sexual exceptionalism and queer secularism are useful concepts in attending to the binaries that underpin progressive discourses of sexuality education. The notion of queer secularism, as I deploy it here, gestures toward particular associations between sexual freedom and autonomy, progressivism, and modernity relating to sexuality education in the US and Australia. I have argued that these associations may be inherently damaging to how comprehensive sexual education is constructed and delivered because they produce a sexuality education that is, in effect, often preaching to the converted. The foreclosure of religion and the normalization of progressivism are, at once, pleasurable and problematic because they reinforce them-and-us binaries. Expanding the reach of comprehensive approaches might necessarily involve questioning attachments to some of the secular norms that sustain progressivism.

NOTES

1. I should add a caveat here that underscores the fact that both comprehensive and abstinence-based approaches teach the value of abstinence.
2. I have no doubt that Ballard's experience with this taxi driver in Newcastle would have been very disturbing, and my intention is not to minimize the gravity of and significance of such acts of homophobia.

REFERENCES

Allen, L. (2004). Beyond the Birds and the Bees: Constituting a Discourse of Erotics in Sexuality Education. *Gender and Education*, 16(2): 151–167.

———. (2012). Pleasure's Perils? Critically Reflecting on Pleasure's Inclusion in Sexuality Education. *Sexualities*, 15(3–4): 455–471.

Barnard, I. (2004). *Queer Race: Cultural Interventions in the Radical Politics of Queer Theory*. New York: Peter Lang.

Cavazos-Rehg, P. A., Krauss, M. J., Spitznagel, E. L., Iguchi, M., Schootman, M., Cottler, L., & Bierut, L. J. (2012). Associations between Sexuality Education in Schools and Adolescent Birthrates: A State-Level Longitudinal Model. *Archives of Pediatric and Adolescent Medicine*, 166(2): 134–140.

Corngold, J. (2013). Moral Pluralism and Sex Education. *Educational Theory*, 63(5): 461–482.

Fields, J. (2008). *Risky Lessons: Sex Education and Social Inequality*. New Brunswick: Rutgers University Press.

Jagose, A. (2012). *Orgasmology*. Durham, North Carolina: Duke University Press.

Jakobsen, J.R., & Pellegrini, A. (2004). *Love the Sin: Sexual Regulation and the Limits of Religious Tolerance*. Boston, Mass.: Beacon Press.

Landry, D.J., Lindberg, L.D., Gemmill, A., Boonstra, H., & Finer, L.B. (2011). Review of the Role of Faith-and Community-Based Organizations in Providing Comprehensive Sexuality Education. *American Journal of Sexuality Education*, 6(1): 75–103.

Lesko, N. (2010). Feeling Abstinent? Feeling Comprehensive? Touching the Affects of Sexuality Curricula. *Sex Education*, 10(3): 281–297.

Lottes, I. L. (2013). Sexual Rights: Meanings, Controversies, and Sexual Health Promotion. *The Journal of Sex Research*, 50(3–4): 367–391.

Mahmood, S. (2005). *Politics of Piety: The Islamic Revival and the Feminist Subject*. Princeton, New Jersey: Princeton University.

McKay, A. (1999). *Sexual Ideology and Schooling: Towards Democratic Sexuality Education*. Albany: State University of New York Press.

Mills, J. (2012). I Should Get Married Early: Culturally Appropriate Comprehensive Sex Education and the Racialization of Somali Masculinity. *Spectrum: A Journal on Black Men*, 1(1): 5–30.

Moran, J.P. (2000). *Teaching Sex: The Shaping of Adolescence in the 20th Century*. Cambridge, Mass.: Harvard University Press.

———. (2003). Sex education and the rise of the new right. *Reviews in American History*, 31(2): 283–289.

Pellegrini, A. (2009). Feeling secular. *Women & Performance: A Journal of Feminist Theory*, 19(2): 205–218.

The Pew Forum on Religion and Public Life. (2007). *Religion in the Public Schools*. Available from http://www.pewforum.org/files/2007/05/religion-public-schools.pdf (Last accessed July 1, 2014).

Puar, J. K. (2007). *Terrorist Assemblages: Homonationalism in Queer Times*. Durham: Duke University Press.

Puar, J.K. (2014). Reading Religion Back into Terrorist Assemblages: Author's Response. *Culture and Religion*, 15(2): 198–210.

Rose, S. (2005). Going Too Far? Sex, Sin and Social Policy. *Social Forces*, 84(2): 1207–1232.

Scott, J.W. (2009, April 23). *Sexularism*. Ursula Hirschman Annual Lecture on Gender and Europe, Florence, Italy.

Stranger-Hall, K. F., & Hall, D. W. (2011). Abstinence-Only Education and Teen Pregnancy Rates: Why We Need Comprehensive Sex Education in the U.S. *PLoS ONE*, 6(10): 1–11.

Taylor, C. (2007). *A Secular Age*. Cambridge, Mass.: Belknap Press.

Tolman, D.L., & McClelland, S.I. (2011). Normative Sexuality Development in Adolescence: A Decade in Review, 2000–2009. *Journal of Research on Adolescence*, 21(1): 242–255.

Whitehead, D. (2005). In pursuit of pleasure: Health education as a means of facilitating the "health journey" of young people. *Health Education*, 105(3): 213–227.

Yang, Z., & Gaydos, L. M. (2010). Reasons for and Challenges of Recent Increases in Teen Birth Rates: A Study of Family Planning Service Policies and Demographic Changes at the State Level. *Journal of Adolescent Health*, 46(6): 517–524.

3 Sexuality Education in Public Schools in Australia and Aotearoa-New Zealand

Mary Lou Rasmussen and Fida Sanjakdar, Monash University; Kathleen Quinlivan, University of Canterbury, Christchurch, New Zealand; Louisa Allen, University of Auckland, New Zealand; Annette Bromdal, University of Southern Queensland; Clive Aspin, Independent Researcher, Sydney, Australia.

> Because the secular is so much part of our modern life, it is not easy to grasp it directly.
>
> (Asad, 2003: 16)

A particular focus of this chapter is public schools in Australia and Aotearoa-New Zealand, drawing on research on cultural and religious difference in sexuality education. Data was collected in four schools, two in each country. Our focus is on culturally and religiously diverse public schools because these are sites where young people from many backgrounds will necessarily come together, and there is no expectation that the curriculum will serve students from a particular group. In choosing this focus we also reasoned that attention to diversity should be a fundamental characteristic of sexuality education as many young people approach adulthood faced with conflicting and confusing messages about sexuality and gender (UNESCO, 2009). Our research illustrates that some young people did perceive conflict—or happy clashes—between the curriculum and what they understood about sexuality, as learned at home and in their peer groups, while other participants perceived the curriculum as in alignment with the values they learned at home. Altogether, our research indicates contemporary school-based sexuality education in Australia and Aotearoa-New Zealand fails to address effectively cultural and religious difference (Sanjakdar, 2009a; Jackson, 2004; Singh, 2001). This tendency to avoid questions of religion and culture in sexuality education is compounded in Australia and Aotearoa-New Zealand by perceived tensions that teachers and students feel are generated by conversations about cultural and religious diversity, particularly within the public sphere (Goldman, 2008; Rasmussen, Mitchell and Harwood, 2007). Failure to consider cultural and religious difference in sexuality education in public schools can result in a rejection of government initiatives in this area and ultimately reduce program effectiveness (Lidstone and Wilmett, 2008).

In this chapter we adapt Jakobsen and Pellegrini's (2008) discussion of key elements that they see as implicated in the "process known as secularization" (4) to consider how they manifest in sexuality education. These elements include rationalization, enlightenment, separation of church and state, freedom, privatization, universalism, and finally, modernization and progress. This analysis will illustrate how these elements of secularization infiltrate research, classroom conversations, and students' own imaginings of sexuality education. First we give some background about the study and three of the schools in which the study was located. These schools are the principal focus of data analysis in this chapter. We then consider these sites in relation to the elements of secularism identified by Jakobsen and Pellegrini (2008).

PUBLIC SCHOOL, SEXUALITY EDUCATION, AND CULTURAL AND RELIGIOUS DIFFERENCE

The schools chosen for the study varied significantly in terms of socioeconomic composition, but they were all coeducational public secondary schools with diverse populations in terms of ethnicity and religious difference. Observations were conducted in sexuality education classrooms over two years[1] (2011–2012). Where possible, we observed the same cohort of students. We also conducted individual interviews with participating students in these classrooms and focus groups. Interviews were conducted with teachers but only in Aotearoa-New Zealand. This chapter draws primarily on data from three locations listed in more detail below.

Central High[2] is located in inner suburban Melbourne, in an area that has experienced high levels of gentrification. Increases in house prices have changed the student demographic and the school curriculum. The school has a highly sought-after gifted and talented program, strong international links as well as music and drama programs. The school also celebrates Rainbow Day each year. On this day there are many of pro-gay posters around the school. In terms of religious diversity, Australian Bureau of Statistics (ABS) data demonstrate that 40 percent of students in this community come from families that identify with no religion, while 40 percent come from Christian backgrounds (predominantly Catholic and Eastern Orthodox). The number of students from families designated as having no religion is significantly above the Australian average. ABS data reports that, on average, 31 percent of students in high schools are listed as having no religion.[3]

Devondale High[4] is located on Melbourne's outer fringe. The suburb in which it is located is about 20 years old with a lot of new immigrant families. The ABS classifies the community as having low to middle socioeconomic status. Unlike Central High, the community of Devondale High is predominantly associated with some religion, according to census data, with approximately 40 percent of students identifying with Christianity, while approximately 30 percent of families in this community identify as Islamic. Both Central High and Devondale High had small populations of Buddhist students (between 2 and 4 percent).

Pacific High, located in an urban center in Aotearoa-New Zealand is a decile[5] four school with a mixed population in terms of socioeconomic status. The school's largest ethnic groups are Maori and Pasifika, though it also has a number of NZ European/Pakeha[6] students as well as new immigrant families from Africa, the Middle East and Southeast Asia. A significant proportion of Maori and Pasifika students identify as Christian.

We now turn to a discussion of how conversations about sexuality education are constructed within the public school classrooms we observed. Given the small number of schools in which we were able to observe, we are clearly not able to make any generalization about the relationship between public schools and the sexuality education curriculum, nor would we wish to generalize about how sexuality education is enacted. Indeed, the complexity of the enactments of sexuality education experienced by the young people within this research, within and across the specific locations studied, underscores the difficulties of making generalizations about sexuality education provision.

RATIONALITY AND THE SEPARATION OF CHURCH AND STATE IN SEXUALITY EDUCATION

> With the evolution of knowledge comes the possibility of differentiating specific tasks into different sections of society, so that, for example, the functions of the church can be separated from those of the state.
>
> (Jakobsen and Pellegrini, 2008: 5)

This quote refers to what Jakobsen and Pellegrini call *social-structural differentiation*, the understanding that certain sorts of knowledge are properly performed within specific contexts. For instance, during the second focus group at Central High, Rasmussen raised the topic of teaching about abstinence as part of sexuality education.[7] Dirk, one of the students in the focus group, strongly argued that abstinence was only acceptable as a topic in sexuality education if a solid evidence base could support this curriculum. In taking this stance Dirk constitutes evidence as important in the field of sexuality education, especially within the context of public schooling. But, for Dirk, this is different in Christian schools, where he thought conversations about abstinence might be admissible. In the research conducted for this study, different students viewed public schools quite distinctly in terms of social-structural differentiation and the types of knowledge that they perceived as admissible in the public sphere.

> **Dirk (Focus Group 2: Central High, May 2012):** But still I think that any school their responsibility is that scientific facts matter, it's not morals and if this . . . organisation [promoting abstinence education] say we want to teach this at your [public] school then . . . before they accept them [the school] should consider right you need to prove that abstinence is the best course for a variety of reasons, it has to be backed up by solid evidence and we have decided this is definitely going to be the best and safest option . . .
>
> I would like to come back to my other argument that something like this because obviously abstinence has a lot of connections to the Christianity so at schools like that then maybe something like that could get across but in a public school there are so many different ethnic just groups in general that they have to focus on things like more evidence of that rather than belief.

Dirk perceives sexuality education as having a specific function within the public school. He perceives belief, specifically beliefs related to abstinence, as something that may be appropriate at a Christian school. However, he perceives public schools as needing to distance themselves from beliefs and morals. He rationalizes this claim based on the assumption that there are many ethnic groups in public schools—and presumably many beliefs about sexuality, and therefore evidence needs to triumph over belief. He also sees evidence about sexuality as needing to be supported by science (not morals or belief) because he perceives this as "the best and safest option." On the contrary, belief is something he perceives as acceptable in a religious school because such schools bring together students on the basis of belief.

How did Dirk develop these beliefs about the place of religious and cultural difference in sexuality education? He seems quite sure that he is on firm ground when he underscores public schools' responsibility to teach the "scientific facts of the matter." Dirk perceives the public school as performing its duty responsibly when it dispenses authoritative pronouncements about sexuality. Drawing on the work of Michel Foucault, Michael Warner (2009) contemplates the role of professors, teachers, and other experts in making pronouncements about sexuality and how these pronouncements determine how sex and sexuality enter the public sphere. Warner (2009) argues that sexuality studies and education about sexuality are often constructed as part of the broader scientific study of populations. It is this association that conditions how expertise about sexuality is authorized and received via attachments to scientificity and evidence—it is this association that appears to underpin Dirk's objection to the appearance of abstinence-based approaches in sexuality education in the public school. Sexuality education, when it is associated in these participants' minds and in curricula with particular types of scientific expertise, thus becomes part of the process of secularization. Students and teachers may see sexuality education as a secular endeavor, especially when located in the public school context, precisely because it is so often constituted as part of the rationalization of certain types of knowledge designed to secure the health of the population and therefore ensure progress (Warner, 2009).

The relationship between sex and secularism is long-standing, but as Warner (2009) points out, secularism has not featured prominently as an area of analysis in sexuality studies. Warner also suggests conflicts between the secular and the religious (a common theme in research on sexuality education) have averted attention from the ways in which sexuality and religion are interrelated. Mark Halstead and Michael Reiss in their book *Values in Sex Education: From Principles to Practice* (2003) also consider the relationship among religion, secularism and sexuality education. They reject the idea that "a Christian perspective on sex education is wholly distinct from a secular one; [they also reject the idea] that a Christian perspective differs only marginally, if at all, from a secular one" (112). By looking at young people's experiences of sexuality education through the frame of cultural and religious difference, we hope to better grasp how sexuality and religion are seen as interrelated and distinct in sexuality education provision in public schools.

In the second focus group Rasmussen conducted at Central High, she decided to raise the topic of arranged marriage in the context of a recent court case in which a 14-year-old girl had appealed to the family court to have her overseas trip cancelled on the grounds that she was going to be married to a 17-year-old man she had not met. We reasoned that this case, which pertained to a girl who was the same age as our participants, might act as a lever for the consideration of how religion might be something of value to discuss in sexuality education, even if only terms of consent. When Rasmussen raised the issue of arranged marriage as a possible subject for discussion within the context of sexuality education, Daniel offered that he had indeed studied this topic at Central High. But he notes that it was introduced to students in the subject of humanities under the banner of human rights. The transcript that follows illustrates how Daniel compartmentalized different types of knowledge by placing conversations about a topic, such as arranged marriage, as outside the bounds of sexuality education:

> Mary: Lou Rasmussen (MLR) (Focus Group 2: Central High, May 2012): So should schools teach about issues on something like arranged marriages, do you think like it's important to have that conversation about that sort of thing at school?
> Daniel: Well we have sort of touched on it when we did humanities this year, when we were doing human rights.

MLR: Can you tell me about what you did?
Daniel: Well that was just one of the issues which we touched on very briefly. It was one of the major topics because we had to write an essay on a certain area of children's rights and I spent a lot of time writing about this, so I know quite a lot on this . . .
MLR: So you have done it in other classes, not in sex education?
Daniel: Not in sex ed no . . . they kind of leave something like this to . . . humanities where it talks about rights as a human being.
MLR: So do you think that this should be covered in sexuality education as well, should it be a part of sexuality education, conversations around stuff like this?
Daniel: It doesn't have much to do with sexuality really. Yeah I would say it's more of a humanities subject, it's someone's rights, it's for a law subject, I wouldn't say it has as much to do with this [sexuality education] because there are all sorts of things you could, like I don't think it's really that relevant, no . . . I think technically it could be touched on, sexual education, but as a main topic it seems to suit better in something like humanities.
MLR: Why are you making that distinction?
Daniel: In my view, I am speaking for all of us here, this isn't really about sort of relationships as such, this is more about sort of cultural and theological and also sort of what decisions what sort of your opinion matters . . . I think a lot more could be learnt and understood about these issues if they were addressed as cultural issues and social issues rather than a sexual issue.

At least for Daniel, it appears that sexuality education is not the location for discussion of cultural issues and social issues. Sexuality education is about sexual issues. In other words, sexuality education is about evidence, not belief or opinion. Conversations about arranged marriages that touch on cultural and theological issues, where opinions matter, are not the stuff of sexuality education. Daniel seeks to make this distinction, we would argue, for the same reasons that Dirk argues that sexuality education needs to be evidence based and not about beliefs or morals. Both Daniel and Dirk see sexuality education at Central High through the frames of rationalization and social-structural differentiation. This is why sexuality education is perceived by these participants to be about evidence and decidedly not about matters of opinion. It is also why they think it is OK to discuss theological and cultural issues at their public schools in the humanities but not in the context of sexuality education. They are differentiating curriculum spaces according to different types of expertise and according to their beliefs about sexuality education and its relationship to evidence. The differentiation that goes on in this conversation is of interest in the context of this book because it illustrates the depth of processes of secularization. The 13- and 14-year-old boys in this discussion group have sophisticated understandings of how sexuality education should be structured within the context of a public school. This informs their perception of different types of knowledge production within different curriculum and schooling contexts.

FREEDOM AND THE PRIVATIZATION OF RELIGION IN THE SEXUALITY EDUCATION CLASSROOM

In the narrative of secularism, outlined by Jakobsen and Pellegrini (2008), they perceive freedom as autonomy and separation from religious authority. They argue that to be autonomous, within a secular framework, is to be free from religion. Jakobsen and Pellegrini (2008) also associate secular conceptions of freedom with the privatization of religion because "in the modern, secular, and enlightened world, religion is contained in the private sphere of personal belief" (5). In three of the four sexuality education classrooms that we observed in the Australian and Aotearoa-New Zealand contexts, explicit discussions of religion were absent. In one of the sites in Aotearoa-New Zealand, a teacher invited sexuality educators into the classroom who utilized an abstinence-based approach—and no reference to nonnormative sexualities.

Participants who identified as having no religion did not tend to see the absence of religion as a problem. Participants, who identified as religious and as having no religion, saw the absence of religion as productive or, alternatively, just the way things are. One participant, Ada, who came from a background with strong religious affiliations perceived the Aotearoa-New Zealand context as predominantly Christian (the public school she attended utilized sexuality educators who adopted a Christian perspective).

Ada appears to be open to the idea of learning about other cultures in the context of sexuality education at her public school:

> Louisa: Allen (Individual Interview, Pacific High, May 2012): What information about different religions and cultures would you like to learn about in sex education class? Would you want to hear about other cultures, apart from, I guess, the dominant Pakeha/Palagi[8]/European one, which is what you get, don't you?
>
> Ada: Right. Yeah, it would be great for general knowledge and that. It would be great. We've got the global village in this century. It would be good to be aware of other places, but for me I guess I don't really need it. At school I've got it everywhere. I've got friends at mosque from [my home country] and this place and that place. I'm very exposed to their cultures. That's fun. That's very fun.

Ada is open to the possibilities that may be present in learning about cultural and religious difference in sexuality education. She also sees learning about other ways of thinking about sexuality education as useful because she perceives general knowledge about sexuality as part of the context of thinking about society as a "global village." But Ada also perceives the need for this as somewhat redundant, given the diversity she experiences both at school (Pacific High is a very multicultural school) and in the classes she attends at mosque on weekends. At her mosque Ada is exposed to conversations about sexuality and cultural difference because of contact with people from diverse cultural groups. For example, while attending mosque she discussed arranged marriages with her peers from different cultural backgrounds. We see potential benefits for young people's general knowledge, and for social cohesion, in having spaces to engage in education about sexuality that explicitly engages with cultural and religious differences. Interestingly though, Ada did not want to publically engage with others at her school about her religion and culture—in case they got it wrong.

Zina, a participant at Devondale High in Melbourne, perceives a disjuncture between what she learns at home and what she learns at school, with the latter being a more scientific approach to sexuality. But Zina doesn't appear to see the privatization of religion as a problem, reasoning that she receives appropriate education regarding how to behave with regard to religion from her parents:

> Zina: (Individual interview Devondale High, June 2012): I guess it's the religious part that is making what that person's told at school thinking okay that's what I'm hearing at home but I'm learning something different at school, this is more scientifically, more like information and facts but this side is more like beliefs and stuff so usually children or kids or teenagers like our age listen to what the parents say usually. Some of them actually take in both sides and think okay that's what I think is right so that's what I believe and think is true but some teenagers are okay I'm confused.
> Fida: Sanakdar (FS): Is it fair for me to say you come from a religious background?
> Zina: I do come from a religious background.
> FS: Do you think learning about sex education from your religious background is important?
> Zina: In a way it is because I really care about my religion and the reputation my religion has. So I'll do what is right but I wouldn't go far you know. Like I'll have my religion in the background of the thing but I'll still take in what I'm told because I think that is right so I'll do what I think is right, what I feel comfortable in and actually in the manner how it's told to me . . .
> FS: Do you find it important for you and useful to learn about the people's religion and their perspectives on sex education?

Zina: I guess it is actually a good topic to discuss because it'll be, because maybe people that have that feeling inside of them will be able to speak up in a conversation like that and feel free to talk about what might have confused them at some stage and maybe what their religion thinks of stuff and how that changes their thoughts around this topic.

In thinking about the place of religion in sexuality education at school, Zina and Ada suggest that religion is not a part of their official classroom conversations. This is noteworthy insofar as both these schools include large proportions of students who identify as coming from religious backgrounds.

Ada is explicit about the possible benefits of bringing discussions of religion into the sexuality education context. Zina sees some potential for conversations where students "feel free to talk," but for Zina this freedom to speak about religion is not seen as a way of gaining freedom from religious authority. Zina keeps the potential for children to think differently from parents open, but she also says children should first listen to their parents. Sometimes she concedes young people may be confused (presumably when knowledge from diverse sources is conflicting), but *usually* (not always) they will listen to their parents. In response to Sanjakdar's question, Zina also appears to wonder if the sexuality education classroom could be a place where students might change their thoughts about sexuality or at least express their confusion between messages learned at home and at school. Although, Zina is careful not to portray herself as confused, and she suggests that she prioritizes the messages of her parents over the facts that she learns at school.

Our observations suggest that the place of religion in sexuality education, at least in these few contexts, was marginal. For Ada, the opportunity to learn about religion in sexuality education would be educative, but is certainly not necessary, and may even be problematic at a public school, which she perceives as predominantly a Christian space. For Zina, opening up space for discussions of religion could be educative—but at the present moment she feels that the sexuality education classroom is not open to conversations about sexuality and belief and rather perceives sexuality education as scientific. Neither Ada nor Zina questions the privatization of religion in their public schools, although they both identify as religious. They may take comfort in the privatization of religion (see Ada's previous comments), and/or they might have learned that religion (or, more precisely, their religion) is something that does not belong in a public school and is better left to spaces outside the school (home or mosque).

In the interviews and focus groups discussed, it is also possible to see what David Seitz refers to as the "performativity of secular freedom" (Seitz, 2014: 85). This performativity crafts participants as understanding public schools as secular places. This is an understanding all these participants have learned; in this way secularism is performative in these young people's lives. It frames their understandings of the relationship between schooling and sexuality through sedimented understandings about the privatization of belief. The participants didn't question the proposition that public schools are spaces that are free of religion—indeed for some participants who identified as religious, this belief was something of a relief. It meant that while at school, they were not expected to enter into dialogues about their religion and thus run the risk of their beliefs being misapprehended, willfully or otherwise. However, some of the young people we interviewed were open to suggestions of other ways of conceptualizing sexuality education. Ada thinks that the opportunity to learn about other culture's views on sexuality would be worthwhile.

In bringing the second focus group at Central High to a close, Rasmussen asked her participants what, if anything, they like would to see more of in their sexuality education classroom. In what we recognize as something of an about-face, which may well be prompted by these gifted learners' desire to please the researcher and get it right (see Quinlivan, forthcoming)—they brought the focus group to a close in the following exchange:

> Rasmussen: (Focus Group 2: Central High, May 2012): What do you want?
> Dirk: I would be very happy, I would quite like to do more cultural stuff, I was saying before that this forced marriage wouldn't fit in to what we do at the moment at all, as it's completely different train of thinking, but if they are re-writing the curriculum I think we should definitely have some more in-depth cultural analysis of issues.
> Daniel: Yes, cultural issues.
> Arthur: And just rather [than] learning that this is ok and this is bad and just have more discussion have a look at it from these sort of perspectives
> James: Yeah how sex is viewed from different cultures and different people.
> Rasmussen: Do you really think you would find this interesting, or are you just saying that to make me happy?
> Dirk: No, it would [be] more interesting. We would find it more interesting. Honestly I would.
> Rasmussen: You would find it more interesting?
> Dirk: Currently the audience finds it completely boring and won't listen to a word.

As stated, we do have some skepticism about this seemingly last-minute conversion to a sexuality education that is more open to conversations about cultural difference. We are clear that we are setting the agenda by doing a project that is framing these issues as important, and the participants in this interaction are clearly picking up on our own agenda in framing this research. We also note that the notion of religion is still unspeakable for these participants at Central High, even as it is somewhat alluded to via the reference to arranged marriage.

We do believe that these incredibly articulate young participants could benefit from a more intellectually engaging sexuality education. Albert, in the first focus group at Central High states, "Well, I'm not really interested in the subject so I don't think I'd have many questions to ask. I don't really care about it." He goes on to assure us he does care about sex—just not the contents of the curriculum. Julie, the only female participant at Central High stated that "in high school [what we learnt] . . . was pretty similar to primary school but I guess that's just because some people learnt different stuff . . . they're not really teaching us much new stuff, going out and stuff." Sexuality education may have the capacity to engage students in complicated conversations that incorporate religious and cultural difference. Such conversations could extend students, religious and nonreligious alike, helping them to think about other ways of imagining relationships, culture, religion, sexuality and their relationships to sexual and religious freedom in public and private spaces. Such conversations could also easily go awry, othering students, particularly students who are religious but not Christian, who voice positions that are perceived as anathema to sexual progressivism.

ENLIGHTENMENT IDEALS AND DEMOCRATIC SEXUALITY EDUCATION

Charles Taylor helps us to clarify the power of secular reason in shaping discourse. He argues:

> Secular reason is a language that everyone speaks, and can argue and be convinced in. Religious languages operate outside of this discourse, by introducing extraneous premises which only believers can accept. So let's all talk the common language.
> . . . Religious reason either comes to the same conclusions as secular reason, but then it is superfluous; or it comes to contrary conclusions, and then it is dangerous and disruptive. This is why it needs to be sidelined. (Taylor, 2008, para. 2 and 3)

This notion of a common language of secular reason informs our discussion of the relationship between secularization, Enlightenment ideals, and democratic imaginings of sexuality education. We recognize common languages being formed within sexuality education that value the place of reason while often troubling the place of religion.

In the *Sex Education Debates*, Nancy Kendall makes these connections explicit, arguing that CSE's

> ... understanding of LGBTQ identities is based on a rationalist ideology that claims to eschew values and embrace science as an unbiased and objective standard for categorizing identities. Though this ideology is itself shaped by and reflects a core set of Enlightenment ideals, it views itself as aiming for objective, value-free, complete and correct scientific information. (2013: 186)

Kendall goes on to identify these Enlightenment ideals as about "truth, justice and individual rights" (226). Kendall recognizes that Enlightenment ideals, fundamental to CSE, are political and ideological.

This view is supported by Alexander McKay, a Canadian scholar, in his book *Sexual Ideology and Schooling: Towards Democratic Sexuality Education* (1999). McKay writes:

> Although the future is uncertain, as it always is in a democracy, we can be confident that if it is critical deliberation and respect for democratic principles that takes us forward, the future will be bright. The rigid imposition of sexual ideology, so long the modus operandi of Western culture, is the author of ignorance, unhappiness, and oppression. Extending the basic principles of democracy to sexuality can advance our culture in significant ways. (1999: 192)

In McKay's reckoning a "democratic sexual landscape" provides the "freedom [to] consciously make knowledgeable choices and respect the rights of others to pursue their own conception of the good life" (191). This argument does resemble a position Rasmussen is taking throughout this book, that sexuality education can be enriched through stronger engagements with diverse religious perspectives.[9] But McKay's conception of a democratic sexuality education is also associated with a belief in the free pursuit of reason, based on knowledge that is not constrained by a particular ideology (permissive or restrictive—to use his characterization). The faith that McKay places in this vision for a democratic sexuality education appears to us to be a product of what Mahmood (2005) terms "the progressive secular imaginary" (2005: xi). It doesn't attend to the ways in which religious discourses are sidelined from this democratic sexual landscape.

Religion does have a role to play in the democratic sexuality education McKay envisages, but religion is necessarily subsumed within the framework of democratic principles. McKay believes in the value of democratic principles in developing sexuality education. But the ideological nature of these democratic principles is not the subject of robust scrutiny in McKay's argument. McKay frames sexuality education debates as ideological—permissive or restrictive—but he does not appear to associate ideology with the Enlightenment itself or associated beliefs in the value of democracy. Different ideologies of sexuality education should be debated, he argues, but when ideologies differ, democratic principles should prevail (1999: 190). As discussed further in Chapter 4 and Chapter 8, this way of seeing secularism (which is aligned with a particular valorization of democratic principles) is perceived to transcend cultural and religious difference, enabling democratic sexuality education to purportedly stand above the fray as arbiter of sexual freedom. Or, in McKay's own words, "[P]olitical liberalism is interested only in preserving the right of individuals to exercise their reason under the conditions of freedom" (123).

Here we part with McKay's Rawlsian-inspired liberalism because we are not confident that "critical deliberation and respect for democratic principles" will guarantee a brighter future or conditions of freedom. Democracy here is situated above ideology, and this belief is underpinned by the idea that deliberation can beget consensus. In this way of seeing, as Charles Taylor points out, "[R]eligious languages operate outside this discourse by introducing extraneous premises that only believers can accept" (2008: para. 2). McKay sees democracy as able to arbitrate questions of religion because "[i]t perhaps goes without saying that, at their very essence, religious beliefs are a matter of faith rather than of concrete observations about the material world" (1999: 104). In this way of seeing, matters of faith—that are constructed as only pertinent to believers—must be subsumed to democratic principles because the latter are based on evidence, and therefore, unlike faith, are equally applicable to all.

We also associate McKay's democratic approach with the belief that effective sexuality education should aim to increase young people's sexual autonomy, concomitantly liberating them from antidemocratic ideologies, whether they be permissive or restrictive. McKay's democratic vision for sexuality education is a progress narrative in which people of different beliefs "have the right to toleration and autonomy with respect to sexual values" (1999: 127). For Jakobsen and Pellegrini, such faith in the value of autonomy is constituted as one of the hallmarks of sexual progressivism:

> If over time secularization allows societies to increase in autonomy, the secularization implies progress, whereas the continuation (or, still worse, the reassertion) of religion maintains constraint and implies stasis or even regression. This temporal division implies a simultaneous moral division. Those societies that are "ahead" are also understood to be "better"—more rational and freer, for example—than those that are "behind." (2008: 6)

We want to push back against McKay's democratic vision for sexuality education, partially because we are not convinced by the value of more secularization (which is implicit within McKay's approach). Like McKay, we understand that religion has a role to play in sexuality education, but we also see this role as highly constrained within McKay's vision because we believe religious beliefs are too easily set aside within a democratic approach—because they can always be dismissed as pertinent only to people of a specific faith.

The distinctions McKay draws between permissive and restrictive approaches have become increasingly murky for us in the course of this research. This also seems to be the case for our participants when they are describing their own attitudes regarding the place of religion in discussions of sexuality education. For instance, in the following excerpt, a participant at Pacific High who identifies as Muslim constructs certain religious ideas as backward:

> Louisa: Allen (LA) (Individual Interview, Pacific High, June 2012): Should schools teach about the issue of arranged marriages?
> Chana: I think that happens somewhere in the Middle East. That would be—that's part of the cultural backwardness. We're told not to force our girls, but they still do it, some still do it.
> LA: What should schools teach about the issue of arranged marriage then? What should they say?
> Chana: That's kind of hard now, because it's like a private, culturalised thing. But I think—I mean, initiatively human-wise we all know that arranged marriage is wrong if no one wants to do it. Or if the girl and the guy are happy with it, then it shouldn't be an issue. As a human, I think we all know that. Otherwise, I don't know what the school should say, because it's an uncomfortable topic. I don't think, me as a teacher, if I was a teacher, I wouldn't want to be comfortable with informing it when there's so many different people in the class . . .
> LA: Do you think students need to be exposed to discussions of such topics?
> Chana: Possibly, yes.

To our minds Chana's ambivalence regarding the introduction of conversations about arranged marriage can be seen as productive. It suggests a way of explicitly introducing conversations about sexuality that incorporate religion and culture. It may also be useful to incorporate conversations that involve discussion of different types of issues associated with marriage within the same context (marriage equality, arranged marriage, or marriage and divorce), as well as thinking explicitly about the links between ideas on marriage and their relationship to notions of progress, enlightenment, and modernity. This excerpt from the interview with Chana also illustrates the difficulties of determining just what is secular and what is religious and how this might properly relate to our sexuality and our sexuality education.

Chana appears to be ambivalent about the subject of arranged marriage. In the exchange she describes it as culturally backward [when it happens somewhere in the Middle East] but also something that is acceptable if done with the consent of participants. She says arranged marriage is private but also suggests that "possibly" conversations about such things have a place in the sexuality education classroom. She worries that the topic would be uncomfortable for the teacher, though we suspect that she is also concerned that such topics might be uncomfortable for her and for her peers. This discomfort might be associated with her feelings of ambivalence about this subject. This discomfort might also reflect increasing levels of harassment of people who are identifiably religious (these levels of harassment that have been further ignited at time of writing by current conflicts in Israel, Gaza, Iraq and Syria).

The significance of arranged marriage as a potential topic for discussion in the sexuality education classroom is underscored by research undertaken by Saeeda Shah and Catherine Conchar in the UK. They argue:

> ... Co-education is perceived as a threat to arranged marriages as it may open other venues of thought and options. The girls in co-education may choose to exercise personal choices, defying collective decisions ... A marriage is perceived as a collective rather than an individual matter. In fact, arranged marriages are not always simply organised by parents, but are often decided under huge pressures from extended families and bradaris [community]. In the collective cultures of these societies, underpinned by the network of arranged marriages, parents often have difficulty in questioning bradari authority (Basit, 1995). (2009: 200).

This research appears to reflect some of the ambivalence voiced by Chana in the interview with Allen. From the perspective of sexuality education, Shah and Conchar's research is instructive insofar as it illustrates how marriage may be seen as something that is first and foremost a collective decision rather than an individual choice. How might discussions about choice and consent in sexuality education take account of arranged marriage in such a way that recognizes that the participants might be somewhere in between—happy and consenting or unhappy and un-consenting? How, for instance, are notions of sexual autonomy to be understood in relation to marriages that are arranged via collective decision making? Can people participating in these types of arranged marriages ever be understood as sexually agentic within the frame of progressive sexuality education? Are such arrangements backward and antidemocratic? Are they the ultimate expression of a democratic sexuality education?

In a small qualitative study titled "Constructions and Experiences of Sexual Health Among Young, Heterosexual, Unmarried Muslim Women Immigrants in Australia," Anneke Wray, Jane Ussher, and Janette Perz (2014) employ a feminist discourse analysis to consider some of the complexities of delivering a sexual health education (within a comprehensive framework) to this particular target group. This group was identified by the researchers as having particularly poor sexual health outcomes combined with reluctance to access sexual and reproductive health services. In conducting this study, the researchers "identified 'purity versus corruption' as the primary construction [the participants utilized to apprehend sexuality], where women positioned their sexual behaviour as that of purity and uninvolvement or corruption through unwedded participation" (76). Wray et al. also note that the lack of sexuality education could not necessarily be held to account for these women's sexual health outcomes as

> . . . many of the women in the present study reported adequate education on sexual health due to many years of schooling within the Australian education system. Thus, poor sexual health knowledge and application is not related to the inability to attain information within the Australian education or healthcare system, *but more closely linked to community regulations and the woman's self-policing.* This confirms previous reports that culture and religion is an important factor influencing women's sexual self-understandings, for both Muslim and Christian minority ethnic migrants (Khoei, Whelan, and Cohen 2008; Rawson and Liamputtong 2010; Ussher et al. 2012). (2014: 86, my emphasis)

All the participants in this study by Wray et al. (2014) are unmarried university students without children (97). At the outset these young women are constructed as enlightened because they are clearly successful students and presumably capable of rational decision making. They conclude their study observing that these young women have clearly not learned the lessons of their adequate sexuality education. Wray et al. appear to be linking religious affiliation, and being an immigrant, with poor sexual health outcomes and diminished capacity for self-sovereignty with regards to sexuality. Such research is endeavoring to identify an important problem, namely poor sexual health outcomes for a group of minority women.

Faced with the conundrum presented by these educated women who refuse to act on sexual knowledge to advance their health outcomes, Wray et al. suggest:

> A major challenge for future sexual-health research is to identify the discourses and material practices behind this resistance to sexual-health knowledge, in order to facilitate sexually-healthy behaviour without the psychological and emotional consequences that are associated with fallen woman[10] status (Hirschman, Impett, and Schooler 2006; Lees 1993). (2014: 86)

The value of the sexual health knowledge being presented to these women does not appear to be the main object of inquiry as a result of this research. Rather, Wray et al. argue these Muslim women need to be dissociated from the negative associations that adhere to the label "fallen woman" to achieve "sexually-healthy behaviour." A line is drawn here between sexually healthy behavior and rejection of fallen women status. This immediately sets up tensions as well as obfuscates the potential health benefits of these women's cultural, religious, and familial affiliations and attachments.

How is it possible to attend to the sexual health of these women without constituting religion as repressive? Sexuality education, in research and practice, has to resist the temptation to argue that

> ... freedom from religion is the answer to the problem. This traditional view plays into the larger Enlightenment narrative in which freedom from religion brings about human liberation. In contrast to this view, however, I argue that our problem is as much secular freedom as it is religious regulation.
>
> (Jakobsen, 2005: 286).

For Janet Jakobsen, freedom is intrinsic to the exercise and imaginings of religion and sexuality. But freedom is always already marked by certain religious and secular imaginings. We cannot imagine sexual freedom as outside or somehow detached from politics, class, culture, religion, and nation. Taking this perspective, it is important to interrogate narratives of the "fallen woman" and to consider how they might regulate participants' or students' sexual freedom. It is also important to interrogate how secular beliefs constitute a powerful competing vision of sexual freedom that might not fully apprehend how fallen woman status mediates women's sexual health.

If cultural and religious differences are intrinsic to how some young people are navigating their sexual lives, ignoring this significance in school-based sexuality education curriculum runs the risk of this education being seen as irrelevant—this seems to be borne out in Wray et al.'s research. These young women, it is noted, have been exposed to a comprehensive sexuality education. The findings from this research project focus on these young women's reticence to take on board the lessons they've learned. Maybe the focus needs to shift to the adequacy of the education they received. Does this sexuality education fathom how these young women understand and enact their sexuality? These findings might prompt the need for sexuality educators and sexuality education curricula that is mindful of these women's sexual decision making and knowledge and how this is related to piety, faith, and belonging. This is recognition that sexual knowledge and sexually healthy behaviors are always things to be negotiated within specific sets of material, moral, ethical, and spiritual conditions.

NO APOLOGIES: UNIVERSALISM AND ABSTINENCE AT CENTRAL HIGH

As part of the second focus group at Central High, Rasmussen played an excerpt from a promotional video advertising the *No Apologies* sexuality education curriculum to participants. *No Apologies*, produced by Focus on the Family Australia,[11] is described on the organization's website as a character-based abstinence education program. The participants at Central High were highly critical of the abstinence-based message depicted in the *No Apologies* video.

> Mary: Lou Rasmussen (MLR) (Focus Group 2: Central High, May 2012): And so what do you think about No Apologies's claim that abstinence until marriage is the best and healthiest sexual decision for teenagers?
> Daniel: Sorry I just can't help laughing, I mean what do you always see on TV shows and stuff, it's like, if they ever mention abstinence? Like someone said isn't that a wedding ring, so it's like, how blessed it was after marriage. I found that abstinence in TV shows they just kind of make fun of it.
> MLR: Look I agree, like I don't think that many people take abstinence very seriously in Australia. I think that's a fair comment. So have you come across any messages like any abstinence messages that people have tried to deliver seriously to you?
> Arthur: No, not at school no.
> MLR: Not at school?
> James: I think that we have probably seen similar messages.
> Arthur: Yeah, that's what I was thinking. But I mean it's just the way that people have been brought up. It's kind of like ok abstinence, huh, that's really stupid. We all do meth here.

The participants at Central High constitute the idea of abstinence education, at least as imagined in Focus on the Family's *No Apologies* video, as laughable. We found Arthur's comment particularly interesting insofar as he portrays the message of abstinence as something you could only really take on board if you were the type of person who was stupid enough to take drugs (meth). The assumption here is that abstinence is really only an option for stupid people.

Debates about abstinence education in public schools have come to Australia, but abstinence-based education has not shared similar government support to that received in the US context. Abstinence education is being taught in some publicly funded Christian schools where staff make the decision to contract the services of sexuality education providers[12] such as those utilizing *No Apologies*. Public schools also use external groups who utilize an abstinence-based message to deliver sexuality education in the Australian context (it is apparent that this has also been the case in some Canadian provinces—see Chapter 8). It is not possible to determine the number of public schools that utilize abstinence-based approaches as this information is not available in the public domain. In Aotearoa-New Zealand we do know that groups utilizing abstinence-based approaches are regularly co-opted to teach sexuality education in a range of school settings.

In introducing this video to these participants, our aim is not to advocate an abstinence-based approach. Rather, Rasmussen was interested in ascertaining her participants' thoughts on a sexuality education program that was not avowedly secular. The participants' reactions make us wonder what it would be like for a student, in the space of sexuality education at Central High, to come out as abstinent.

In the introduction to *Secularisms*, Jakobsen and Pellegrini argue that, within the context of the European Enlightenment, universalism develops through the emergence of the idea that reason "transcends religion and is universally valid" (2008: 5). Reason is seen as distinct from religion within this framing because

> . . . although many religions make universal claims, these claims are themselves particular to the adherents of that religion, whereas reason, shared by all human beings, transcends such cultural particularities. This form of reason, liberated from the constraints of religious dogma, opens the door to the settlement of disagreement through reasoned debate rather than enforced belief. (2008: 5)

We argue that this notion of reason as something that is universal continues to play an important role in the production and imagination of progressive sexuality education. Such a perspective also fails to attend to the ways in which people utilize faith to reason. CSE is often purveyed, we argue, as liberated from the constraints of religious dogma and is therefore reasonable. The acceptance of this logic, Jakobsen and Pellegrini argue, "remains the site of manifold academic and political investments" (2008: 6). How do some of these academic and political investments about the value of reason and the problem of enforced belief play out in sexuality education?

Sex educators are trained to believe that they are doing good work, that this work is well informed, and that it can be effective and bring about positive social change (Moran, 2000). Part of this belief may be associated with educators' and students' association of a comprehensive approach to sexuality education with reason and evidence. Jeffrey Moran articulates this move toward a more evidence-based approach and away from a focus on morality in his book *Teaching Sex: The Shaping of Adolescence in the Twentieth Century*. Moran identifies the manifestation of moral neutrality in sexuality education as having at least three characteristics. First, "moral neutrality [associated with the comprehensive approach] seemed an attempt to label religious considerations irrelevant" (2000: 192). Second, urging young people to make their own moral decisions "implicitly suggests that adolescents need not accept their parents authority as absolute" (192). Third, sex educators "seemed to exemplify the moral bankruptcy of the elite establishment" (193). According to Moran, this shift to moral neutrality, engineered by Mary Calderone and Sex Information and Education Council of the United States (SIECUS) became the "official pedagogical basis of the dialogue-centred sex education course" (192), a shift that was made as a way of "sidestepping moral and religious controversy" (192) and saving teachers the problem of determining which particular morality should be taught. Moran is making these observations looking back to sexuality education provisions in the US in the 1960s and 1970s. As Moran indicates, the strength of this approach is sometimes predicated on the fact that this style of sexuality education is perceived as universal because it is "liberated from the constraints of religious dogma" (Jakobsen and Pellegrini, 2008: 5).

Referring to a period 40 years later, in her book *The Sex Education Debates*, Nancy Kendall observes:

> CSE approaches value universal models of the rational individual and of scientific truth, which lead, conceptually, to a belief that all students should receive the same "complete and correct" CSE programming. What constitutes "complete and correct" information in CSE programs is determined in relation to Enlightenment ideals of rationality, science, and truth. CSE approaches are also shaped by support for universal human rights and progressive and politically liberal ideals related to multiculturalism and respect for diversity, which lead to a desire to acknowledge difference and provide programming that meets the diverse needs of students with different life experiences, language capacities, sociocultural norms, economic backgrounds and so forth. (Kendall, 2013: 123)

By rehearsing these arguments, which are clearly not new, we want to underscore the association between comprehensive sexuality education, progressivism, and Enlightenment ideals—an association that is well entrenched and well documented.

Our belief is that the consequences of these associations *for addressing the intersections among culture, religion, and sexuality education* have not been sufficiently scrutinised, though they have oft been identified. In conducting the empirical research that informs this chapter, we wanted to investigate further how understandings about cultural and religious difference are always and already mediated by secularism within sexuality education. Religious or nonreligious, there is no escaping secularism's firm embrace when imagining the project of sexuality education. We see sex education's secular associations as sedimented and various, and in this chapter we have tried to highlight some of the implications that ensue from continued imaginings of sexuality education as a progressive project.

CONCLUSION

Our research suggests that, at least in the public schools in Australia and Aotearoa-New Zealand in which we observed, religious and cultural difference were often not seen as legitimate parts of comprehensive sexuality education. This is because religious and cultural differences are largely perceived as superfluous to the delivery of quality sexuality education, and this belief reinforces an understanding of religion as extraneous to sexuality education.

Comprehensive sexuality education (in practice and research) is largely perceived to represent a universal consensus on what constitutes a reasonable approach. To be clear, we understand that the absence of religion in sexuality education is by no means universal. We also recognize that there are attempts to bring religious questions into sexuality education, but we argue that these attempts to admit religion will likely only affirm religious reason that "comes to the same conclusions as secular reason" (Taylor, 2008: para 3). This is apparent in McKay's vision for a democratic sexuality education, and in our own interactions with participants—whether they identified as religious or nonreligious—these young people were often wary of engaging in conversations about religion in the context of sexuality education in public schools.

These findings might suggest the value of working toward an understanding and vision of sexuality education that is inclusive of differing religious perspectives, just as we have argued that sexuality education should be inclusive of diverse forms of embodiment, sexuality, and gender identities. However, we are mindful that the prospects for conducting conversations about sexuality that are respectful of religious and sexual freedom are not particularly positive, at least within the contemporary context of public schooling.

NOTES

1. All names are pseudonyms. During our observations in 2012, Central High did not provide sexuality education for the year nine group. Observations were only conducted at Pacific High for one year. For a discussion of the ethical challenges of negotiating research on sexuality education, see Allen, Rasmussen, Quinlivan, Aspin, Sanjakdar, and Bromdal (2014).
2. Central High participants were five males and one female. Only one male identified as religious—he listed his religion as Buddhist (four of the participants were Anglo, one male was Thai-Australian, and one male was of African ancestry).
3. See Australian Bureau of Statistics (2013), 4102.0—Australian Social Trends.
4. Devondale High participants were all female, and all had religious affiliations.
5. Aotearoa-New Zealand schools in decile one have the highest proportion of students from low socioeconomic backgrounds, while schools in decile ten have the highest proportion of students from high socioeconomic backgrounds.

6. This designation is used by the New Zealand government.
7. The participants in this focus group are boys in year nine (age 13 or 14). They were all part of an accelerated learning program. The conversations we had about sexuality education were wide ranging.
8. This is a Polynesian term for "the White man."
9. The research team is in some disagreement about the extent to which the arguments through the text and this chapter diverge from or resemble McKay's position. These different readings of McKay's argument speak to the challenges of identifying just what secularism is and how it shapes scholarship in sexuality education.
10. In this context, the notion of a "fallen woman" refers to a woman's perceived sexual deviance and loss of purity and innocence in the eyes of God.
11. This is clearly an offshoot of the US organization of the same name, using similar branding. The *No Apologies* curriculum also comes from the US.
12. A report in *The Age* newspaper in 2008 states that more than 5,000 Australian teens have completed the *No Apologies* program created by Focus on the Family (see Bachelard, 2008).

REFERENCES

Allen, L. E., Rasmussen, M. L., Quinlivan, K. A., Aspin, C., Sanjakdar, F., & Brömdal, A. C. G. (2014). Who's Afraid of Sex at School? The Politics of Researching Culture, Religion and Sexuality at School. *International Journal of Research and Method in Education*, 37(1): 31–43.

Asad, T. (2003). *Formations of the Secular: Christianity, Islam, Modernity*. Stanford, CA: Stanford University Press.

Australian Bureau of Statistics. (2013). *4102.0 — Australian Social Trends*, November 2013. Canberra, Australia. Available from http://www.abs.gov.au/ausstats/abs@.nsf/Lookup/4102.0Main+Features30Nov+2013#religionandschool (Last accessed February 19, 2015).

Bachelard, M. (2008). At the Crossroads? *The Age Newspaper*, February 25. Available from: http://www.theage.com.au/news/in-depth/religious-schools-at-the-crossroads/2008/02/24/1203788145887.html?page=fullpage (Last accessed February 19th, 2015).

Goldman, J. (2008). Responding to Parental Objections to School Sexuality Education: A Selection of 12 Objections. *Sex Education*, 8(4): 415–438.

Halstead, J. M., & Reiss, M. J. (2003). *Values in Sex Education: From Principles to Practice*. London: Routledge.

Jackson, S. (2004). Identifying Future Research Needs for the Promotion of Young People's Sexual Health in New Zealand. *Social Policy Journal of New Zealand*, 21: 123–137.

Jakobsen, J. R. (2005). Sex + Freedom = Regulation: WHY? *Social Text*, 23(3–4): 84–85, 285–308.

Jakobsen, J. R., & Pellegrini, A. (Eds.). (2008). *Secularisms*. Durham and London: Duke University Press.

Kendall, N. (2013). *The Sex Education Debates*. Chicago: University of Chicago Press.

Lidstone, J., & Wilmett, A. (2008). Sex education or indoctrination? Experiences of sexuality education in Catholic schools. Germany: VDM Verlag.

Mahmood, S. (2005). *Politics of Piety: The Islamic Revival and the Feminist Subject*. Princeton, New Jersey: Princeton University.

McKay, A. (1999). *Sexual Ideology and Schooling: Towards Democratic Sexuality Education*. Albany: State University of New York Press.

Moran, J.P. (2000). *Teaching Sex: The Shaping of Adolescence in the 20th Century*. Cambridge, Mass.: Harvard University Press.

Quinlivan, K. (forthcoming). Dumbing Down Sexuality Education in an Age of Anxiety: Mapping the Production of the 'Getting It Right' Assemblage in a High School Sexuality Education Classroom. In L. Allan & M. L. Rasmussen (Eds.), *International Handbook of Sexuality Education*. London: Routledge.

Rasmussen, M., Mitchell, J., & Harwood, V. (2007). The Queer Story of the Heterosexual Questionnaire. In N. Rodriguez & W. Pinar (Eds.), *Queering Straight Teachers: Discourse and Identity in Teacher Education* (pp. 95–114). New York: Peter Lang.

Sanjakdar, F. (2009a). 'Teacher Talk': The Problems, Perspectives and Possibilities of Developing a Comprehensive Sexual Health Education Curriculum for Australian Muslim Students. *Sex Education: Sexuality, Society and Learning*, 9(3): 261–275.

Seitz, D. (2014). Unpacking Queer Secularity: Queer Kids, Schools and Secularism in Toronto, Ontario, Canada. In Y. Taylor & R. Snowden (Eds.), *Queering Religion: Religious Queers* (Routledge Studies in Religion) (pp. 85–100). London: Routledge.

Shah, S., & Conchar, C. (2009). Why Single-Sex Schools? Discourses of Culture/Faith and Achievement. *Cambridge Journal of Education*, 39(2): 191–204.

Singh, P. (2001). Speaking about Cultural Difference and School Disadvantage. An Interview Study of 'Samoan' Paraprofessionals in Designated Disadvantaged Secondary Schools in Australia. *British Journal of Sociology of Education*, 22(3): 317–337.

Taylor, C. (2008). Secularism and Critique. *The Immanent Frame: Secularism, religion, and the public sphere*. Available from http://blogs.ssrc.org/tif/2008/04/24/secularism-and-critique/ (Last accessed October 3, 2014).

UNESCO. (2009). *International Guidelines on Sexuality Education: An Evidence Informed Approach to Effective Sex, Relationships and HIV/STI Education*. Paris, France: UNESCO. Available from http://www.refworld.org/docid/4a69b8902.html (Last accessed November 5, 2014).

Warner, M. (2009). Who Wants to Know? *Great Issue Forum, The Graduate Centre, The City University of New York*. Available from http://www.greatissuesforum.org/index.php?option=com_content&view=article&id=98 (Last accessed 6 January, 2014)

Wray, A., Ussher, J. M., & Perz, J. (2014). Constructions and Experiences of Sexual Health among Young, Heterosexual, Unmarried Muslim Women Immigrants in Australia. *Culture, Health & Sexuality: An International Journal for Research, Intervention and Care*, 16(1): 76–89.

4 Sex Panics, Sexuality Education, and Secular Explanations

Scholars of sexuality education have explored the notion of *moral panic* to understand religious opposition to sexuality education programs. By considering an array of different accounts of moral panics related to sexuality education, my aim is to consider how researchers account for religious concerns associated with moral panics and how these accounts might be shaped by secularism. I consider how beliefs about what constitutes effective sexuality education permeate all discourses related to moral panics, including those discourses designed to diagnose and neutralize panics.

I begin by interrogating different conceptualizations of moral panic in academic and popular discourse and proceed to a discussion of moral panic in the field of sexuality education, specifically focusing on the work of US researcher Janice Irvine (2006, 2007). I also consider some research on South Australian controversies related to sexuality education in schools (Gibson, 2007; Johnson, 2006; Peppard, 2008). Do such accounts of moral panics in sexuality education downplay the significance of religion and belief? Are moral panics too easily utilized by progressive researchers to displace and undermine would-be religious objections to sexuality education?

MORAL PANICS AND SEX PANICS

The British Journal of Criminology has devoted a special issue to the notion of moral panics. In the introduction to this issue, Nachman Ben-Yehuda (2009) provides a brief introduction on the history of this idea in a foreword titled "Moral Panics—36 Years On." Ben-Yehuda notes that the concept of moral panic was popularized by Stanley Cohen (1972) in his famous book *Folk Devils and Moral Panics: The Creation of the Mods and Rockers* and that "the concept broadly refers to the creation of a situation in which exaggerated fear is manufactured about topics that are seen (or claimed) to have a moral component" (2009: 1). In his text *Moral Panics*, Kenneth Thompson (1998) writes that moral panics have several components. He argues that, in the context of a moral panic, something or someone is defined as a threat to values or interests; this threat is easily identifiable by the media;

there is a rapid buildup of concern and a response from authorities or opinion makers; and the panic recedes or results in social change (8). For Thompson, the panic is designated as moral precisely to indicate that the perceived threat is not to something mundane—such as economic output or educational standards—but a threat to the social order itself (8). Within this schema, Cohen (1972) characterized the threat and those portrayed as its perpetrators as "folk devils." Thompson (1998) goes on to argue "it would be wrong to assume that the motive of actors involved in generating a moral panic . . . is that of cynical manipulation for ulterior ends; they may genuinely believe what they say. (Although there might be a happy coincidence of principle and interest.)" (8, 9). It is this last claim, regarding authenticity in relation to the construct of moral panics that I want to scrutinize further.

Determinations of when to call something a moral panic cannot be separated from the political leanings of the person making the judgment. Thompson (1998) argues that determining whether or not something might be designated as a moral panic is not always clear-cut and that this designation might, in certain instances (he provides the examples of feminist campaigns against pornography), be inappropriate. Are there instances in research on sexuality education when the designation of events as moral panics may be inappropriate?

Answering this question is challenging because how is it possible to determine whether or not public concerns that underpin a panic are manufactured or authentic? Paul Jones (1997, cited in Poynting and Morgan, 2007), suggests "those who deploy the moral panic model in their analysis might overestimate the media's ability to shape public opinion and have failed to recognize that moral panics will only take off if they articulate real public concerns that exist prior to media-beat ups" (4). This conceptualization of moral panics is particularly pertinent because it highlights the notion that objections cast as moral panics may articulate views that exist prior to the production of the moral panic.

In 1984 Carol Vance coined the phrase *sex panic*. In this chapter I am pushing back against the utility of sex or moral panic as "an ideal concept for considering the fierce battles over sexuality in the United States" (Irvine, 2006: 82). For Vance, a sex panic is apparent when "irrational fears about sexuality are mobilized by the effective use of alarming symbols . . . [I]n order to operate, sex panics mobilize fear of pollution in an attempt to draw firm boundaries between legitimate and deviant forms of sexuality and individuals" (434, 435). I concur with Vance that sex panics might involve irrational fears (I am sure they often do). But are sex panics better understood as something more than the mobilization of irrational fears about sexuality? While potentially convenient from a progressive perspective, I wonder if Vance's argument really addresses the complexities underpinning sex panics.

In his article "Sex, Panic, Nation," Bruce Burgett (2009) situates moral panics as something in which academics have their own particular investments, and he suggests that these require further interrogation. What investments might researchers in sexuality education have in characterizing an event as a sex panic? Looking at the role of sex panics in the US context, Burgett asks:

> What happens if we reject the panic hypothesis as our starting point as we seek alternative means of approaching the histories of sex and sexuality? What happens, in other words, if we begin by thinking more skeptically about why activist-oriented literary historians and cultural critics are so willing to attribute panic to persons, populations, and publics when it comes to matters of sex? What is gained and lost when we talk, write, and theorize in these terms about social formations and forms of collective agency? (2009: 68)

In addition to asking literary historians and cultural critics of sexuality to think again about the ways in which sex panics are mobilized in their research, Burgett (2009) also offers a provocation to think more critically and creatively about the epistemologies that we have inherited from the historical archives we research and assemble. This forces us to question familiar couplings of nation and sex or, I would add, religion and sex. Burgett also cites Cohen's (2002) own discomfort with his original theorizing on the notion of moral panic and his unease with his prior tendency to assert that better reporting of issues might lead to more rational conclusions. Such a stance seeks out and privileges rationality; this is suggestive of moral panics' secular underpinnings.

The tendency to construct sex panics as irrational has at least two negative effects. First, it situates people who strive to draw firm boundaries between legitimate and deviant forms of sexuality as irrational and therefore as somehow inhabiting a space outside the bounds of rational debate on issues related to sex. Second, it situates morality as associated with conservative views on sexuality. Moral debates about sex and sexuality education consequently become divided between those who have morals and those professionals who work in the field of sexuality education. This constructs a binary between the rational and the irrational, those who rely on evidence-based arguments and those who do not.

Janice Irvine has made much use of the notion of moral panic in researching sexuality education, but her definition is somewhat different from that of Vance (1984). Irvine (2006) describes moral panics (or sex panics, as she later terms them) as "recursive conflicts over sexual issues" (82). For Irvine (2002), the moral panic, as observed in academic discourse, has three stages:

> First a group, person, or issue emerges to become defined as a social threat. Media representations then stylise this alleged threat in a simplistic and stereotypical way, fueling intense public concern. Next, moral entrepreneurs of various types devise coping mechanisms and solutions. The perceived threat eventually diminishes and the panic recedes. (82)

Irvine (2002) endeavours to complicate this reading of moral panic. I will address Irvine's critique of moral or sex panic in more detail later in this chapter; suffice to say that she is critical of the way in which the emotions that emerge within these panics are accounted for in academic research. While Irvine is critical of how moral panics in sexuality education are currently interpreted, she still finds it valuable to deploy the term in understanding recursive battles over sexuality education in the US.

Irvine is not alone in her critique of the notion of moral panic. For instance, Ben-Yehuda (2009) points to the

> need to re-think possibilities for the generalizability of moral panics in societies that have become fragmented and multicultural. The original model seemed to have assumed a more or less monolithic moral culture. But what happens to moral panics in multi-cultural societies where morality itself is constantly contested and negotiated? . . . [M]oral panics are about struggles for moral hegemony over interpretation of the legitimacy (or not) of prevailing social arrangements and material interests. And, as well as being local, today they may also be cross-national or even global. (2, 3)

Ben-Yehuda's observations about the intersections between moral panic and multiculturalism are important in considering how we might account for and characterise conflicting views on sexuality education. Heated debates about the content of sexuality education are surely to be expected, especially within societies such as Australia and the US, where there can be no easy agreement about whose morality should be reflected in the curriculum. Below, I offer some examples of Australian media reporting that may be constituted as suggestive of a moral panic on sexuality education.

"FOLK DEVILS," SEXUALITY EDUCATION, AND MORAL ENTREPRENEURS

Around Australia, news reports on the subject of sexuality education that might be characterized by the concept of moral panic appear intermittently (Devine, 2008; Hutchens, 2014; Martain, 2012). For instance, in 2009 the Victorian Branch of the Australian Medical Association (AMA) made a submission to the state budget to request that the state government increase the size and scope of its sexuality education curriculum. In an article in *The Age*, a local broadsheet titled "Push for Sex Ed From Age 10," Jill Stark quotes Kit Fairley, professor of sexual health at the University of Melbourne, responding favorably to this initiative:

> "Parents need to understand that sexuality education in schools is of benefit to their children. It does lower teenage pregnancy rates, it does

not increase them, and it does not encourage people to have sex at an earlier age. The way parents protect their children is by making sure they're informed' . . . (Fairley in Stark, 2009a)

In Australia, there is strong support within the health community for comprehensive sexuality education. This support has been widespread within the domains of public health and public education. The AMA's (2009) budget submission in support of CSE made the news not because of its support for CSE but because it advocates sexuality education for primary school students.

A statewide newspaper reported this issue as, "AMA seeks sex lessons for 10-year-olds." The Victorian AMA vice president is quoted in this piece saying that it is "too late to begin sex education" when children are already sexually active and that "it must be taught before puberty." Furthermore, Dr. Wainer says,

"We need to stop pussyfooting around with language . . . We need to make it really clear what we're talking about. If we're discussing the risk of sexually transmitted infections through fellatio, we need to make sure that these young people understand we're talking about blow jobs . . . We need to talk about what chlamydia is, how herpes is contracted, the risk factors for anal sex, vaginal sex, oral sex. We need to teach young people that some people can carry STIs without exhibiting symptoms . . . In some circumstances the use of educational images will be appropriate, for example to show older teenagers the effects of sexually transmitted infections."

(Stark, 2009a)

Most sexuality educators in Australian public schools are not reluctant to talk about sexuality and risk in the fashion described by Wainer (Leahy, 2014), although such discussions would currently take place when students are age 12 to 15, in early secondary school rather than primary school.

In response to the Australian Medical Association (AMA), journalist Jill Stark (2009b) quotes Nicholas Tonti-Filippini, a Catholic ethicist and fellow of the John Paul II Institute for Marriage and Family. Reportedly, Tonti-Filippini is horrified about the plan, calling it "child sexual abuse" and promises "to call the police if any teacher dared discuss intercourse with his children at such a young age." In the context of this book, it is important to note that Tonti-Filippini is not antisex education. He has written about the subject of sexuality education in a different register, arguing in favor of age-appropriate sexuality education that combines an abstinence-based approach with the facts in the context of "a holistic understanding of the human person and human relationships" (Tonti-Filippini and McConnell, 2007: 179). Tonti-Filippini's other writings on this subject are significant in thinking about the role he plays in such debates because they complicate his characterization primarily as a moral entrepreneur as well as the ideological juxtapositions that such media reporting inevitably entrenches.

Tonti-Filippini's portrayal of the AMA's proposal as a form of child abuse can be suggestive of a moral panic—he clearly attacks sex educators with "stigmatizing rhetoric" (Irvine, 2006: 83) and depicts the sexuality program and its advocates as a kind of "folk devil"—effectively labeling teachers who implement CSE as child abusers. Tonti-Filippini's comments need to be interpreted as playing to the media debate. He is no doubt aware that the use of such language will ensure that his objections to the AMA's position on sexuality education are aired as part of the debate in which he is trying to participate. Tonti-Filippini wasn't alone in his condemnation of the AMA's recommendations.

Daryl McLure wrote an article in the *Geelong Advertiser*[1] about the AMA proposal, provocatively titled "AMA Plans Would Lead to . . . Gutter Sex Ed" (McLure, 2009: 31). In the article, McLure (2009) notes:

> The AMA is concerned about an "alarmingly high" rate of teenage pregnancy and sexually-transmitted infections. Gee, we've sure come a long way with sexuality education since the 1970s, haven't we? So, what's our new approach going to be? The AMA's answer, according to *The Age*, is to introduce 10-year-olds to topics such as masturbation, anal sex, date rape and oral sex in classes using the language of the gutter. I presume there is much more, hope that there is more, than this. Is this really the best we can offer after 30 years? The same arguments used a generation ago are being trotted out to support an obviously failed policy. These people are condemned out of their own mouths. If there is concern, revisit the issue but perhaps within a religious and/or moral framework explaining to children that sex is much more than just a physical, animal coupling with a few human variations thrown in. (31)

Sexuality education is seen by Tonti-Filippini and McLure to have a moral component, and the association of sexuality education with the gutter in the title of McLure's piece attempts to constitute the style of sexuality education advocated by the AMA as dirty and inappropriate for young people. The image of the gutter may also be intended to amplify the alarm McLure's readers might feel after reading about the AMA's proposal in his article.

Based on Ben-Yehuda's (2009) discussion, at least two aspects of the concept of moral panic come into play in Tonti-Filippini and McLure's comments: there is exaggerated discussion of the potential content and consequences of sexuality education; and sexuality education is constituted as part of a battle over moral hegemony. McLure (2009) goes on to argue that "Australian Islamic schools have rejected the secular approach to sexuality education, I suspect because of its almost anything goes element. I think many Christians agree" (McLure, 2009). For McLure, different approaches to sexuality education are indicative of different values, and he is specifically critical of what he terms the "secular approach to sexuality education." It is noteworthy that McLure utilizes the notion of secularism explicitly in making his argument against this "approach." While I believe secularisms are shaping many debates in sexuality education, it is rare to see this association with secularism made explicit.

McLure's condemnation of the AMA was echoed by another blogger, called *The Secular Heretic* (2009), who expressed concern about the AMA's proposal, writing:

> While I agree that sexuality education is a good thing, the important issue is what type of sexuality education the AMA is suggesting. Are they advocating an abstinence education type program where children learn about the purpose and meaning of sex and its place within marriage or is there a focus on contraceptives and the use of sex as a form of entertainment? Due to the widespread use of birth control, more and more people are having sex without intending to have children. Sex out of wedlock has become far more common, and more sex means more babies. (para. 2)

The language used in the blog, and in McLure's newspaper article, situates sexuality education as an issue closely related to morality, religion, and particular conceptions of what constitutes age-appropriate provision. McLure's (2009) reference to Islamic schools is also noteworthy because of its attempt to suggest agreement across religious groups about the inappropriate nature of secular sexuality education. It is easy to dismiss such journalism as the work of moral entrepreneurs, but I think that the concerns voiced by these commentators, especially Tonti-Filippini, are authentic—when taken in the context of his other writing. The overall character of these responses to the provision of comprehensive school-based sexuality education in Australia (and overseas) is not new, and this small sample is not meant to be all-inclusive. It is offered as an indication of some of the content included in such debates.

In the analyzed newspaper articles and blog, opponents of CSE depict it as problematic because it is secular and therefore amoral. In contrast to this, Tonti-Filippini (2007) constructs his vision for sexuality education as one in which "the facts" are presented as but one part of a holistic approach to sexuality education. McLure (2009) suggests that issues might be relevant but only if presented within the context of "a religious and/or moral framework." *The Secular Heretic* (2009) depicts the comprehensive approach as equating sexuality with entertainment rather than something that has purpose. In my reading of these commentaries, there is a deliberate attempt to construct secular sexuality education as something which is value free, a charge rejected by advocates of CSE (Kendall, 2013; Lamb, 2013). While

CSE is clearly not value free, the repetition of this claim suggests that these Australian commentators still think it has political power.

Nancy Kendall, in her book *The Sex Education Debates* (2013) writes that US advocates of Abstinence Only Until Marriage Education (AOUME) "draw on public health rationales to argue for AOUME approaches. [This is because] For members of the New Christian Right, AOUME is not fundamentally (public) health education but moral education" (5). She believes AOUME advocates adopt this "way of speaking about sex education . . . [because it is] viewed as powerful in shaping public opinion and access to public institutions" (194). CSE opponents believe that to be heard, there is a need to fashion arguments in a language that has power in the realm of secular politics.

Paradoxically, the repetition of the scholarly discourse of moral panic may also work to reinforce the association between morality and conservative perspectives on sexuality education, reinforcing a popular understanding of CE as value free—"just the facts." This fraught association with morality clearly presents different challenges for advocates of CSE and its opponents. Nancy Kendall (2013) conceives as sex education programs (comprehensive and abstinence based) as competing "morality tales" where CSE advocates focus on rights, rigor, evidence, and health outcomes, with AOUME mirroring this but also focusing on moral dangers. In observations I have undertaken in sexuality education classrooms in Australian public schools, the focus is squarely on health risks rather than morality.

While Australia does have a history of contestation over sexuality education, these contestations do not rival US contests in frequency or intensity. Partially, this may be because many parents in Australia opt to send their children to (partially publically funded independent and religious schools. School curricula are also less politicized at the local level, with state (and, more recently, the federal) government responsible for authoring curriculum. Though, the parlous state of sexuality education in Australian schools suggests that opponents have had some success in ensuring that it does not play a significant role in the education of young people about sexuality (Aggleton, 2013).

AUTHENTICITY VERSUS IRRATIONALITY: ANALYZING THE POLITICS OF EMOTIONS IN SEX PANICS

In this section I consider some of Janice Irvine's research on sex panics in debates about sexuality education in the US. As indicated in previous sections, the educational and political context of sexuality education is quite different in the US and Australia, though as I demonstrate later in this section, Irvine's work has been significant in shaping some Australian research on sex panics.

In "Emotional Scripts of Sex Panics," Janice Irvine (2006) contends that discourses related to sex panics have focused too much on issues related to sex and morality and that they have not paid enough attention to the emotions associated with the "panic." Irvine (2006) argues that sex panics in education (in the US) should not be seen as authentic expressions of public outrage. To her mind, they might be better perceived as engineered by moral entrepreneurs. She perceives them, in essence, as a crafted piece of political theater and argues they are misunderstood when construed as the result of grassroots outrage or "spontaneous uprisings of anger and fear" (85).

Highlighting the role moral entrepreneurs play in the production of sex panics, Irvine suggests that "[i]n local sex panics[2]... emotionality is neither mindless nor simply spontaneous; rather it is normative behavior produced in response to emotional scripts" (84). She believes moral entrepreneurs have been developing tactics "strategically triggered to erode sexual rights" (85). These tactics have been successful, particularly within the US context, Irvine argues, because they create a "highly emotional political climate in which it is difficult to speak in support of sexuality education" (2006: 86).

For Irvine, moral panics are more political than moral. In "Transient Feelings: Sex Panics and the Politics of Emotions" (2007), Irvine questions the "authenticity of collective outrage [which] suggests that individuals respond to sex panic scripts because of deep religious and political predispositions" (25). For Irvine, the alignment of sex panics with religious dispositions makes them appear authentic and "diverts attention from those who both foster and benefit from panics ... Mapping transient feelings in space and time reveals the 'panic' as contestation among emotional publics" (31). Irvine's larger goal seems to be a questioning of the religious right's moral authority by emphasizing the political aspect of emotions in sex panics.

In the context of this discussion of secularism and progressive sexuality education, I draw attention to Irvine's (2007) analysis of sex panics because to my mind this analysis reinforces the idea that sexuality education is a battleground between competing religious and secular perspectives. This is borne out in the ways in which sexuality researchers have taken up Irvine's research to critique Australian sex panics. Bruce Johnson (2006), Sally Gibson (2007) and Judith Peppard (2008) have all drawn on the notion of moral panic to interpret debates about sexuality education in the South Australian context. Gibson (2007) argues that the battle over sexuality education "needs to be understood as part of the globalization of the 'family values' movement, and indicates the close links between Christian right groups in the USA and similar groups in Australia" (240). Both Peppard and Gibson explicitly draw on the work of Irvine in their analysis of these "culture wars."

Strong similarities exist in the strategies and tactics utilized in battles over sexuality education in these two countries, prompting Gibson (2007) to argue convincingly that this globalization of family values "should not be viewed in isolation from the global movement by Christian Right groups to challenge social change" (244). Gibson argues further that the creation of fear and panic related to sexuality education is a deliberate political strategy to assert influence on the secular state. While the concerns "appear legitimate," Gibson argues, they are actually aimed at deliberately invoking panic that can be used for political ends" (246). It is here that it is possible to see how Christian groups' opposition to sexuality education becomes constructed as illegitimate through the invocation of moral panic discourse: opposition by Christian groups is cast as a political agenda and therefore illegitimate.

To be clear, I do concur with Irvine (2006) and Gibson's (2007) argument that sex panics are utilized as an effective political tool by the religious right, especially in the US.[3] However, I believe these sex panics are misunderstood if they are reduced to being seen primarily as political theater. Debates about how sexuality education is constructed are bound to be ongoing; however, the attempt to construct opposition to sexuality education as a moral panic and a strategic, political endeavor to "erode sexual rights" fails to capture the different objections and concerns that characterize opposition to comprehensive sexuality education. Disputes about abortion, contraception, and homosexuality in sexuality education reflect diverse moral and political attachments that are only partially explained via the discourse of moral panic.

MORAL PANICS, SEXUAL CITIZENSHIP, AND SECULARISM

Another move I want to trace in debates about sex panics is how they relate to perceptions of sexual citizenship. Irvine (2007) argues:

> Sex panics, such as those over sexuality education, are a form of citizenship politics. These struggles determine which sexualities will be recognized and valued, what will be spoken, and what remains excluded and silenced. Sex panics may buttress state regulatory power by implementing policy or legislation that restricts sexual rights. This has certainly been the case with comprehensive sexuality education, for which the space is shrinking in US public schools. Advocacy groups now argue that access to sexual knowledge is not simply an individual privilege or health concern but a fundamental element of citizenship. (24)

Irvine wants citizenship, not morality, to become the locus of struggle over sexuality education. In this way Irvine attempts to shift the debate away from feelings as *authentic and private* to feelings as *political and public*. By constituting emotions as public (not private), Irvine sets up a contestation among emotional publics. We may see resistance, reversals, and backlashes by citizens both locally and nationally, suggesting that while moral regulation through panics is formidable, it is not inevitable or irrevocable. As such, sex panics are potentially open spaces for progressive political intervention.

Irvine utilizes the notion of emotional publics to argue that sex panics are a legitimate site of progressive political organizing. Such organizing is not irreverent, she suggests, but a necessary tactic in the face of a powerful political foe.

In a piece titled "The Ruse of 'Secular Humanism'" (2008), Michael Warner warns against carving up sexuality into spaces that are perceived as Christian and the inversion of Christianity (or, in the language of this book, religious and progressive) because

> [a]t present we are again seeing a rise in anti-secular rhetoric in which sexuality is taken to be indicative of the secular order. But that rhetoric is now globalizing; it is no longer the idiom of American evangelicals alone. These struggles, and the need to understand them, are likely to deepen. (para. 13)

I worry that Irvine's analysis of sex panic might be construed as carving out secular progressives as pro-sex and potentially antireligion. Adopting such an approach is not only misguided (because sex is not the preserve of secularists), but it also plays into the hands of those would cast secularists as antireligious. For ideas associated with CSE to have purchase beyond liberal secular audiences, they have to work to disturb this association, not reinforce it. This is also recognition, as Warner presciently warns, that strategies that conflate secularisms and sexuality are likely to have unintended consequences—such associations could therefore limit the reach and reception of comprehensive approaches to sexuality education beyond US borders.

Rather than conceive of sex panics as another space where progressives can intervene in the battles over sex education, my inclination is to interrogate how the notion of sex panics are underpinned by the logic of liberal democracy. Talal Asad (2003) suggests that within the frame of secularism that underpins liberal democracies "there is no space in which all citizens can negotiate freely and equally with one another" (2003: 4). This is not a particularly new insight, but I think it is pertinent in analyzing Irvine's (2006, 2007) study of sex panics. *It is recognition that liberalism can't always settle disputes about sexuality, yet progressive sexuality educators tend to put a lot of faith in liberal discourses of democracy and citizenship* (Kendall, 2013; McKay, 1998). Opponents of CSE reject this vision of sexual citizenship; they are keenly aware of the limitations of this approach in settling disputes over sexuality education.

Talal Asad (2003) argues the need to scrutinize what is gained and what is lost in this move to claim an issue as one pertaining to citizenship. He writes that within a secular frame citizenship claims

> ... must transcend the different identities built on class, gender and religion, replacing conflicting perspectives by unifying experience. In an important sense, this transcendent mediation is secularism. Secularism

is not simply an intellectual answer to a question about social peace and toleration. It is an enactment by which a political medium (representation of citizenship) redefines and transcends particular and differentiating practices of the self that are articulated through class, gender, and religion [and sexuality]. (5)

Asad (2003) sees the invocation of citizenship as problematic when citizenship is construed as something that transcends other conflicts. Within the frame of liberal narratives of citizenship, the mythology states that *we might disagree about abortion, homosexuality, or premarital sex, but as equal citizens we are allowed to state these disagreements and have these heard*. The mechanisms of citizenship such as liberal democracy, equal rights, and dialogue (even if they are not always fulfilled) provide the conditions for social peace and tolerance, imperfect as they are.

Drawing on Asad, it is possible to see how secularism and notions of sexual citizenship are interrelated. Both are founded on the idea that debates about personal and public matters related to sexuality can and should be staged using these political mediums—*not through recourse to religion and morality*. In a paper titled "Secular Privilege, Religious Disadvantage," Linda Woodhead (2008) suggests: "The danger here is that 'religion' [especially religion that is identified as nonnormative] becomes a marker of the subjugated other, whilst the privileged become the possessors of pure truth, transparent rationality, and the engines of progress" (Woodhead, 2008: 57).

Some evangelicals' sense of themselves as subjugated other is apparent in Gail Bederman's review of Irvine's (2002) earlier work, *Talk About Sex: The Battles Over Sexuality Education*. In this review it is also possible to see the potential difficulty of distinguishing between public and private emotions. Bederman (2003) writes:

> Many secular Americans find it hard to believe that intelligent, thoughtful people believe in a supernatural God, particularly one whose church seems to advocate 'irrational' ideas about things like sex. Comprehensive sex educators seem to have suffered from this kind of blind spot. Even Irvine herself, despite a clear effort to discuss the nuances of contemporary evangelicalism, tends to explain parents' opposition to comprehensive sexuality education as arising from irrational 'fears and confusions' rather than from thoughtful, principled conclusions. (6)

In these articles on emotions and sex panics, Irvine's (2002) argument has shifted from the one critiqued by Bederman (2003). Irvine is suggesting in her later work that conservative commentaries on CSE are not irrational but rather skillfully engineered to develop a sex panic. I suspect that for Bederman, this latter distinction by Irvine would not offer much comfort. This is because beliefs that may be constituted by Irvine as attributable to a sex panic appear to be personal and authentic for Bederman. Bederman is not naïve about the difficulties associated with resolving conflicts related to sexuality education, observing that "most conservative Christians would not have adopted sex educators' views even if they had understood them. Yet had the mutual misunderstandings been less profound, the debates might have been less bitter and divisive." (2003: 6). To my mind, conservatives will likely read the notion of sex panic offered by Irvine as a failure to engage with the irrationality of belief.

More broadly, Linda Woodhead (2008) argues:

> If religion is particularly significant for the disprivileged, it is often the disprivileged within the disprivileged groups, or the 'minorities within minorities' (Bader, 2007: 30) for whom it is most essential. This is the opposite observation to the feminist and enlightened liberal observation that it is minorities within minorities who are most in need of the protection of state backed human rights legislation. In my view both observations are true, and it is only by holding them both together that we can be responsive to the complexity of the situation of vulnerable individuals in societies in which material and cultural resources are not equally distributed (i.e. all real world societies). (55)

In thinking about the implications of Woodhead's claims for sexuality education, it is necessary to see religion as essential to some young people lives—and to their sexual selves. At the same time, it is necessary to see young people as having sexual rights. Religion may be an essential component of how young people who experience significant disadvantage because of poverty or cultural and religious difference make sense of their sexuality. Therefore, an important question for all scholars in sexuality education is how to hold both these things together without perceiving either as the most enlightened or progressive.

CONCLUSION

Secularism, Marie Griffith and Melani McAlister (2007) argue, is made up of contemporary and contradictory forces:

> There is at the very least a tension between the valorization of secularism, when comparisons to Islam are at hand, and the simultaneous call for more religion in the public sphere, where US politics is concerned. Different interests are at stake in different conflicts, so that what appears to be an infringement of religious rights to one party in a particular case may look like crucial protections from religion to another. (530)

The differing allegiances to secularism in a range of contemporary US political contexts—local, national and international—is a useful reminder that secularism is not easy to pin down and that its allegiances are fickle. This is also true in the field of sexuality education. Irvine argues sex panics are, fundamentally, a sophisticated attack on comprehensive sexuality education. For Bederman, opposition to sexuality education is misunderstood when it is constituted as political rather than principled, within the frame of secular judgment. Different feelings toward and analysis of the relationships among religion, sexuality, politics, and the state are at stake in both these readings.

In a discussion of the role of secularism in forming multicultural coalitions, Tariq Modood (2008) argues the necessity of avoiding transcendent and missionary forms of secularism that see secularists as standing Olympian-style above the fray and needed as the reasonable peacekeepers (51). Is this how academic research positions itself, as the missionary looking down from above? What is the role that academic research plays within these battles, and how does academic research related to sex panics in sexuality education contribute to and sustain these conflicts?

Reading sex panics as irrational and ultimately inauthentic is, I have argued, a result of ideological interactions between moral panic and sex panic. Jock Young (2009), the researcher who coined the term *moral panic* (Ben-Yehuda, 2009: 1), characterizes moral panics as "a mistake in reason" (14) but also as indicative of an authentic expression of emotion. Irvine's (2006) take on moral panics is somewhat different; she argues that sex panics are best understood as manufactured by moral entrepreneurs for political ends and that they are therefore not indicative of authentic emotion. Irvine perceives emotions manifest in these panics as normative behavior produced in response to emotional scripts (84). *While these researchers differ on how emotions might be understood within moral panics, both constitute moral panics as operating to stall progress.*

For Irvine (2006), progress is stalled by the operation of political tactics that work to demonize CSE curricula and its advocates. In Young's (2009) analysis, progress is stalled by authentic expression of emotions that may be a mistake in reason. In both these explanations, the reactions that occur within the context of a moral panic are suspect, or antiprogressive. For Irvine (2006), they are suspect because they are political and not authentic, while for Young (2009), moral panics are marked by a lack of reason. Within this frame of analysis, opponents of sexuality education may be constructed as antiprogressive because their emotional response is unreasonable. Alternatively, their motives may be seen as politically agenda driven and crafted theater.

In the US political climate in which it was produced, Irvine's approach can be seen as a political strategy—one designed to counter the very strong religious influence on public policy related to sexuality education during the era of the Bush administration and beyond. In contemplating the politics of sex or moral panic, it is my hope that researchers can develop new strategies for accounting for religious opposition to the implementation of CSE. Such an approach could result in a more fruitful engagement with religion in sexuality education.

NOTES

1. Geelong is the largest regional city in Victoria and the *Geelong Advertiser* is the daily tabloid newspaper of the region.
2. Irvine use the term *local* here to refer to "hostilities that erupt in communities debating a particular curriculum or program" (2006: 83).
3. Moral panics regarding sexuality are also a powerful political tool in the Australian context. I have recently written about the Northern Territory Emergency Response (NTER), which is ongoing and originally initiated by the Howard Liberal government in August 2007. This is a public pedagogy of sexuality education constructed on a sex panic that situates indigenous people in remote areas of Australia as inhabiting spaces that are depicted as culturally backward, sexually dangerous, and particularly problematic for children and young people (Rasmussen, forthcoming).

REFERENCES

Aggleton, P. (2013). Let's Talk about Sex—Openly and with Respect. *The Age*, November 20. Available from http://www.theage.com.au/comment/lets-talk-about-sex—openly-and-with-respect-20131120–2xuz4.html#ixzz38KuEe3Gg (Last accessed July 27, 2014).

Asad, T. (2003). *Formations of the Secular: Christianity, Islam, Modernity*. Stanford, CA: Stanford University Press.

Bederman, G. (2003). Review: Across the Great Divide. *The Women's Review of Books*, 20(5): 6–7.

Ben-Yehuda, N. (2009). Foreword: Moral Panics—36 Years On. *British Journal of Criminology*, 49(1): 1–3.

Burgett, B. (2009). Sex, Panic, Nation. *American Literary History*, 21(1): 67–86.

Cohen, S. (1972). *Folk Devils and Moral Panics: The Making of Mods and Rockers*. London: MacGibbon and Kee.

———. (2002). *Folk Devils and Moral Panics* (3rd ed.). New York: Routledge.

Devine, M. (2008). Saturated with Sex: The Campaign to Save Young Minds. *Sydney Morning Herald*, May 22, 2008. (Last accessed November 11, 2014, from NewsBank on-line database, Access World News).

Gibson, S. (2007). The Language of the Right: Sex Education Debates in South Australia. *Sex Education: Sexuality, Society and Learning*, 7(3): 239–250.

Griffith, R. M., & McAlister, M. (2007). Introduction: Is the Public Square Still Naked? *American Quarterly*, 59(3): 527–563.

Hutchens, G. (2014). Parents Oppose Gay Sex Lessons, Says Pyne's Man—Schools—Call to Cut Homosexual Content. *Sydney Morning Herald*, February 2, 2014 (Last accessed November 11, 2014, from NewsBank on-line database Access World News).

Irvine, J. (2002). *Talk about Sex: The Battles Over Sex Education in the United States*. California: University of California Press.

———. (2006). Emotional Scripts of Sex Panics. *Sexuality Research and Social Policy*, 3(3): 82–94.

———. (2007). Transient Feelings: Sex Panics and the Politics of Emotions. *GLQ*, 14(1): 1–40.

Johnson, B. (2006). *Being Caught in a "Moral Panic": The Case of the Sexual Health and Relationships Education Project in South Australia*', paper presented at the University of South Australia, Division of Education, Arts and Social Sciences, Research Forum.

Kendall, N. (2013). *The Sex Education Debates*. Chicago: University of Chicago Press.

Lamb, S. (2013). Just the Facts? The Separation of Sex Education from Moral Education. *Educational Theory*, 63(5): 443–460.
Leahy, D. (2014). Assembling a Health[y] Subject: Risky and Shameful Pedagogies in Health Education. *Critical Public Health*, 24(2): 171–181.
Martain, T. (2012). New Sex Classes Stir Debate Heat. *Sunday Tasmanian*, October 21, 2012. (Last accessed, November 11, 2014 from NewsBank on-line database Access World News).
McKay, A. (1998). *Sexual Ideology and Schooling: Towards Democratic Sexuality Education*. Albany: State University of New York Press.
McLure, D. (2009). AMA Plans Would Lead to . . . Gutter Sex Ed. *Geelong Advertiser*, January 19, p. 31.
Modood, T. (2008). A Basis for and Two Obstacles in the Way of a Multiculturalist Coalition. *The British Journal of Sociology*, 59(1): 47–52.
Peppard, J. (2008). Culture Wars in South Australia: The Sex Education Debates. *Australian Journal of Social Issues*, 43(3): 499–516.
Poynting, S., and Morgan, G. (2007). Introduction. In S. Poynting & G. Morgan (Eds.), *Outrageous: Moral Panics in Australia* (pp. 1–10). Hobart: Australian Clearinghouse for Youth Studies.
Rasmussen, M. L. (2015). Sex Education, Bodily Orientations and the Northern Territory Intervention. In S. R. Poyntz & J. Kennelly (Eds.), *Phenomenology of Youth Cultures and Globalization: Lifeworlds and Surplus Meanings in Changing Times* (Routledge Studies in Social and Political Thought) (pp. 183–211). New York: Routledge.
Stark, J. (2009a). AMA Seeks Sex Lessons for 10-year-olds. *The Age*, January 11, 2009. Available from http://www.theage.com.au/national/ama-seeks-sex-lessons-for-10yearolds-20090110-7e1m.html. (Last accessed July 30, 2014).
———. (2009b). Sounds Good, but Does Sex Ed Actually Work? *The Age*, January 18, 2009. Available from http://www.theage.com.au/national/sounds-good-but-does-sex-ed-actually-work-20090117-7jmb.html (Last accessed July 30, 2014).
The Secular Heretic. (2009). *Australian Medical Association Wants More Sexuality Education for Victoria*. Available from http://secularheretic-st.blogspot.com/2009/01/australian-medical-association-wants.html (Last accessed January 9, 2009).
Thompson, K. (1998). *Moral Panics*. Hoboken, NJ: Routledge.
Tonti-Filippini, N., & McConnell, H. (2007). Understand, Appreciate, Protect: Effective Education in Sexuality. In J. Fleming and N. Tonti-Filippini, *Common Ground: Seeking an Australian Consensus on Abortion and Sex Education* (pp. 153–81). Sydney: St Pauls Publications.
Vance, C. (Ed.). (1984). *Pleasure and Danger: Exploring Female Sexuality*. Boston: Routledge & Kegan Paul.
Warner, M. (2008). The Ruse of "Secular Humanism". *The Immanent Frame* website. Available from http://blogs.ssrc.org/tif/2008/09/22/the-ruse-of-secular-humanism/ (Last accessed February 22, 2015).
Woodhead, L. (2008). Secular Privilege, Religious Disadvantage. *The British Journal of Sociology*, 59(1): 53–58.
Young, J. (2009). Moral Panic: Its Origins in Resistance, Ressentiment and the Translation of Fantasy into Reality. *British Journal of Criminology*, 49(1): 4–16.

5 Pleasure/Desire, Secularism, and Sexuality Education

In this chapter I interrogate the politics of pleasure and desire in research that is supportive of CSE as formulated by scholars who might be supportive of, or at least sympathetic to, CSE (Addison, 2006; Connell, 2005; Elliot, 2003; Fine, 1988). This marks a deliberate shift away from research that is focused on religious objections to CSE. I adopt this approach because I am concerned that culture, religion, and morality are too often constructed as somehow outside the bounds of CSE.

In an article on gender and heteronormativity, Robyn Weigman (2006) argues that "gender is always made and remade *according to the political desire that seeks it* in the first place" (99, emphasis in original). This suggests there is not a position on gender that one might take that is somehow outside politics. In an article critiquing feminist ideals related to adolescent sexuality education, Sharon Lamb (2010a) demonstrates how feminist political desires have shaped the field of sexuality education in problematic ways. By emphasizing particular understandings of pleasure, desire, and the "good" these "may have different historical meanings for girls from diverse backgrounds . . . [and] may undermine other important goals of feminism" (294). Weigman prompts me to ask, what is the political desire that makes and remakes CSE?

Consequently, this chapter is a critical consideration of the role of pleasure and desire in sexuality education. Researchers in sexuality education have written a lot about the value of pleasure and desire in sexuality education and argue the need for a clearer focus (Fine, 1988; Fine & McClelland, 2006; Ingham, 2005; Lamb, 1997, 2010a; Whitehead, 2005). Much of this research is broadly aligned, although not uncritically, with CSE. As I discussed in the introduction, CSE has particular characteristics. Educational research that underpins CSE embraces sexual diversity, interrogates heteronormativity, and focuses on reducing unplanned pregnancy and exploring young people's understandings of pleasure and desire. Researchers supportive of CSE perceive young people as agentic sexual subjects with specific rights and responsibilities (Alagari, Collins, Morin, and Summers, 2002; Lesko, 2010).

In the second half of the chapter, I analyse writings from Aotearoa-New Zealand, the UK, and Australia that have been influenced by US scholarship and emphasize the value of pleasure and desire within sexuality education. I also consider how notions of health and morality are deployed as framing devices in this work. This chapter contributes to a growing body of scholarship that scrutinizes research supportive of CSE and progressive scholarship on sexuality education (for some other critiques of the comprehensive approach see Irvine, 2002; Lamb, 2010a; Lesko, 2010; Luker, 2006).

Given successive US administrations' financial and moral support of Abstinence Only Until Marriage (AOUM) programmes that teach students to abstain from sex until marriage, it is not surprising that researchers have focused on the problems with the abstinence approach (Kantor, Santelli, Teitler, and Balmer, 2008; Mayo, 2008; Vergari, 2000). However, in opposing AOUM programs, I am arguing that researchers have reinforced certain secular logics associated with sexuality education. My aim is to complicate the role of pleasure and desire in research and practice related to CSE. Joan Scott (2009), as I note in the introduction, has called for a critique of the "'idealized secular'—the notion that sexual emancipation is the fruit of secularism" (6). In this chapter my focus is on how secularism has come to be associated with particular ideals such as autonomy, pleasure, and sexual freedom. Joan Scott (2009) argues these ideals may be uncritically mobilized in feminist research, and I consider how these ideals are mobilized in sexuality education research.

"THICK DESIRE" IN SEXUALITY EDUCATION

In a 2006 paper titled, "Sexuality Education and Desire: Still Missing After All These Years," Michelle Fine and Sarah McClelland revisit Fine's seminal 1988 article, "Sexuality, Schooling, and Adolescent Females: The Missing Discourse of Desire." Both of these articles focus on how school-based sexuality education operates to constrain the agency of young people, especially young women, who are already marginalized in society. In the earlier piece, Fine (1988) famously argues:

> A *discourse of desire*, remains a whisper inside the official work of U.S. public schools . . . The naming of desire, pleasure, or sexual entitlement, particularly for females, barely exists in the formal agenda of public schooling on sexuality . . . A genuine discourse of desire would invite adolescents to explore what feels good and bad, desirable and undesirable, grounded in experience, needs, and limits. Such a discourse would release females from a position of receptivity, enable an analysis of the dialectics of victimization and pleasure, and would pose female adolescents as subjects of sexuality, initiators as well as negotiators. (1998: 33, emphasis in original)

Fine's claims for the benefits of putting pleasure and desire into the curriculum have been influential in structuring research on sexuality education. Her ideas about pleasure, desire, and sexuality clearly struck a chord with many feminist scholars in this area of research because they refused to construct young women as passive sexual subjects disengaged from pleasure and desire. Fine's work has also been influential on my own thinking about pleasure and desire in sexuality education. I have previously argued for a movement away from a focus on homophobia and gay and lesbian youth as always already "at risk" toward a greater emphasis on pleasure, subversion, and insubordination (Rasmussen, 2004; Rasmussen, Rofes, and Talburt, 2004).

In "Sexuality Education and Desire," Fine and McClelland (2006) continue to focus on young women's access to sexuality education, but the focus is deliberately on "poor and working-class youth, teens with disabilities, Black and Latino adolescents, and lesbian/gay/bisexual and transgender youth" as those most severely impacted by the politics of AOUM movements. Fine and McClelland also situate their analysis of existing programs "within a human rights framework" (298). It is within this context that Fine and McClelland (2006) outline what they call "thick desire."

Inspired in part by Martha Nussbaum (2003) and Arjun Appadurai (2001, 2004), thick desire encourages young women to *"imagine themselves as sexual beings capable of pleasure and cautious about burden without carrying the undue burden of social, medical and reproductive consequences"* (301, with my emphasis). In advocating schools as places in which thick desire could and should flourish, Fine and McClelland (2006) argue that young people need to be taught "skills to express political and sexual agency . . . in order to undertake critical analysis, trusting conversation, and help-seeking, and finally, to negotiate risk and pursue pleasure" (327). Fine and McClelland's vision for what they have termed "critical sexuality research"[1] foregrounds the interrelationship among "economic, social, and corporeal struggles" (326).

The politics that adhere to thick desire may be construed as part of a broader political movement supportive of CSE. Within this approach, the agency of individual young people and their rights to engage in sex for pleasure are no longer foregrounded (in an important shift from Fine's earlier work)—the focus is now on locating young people within broader struggles that shape their sexual subjectivities and capacities. Here Fine and McClelland (2006) place emphasis on developing young people's skills in critical analysis, so they can become critical consumers of information about their sexual health. For Fine and McClelland, thick desire is a framework for "policies and research that recognise how macro-structures, public institutions, practices and relationships affect 'personal decisions,' particularly for those without private supports and buffers" (328). There is still an emphasis on how young people can be encouraged to think of themselves as sexually agentic, weighing up conflicting discourses and deciding what is best for them. However, this framework also emphasizes the ways in which unequal structures modify young people's capacity for agency.

THE PROBLEM OF THICK DESIRE

In focusing on the construction of this notion of thick desire, my aim is to consider the relationship between desire and certain formations of sexularism (Scott, 2009). For Scott, sexularism is

> [t]he most frequent assumption that secularism encourages the free expression of sexuality and it thereby ends the oppression of women because it removes transcendence as the foundation for social norms and treats people as autonomous individuals, agents capable of crafting their own destiny. (2009: 1)

The vision of thick desire and critical studies in sexuality, as articulated by Fine and McClelland (2006), is, I will argue, characterized by the frame of sexularism. In the logic of Fine and McClelland's (2006) argument, readers are introduced to two kinds of desire. I have already introduced their vision of thick desire, and they suggest that the alternative to thick desire is "the unbridled desire of the state and the religious Right to recreate public education in their own image" (325). This bifurcation of the field of sexuality education into two kinds of desire is a problem because it narrows the frame through which we might interpret the many competing desires within the field of sexuality education. How does such an imagining of sexuality education account for opposition to CSE that is not authored by the state or the religious right? In the US, it is apparent that complex moral and religious issues can be found in debates over abstinence versus CSE (Alagari et al., 2002; Irvine, 2002; Lamb, 2010b; Luker, 2006). However, the focus of this chapter is not on religious objections to CSE but on the politics of pleasure and desire in research that is supportive of CSE. In considering the politics that adhere to thick desire, I am undertaking this reading as a researcher who has been supportive of such an approach. But in this book I am arguing that advocates of CSE, myself included, have been disingenuous about how beliefs about progressivism shape our imaginings of CSE. One problem of thick desire, and the progressive approach more broadly, is the binaries it enacts in relation to desire.

For instance, when Fine and McClelland (2006) imagine social contexts that might allow this thick desire to flourish or to be extinguished, they argue that "[e]nabling conditions for thick desire ossify as *public assistance* and are replaced with *punishing morality* as neo-liberalism and fundamentalism frame public educational policy" (301, emphasis in original). In framing their argument about the enabling and disabling conditions of thick desire, Fine and McClelland cite and re-inscribe a political division in which

Pleasure/Desire, Secularism, and Sexuality Education 91

"*punishing morality*" is associated with "neo-liberalism and fundamentalism" (301, emphasis in original). This association also has the effect of dialogically separating neoliberalism and fundamentalism from thick desire, at least as Fine and McClelland construct it. In this configuration there is a strong implication that moralizing about sexuality education is something to be associated with neoliberalism and fundamentalism. In the same move, thick desire becomes dissociated from morality.

I want to advocate for thick desire while simultaneously recognizing that my own critical views on sexuality education (see Rasmussen, 2006) can be viewed by some as dogmatic and unreasonable and that this debate must admit to its own forms of moralizing and to more than "two kinds of desire" (Fine and McClelland, 2006: 325). In her vision of a sexual ethics curriculum, Lamb (2010b) argues for the importance of incorporating teaching about religions and religious practices. This is an important distinction because it explicitly argues the value of incorporating conversations about belief and morality within the context of sexuality education.

In strongly protesting the "moralizing ideology" in public policy related to sexuality education (301), Fine and McClelland (2006) demonstrate how policies related to high stakes testing and juvenile incarceration intersect with the provision of sexuality education. In a section of their paper titled "Developmental Contexts for Thick Desire: Public Institutions and 'Private' Choices," there is a detailed discussion of the ways in which government policy can operate to construct certain young people (Black, Latino, poor, and working class) as irresponsible and more likely to make poor personal choices (301). Fine and McClelland are concerned that "the argument for abstinence only until marriage is beginning to assert a kind of natural cultural authority, in schools and out" (299) because "social policy, ideology, and educational practice are being aligned for abstinence, for heterosexual marriage, and against critical education about power, desires or dangers" (299). The focus of their critique is on the way moralizing discourses operate to privatize "bad" choices, absolving public institutions from responsibility for poor sexual health outcomes. I find this elaboration of public policy decisions borne from moralizing ideology compelling. I am convinced by the argument that public policy in the contemporary US has been constructed in such a way as to reinforce the marginalization of young people (Black, Latino, poor, and working class). I do not seek to refute this claim.

But CSE may also be involved in the marginalization of young newly arrived African migrants who are pro-abstinence and conservative on subjects of women's and gay rights. Critiques of the punishing morality of the religious right can also make it difficult for advocates of CSE to engage young people who don't share their beliefs about progressivism (Mills, 2012). This is apparent in Jesse Mills's (2012) study of a CSE program in San Diego, California (see Chapter 2 for a more detailed description of Mills's analysis of this program). Mills is critical of the educators and funders behind the program because he felt they didn't sufficiently engage with the cultural and religious beliefs of the young African men who were the principal focus of the project. Rather, program workers tended to stick to progressive scripts about sexuality education, pleasure, and desire and didn't grapple with the young men's beliefs, informed by their Islamic faith, about polygamy, homosexuality, and women.

This situation arises partially because progressive sexuality education is cast not as moralizing but as reasonable. It is cast as reasonable because it seeks to separate itself from morality and religion. And, it is cast as reasonable because it is associated with the public cause of human rights—it is pro-gay, pro-women's rights. These distinctions between reason and morality are strongly associated with the idea that CSE, at its best, is evidence based and/or associated with what is considered to a more universal appeal to rights.

As one looks to other international contexts (Australia—Rasmussen, 2006; Netherlands—Mepschen, Duyvendak, and Tonkens, 2010), it is apparent that secularism in CSE, like AOUM in the US, can be a way of thinking about sexuality that can also "assert a kind of natural authority, in schools and out" (Fine and McClelland, 2006: 299). My point is that natural cultural authority is not static and CSE can assert authority that parents, lobbyists, and school communities may perceive as a troubling form or moralizing (Gibson, 2007; Halstead, 1999; Mills, 2012).

I am attempting to make two points about CSE and natural cultural authority. First, natural cultural authority may be more apparent when it is at odds with your own politics of pleasure and desire. As a researcher who has lived and worked in country contexts where CSE is perceived to be under threat (US) and where CSE is consistently implemented as state government policy (Victoria, Australia), it is apparent to me that the politics (or lack thereof) associated with CSE are important to interrogate. Second, when "social policy, ideology, and educational practice are being aligned" in favor of thick desire, there will be religious groups or lobbyists within the community who voice legitimate concerns about such a perspective and further consideration needs to be given to how to respond to those concerns. I am arguing that research and practice associated with CSE needs to pay attention to pleasure and desire, to macrostructures, and to cultural and religious difference to develop understanding on how these things intersect in research and in practice.

HEALTH VERSUS MORALITY: FRAMING PLEASURE AND DESIRE

In this section of the chapter, I want to consider how pleasure and desire are framed in relation to the sexuality education research undertaken in other Western contexts, namely Australia, Aotearoa-New Zealand, and Canada. My goal is to demonstrate how particular understandings of the roles of pleasure and desire have become naturalized in research in the field of sexuality education. I also consider how discourses of health and morality have been situated in scholarly debates about the content of school-based sexuality education.

In his text, *Formations of the Secular*, Talal Asad (2003) makes the point that the secular and the religious share a particular relationship when they are collocated, a relationship that consigns religion to the domain of the private. So, in debates about sexuality education influenced by secularism, we might hear arguments that religion has no place in sexuality education in public schools. This argument rests on an assumption that religion rightly belongs in the private sphere. However, as influenced by Asad, I argue that what constitutes a religious or secular discourse in the domain of sexuality education is not straightforward because the public and the private are never so easily separated as the previous argument would suggest.

Distinctions between the public and private are often impossible to sustain when secular formations are placed under detailed scrutiny. For instance, in arguments that do favor more CSE, one can see how a certain "series of particular oppositions" arise—oppositions, as Asad indicates, that may be linked to particular secular formations that put religion and the public in their "proper" places (25). Significantly, in the context of this chapter, Fine and McClelland (2007) have also affirmed the value of adolescent sexuality education in European countries (unlike the US), where it is not constructed as a political or religious issue "but as a health issue, with healthy sexual development the desired outcome of sexuality education" (1000). In the field of sexuality education, these oppositions might be characterized as taking the following shapes: morality versus health, human rights versus religious rights, and reason (science) versus faith. These oppositions, which are further elaborated in the section, have come implicitly to frame arguments for and against pleasure and desire in sexuality education. It is this structuring, which can be implied or explicit, that often constructs health, pleasure, and erotics as distinct from or an anathema to religious and ethical issues.

I begin with an article from Aotearoa-New Zealand that illustrates this tendency to frame health and morality as necessarily opposed—Kim Elliot's (2003) "The Hostile Vagina: Reading Vaginal Discourse in a School Health Text." Elliot draws on Fine's earlier work in a discussion of sexuality education, which "confirms the missing discourses of erotics and desire (Allen, 2001; Burns 2000; Fine, 1992) in school-based sexuality education and the heterosexist viewpoint (Hughes, 1996; Quinlivan, 1996) of many school curricula in Aotearoa/New Zealand" (133). Going on to argue for a more complex rendering of gender and sexuality in the sexuality education classroom, Elliot (2003) also says:

> A key dilemma that has characterised this area for many years revolves around whether policy-makers are primarily concerned with morality or health . . . Sexuality education based on fear, fear of public opinion,

of social consequence, of fundamentalist intolerance, of political pressure, of sharing power, of reduced school roles is unlikely to truly educate in the way that the Ministry of Education advocates. (2003: 142, my emphasis)

Here, Elliot names what she sees as a key dilemma in sexuality education—the extent to which moral claims might be advanced versus the prioritizing of young people's health. In this logic, one can't be concerned with health and morality; it is necessary to choose one or the other. In this way of seeing, fundamentalism and morality are conjoined in a negative relationship and associated with intolerant fundamentalists. Conversely, those who can realize the New Zealand Government Ministry of Education's vision for sexuality education are constructed as above politics and religion. Those on the side of health are also situated as youth advocates because they are supportive of offering young people the opportunity to clarify their own values in relation to sexuality. CSE researchers are inevitably ensconced in moral and ethical dilemmas, but the politics of these positions—and how they might differ between researcher and country contexts—has not been the subject of much scrutiny.

What is noteworthy in Elliot's analysis of the health-versus-morality dilemma is the elision of the author's own political desires, though one might assume that these are in sympathetic alignment with the Ministry of Education curriculum. This health-versus-morality argument developed by Elliot is reminiscent of Fine and McClelland's (2006) discussion of thick desire in which "the press for abstinence only education" is constructed as a "further violation of human rights" (305). Such research (that constructs abstinence-based education as antihuman rights, anti-young people, and anti-health) is a powerful framing device in scholarship on sexuality education. It is also performative insofar as it reinscribes certain normative beliefs among progressive scholars, across different country contexts, about what is and is not morally acceptable within CSE.

Researchers supportive of CSE also have a tendency to downplay the complexities associated with competing moral claims and rights discourses that clearly permeate this field. For instance, Elliot suggests that we need to teach young people to decode culture critically in "order to clarify which perspectives are most appropriate guides in their own lives" (2003: 142). Such a position assumes some agreement that young people are best placed to make decisions about their sexual lives. The significance of the role of parents, religion, spirituality, and community are not mentioned in this vision; the focus is on the human rights of young people. These debates tend to reinforce a politics of pleasure and desire that reinscribe comprehensive-versus-abstinence binaries (Irvine, 2002, 2006, 2007; Luker, 2006), though clearly some researchers do seriously attend to claims regarding religion (Halstead, 1999; Sands, 2000), morality, and sexuality education (Lamb, 2010b; Vergari, 2000).

Researchers in sexuality education who perceive themselves as progressive have a tendency to undertake research that already has in mind certain notions of how CSE should be constituted. So, advocates of CSE who perceive morality as getting in the way of a more progressive or health-focused manifestation of sexuality education manifest the sexularism that Scott describes. Sexularism, Scott (2009) argues, likes to think of itself as "synonymous with progress, emancipation, and freedom from the strictures of religiously-based traditionalism" (3). I do not think that sexuality education researchers imagine a world free of religion. I am describing a form of secular logic, which conjoins advocating for pleasure and desire in the field of sexuality education with progress and freedom, while simultaneously constructing freedom as the rejection of morality. I think that this logic does underpin some research on sexuality education but that it is not something that researchers necessarily do deliberately. Partially, this logic has made a call for more pleasure in sexuality education a habit of thought that has come to be seen as an innately progressive maneuver in research on sexuality education.

PLEASURE/DESIRE AND AUTONOMY IN SEXUALITY EDUCATION

Arguments that focus on the fundamental importance of the autonomy of young people in the domain of sexuality education can be found in health and medical discourses, philosophical discussions, and more generally, in progressive research on sexuality education. Sue Morgan, in a discussion of relationships among religion, sex, and modernity in Britain in the 20th century, contends that notions of autonomy tend to be linked with secularism. She points to the transition brought about by

> ... psychologized readings of subjectivity in which meaning and authority resided not in some transcendental, divine adjudicator but in the secular, autonomous self. As historians of sexuality have made clear, in the Foucauldian paradigm the "core essence" of the increasingly therapeutic model of modern selfhood and the key to individual personality were no longer defined by religious belief but by sexual desire ... This secularization or, more specifically, this de-Christianization metanarrative, with its central shift from religious to scientific forms of authority, has retained a remarkable explanatory power in the histories of both religion and sexuality. (Morgan, 2013: 155)

Morgan's discussion of shifts in understanding of sexual autonomy is useful because it helps to situate contemporary understandings of pleasure and autonomy in sexuality education as part of a long history of progressivism and secularization, which retains "a remarkable explanatory power" (155).

This secularization of pleasure and autonomy is evident in an article by Erin Connell (2005), "Desire as Interruption: Young Women and Sexuality

Education in Ontario, Canada," where she argues for more pleasure and desire in sexuality education on the grounds that this is integral to the production of young women's agency. Connell characterizes Fine's early discussion of desire as a "genuine discourse" that perceives desire as

> a complex object that can invoke multiple understandings and meanings, [but] what is key in this discourse is the ability for adolescents to explore what feels good and bad, desirable and undesirable . . . [Discussions of desire] would also release females from positions of receptivity—women would be the subjects of sexuality, as well as initiators and negotiators. Such a discourse would enable an analysis of the dialectics of victimization/danger and pleasure/desire. (2005: 257)

In "Sexuality, Schooling, and Adolescent Females: The Missing Discourse of Desire," Fine (1988) argues that by teaching about desire, public schools could develop contexts in which "young women could breathe life into positions of social critique and experience entitlement rather than victimisation, autonomy rather than terror" (50). In Fine's theorization of the "missing discourse of desire," empowerment is firmly associated with autonomy and desire. Like Lamb (2010a), I am concerned about the power that has been invested in the liberatory capacities of pleasure and desire, following on from Fine (1988). The power that researchers in sexuality education have invested in the capacity of pleasure and desire to empower individual young people might be read as a form of "queer exceptionalism" (Puar, 2007), a process that posits "queerness as an exemplary or liberatory site devoid of nationalist and [secular] impulses" (173). Within the logic of this discourse, a focus on pleasure and desire is constructed as a universal good, something that we can all agree on, something genuine. In this way, advocates of pleasure and desire often fail to seriously wrestle with objections to adolescents exploring "what feels good and bad, desirable and undesirable" (Connell, 2005: 257). To my mind, this style of thought also reinforces particular understandings of autonomy and does not adequately engage with kinship, spirituality, and religion (Mills, 2012; Povinelli, 2006).

The right of young people to be the authors of their own sexual destiny is often supported within research on sexuality education embedded in health and medical discourse. Dean Whitehead's (2005) article, "In Pursuit of Pleasure: Health Education as a Means of Facilitating the 'Health Journey' of Young People," illustrates this approach. Whitehead argues that "nowadays, some young people feel that it is their fundamental right to go on their health journey unimpeded, in that they can 'enjoy' it is part of an intrinsic developmental experience" (214). In this argument, young people's rights are entwined with developmental discourse to construct a picture of them as propelled upon a journey of discovery. Whitehead (2005) notes further that in the context of such an approach, labeling behaviour as "delinquent or maladjusted" is ill-advised because such experimentation is "important

Pleasure/Desire, Secularism, and Sexuality Education 97

for young people's development" (215). Whitehead concludes his paper by arguing that

> a more realistic, ethical and humanistic approach lies in facilitating supportive learning environments where the young person may indulge in potentially health-damaging behaviours, but does so from an informed position and within the safest parameters possible. (2005: 222)

For Whitehead, an ethical approach to sexuality education is one that recognizes young people's propensity for risky behavior. Young people's right to experiment without judgment is key to this approach. In this framework, scientific knowledge about risk, pleasure, and resistance is gathered to advocate a "more realistic, ethical and humanistic approach" to sexuality education. Such an approach is also, according to Whitehead (2005), compatible with young people's own thinking because *"good sex has become a key life goal and a source of personal fulfillment: sex as secular salvation"* (Jackson and Scott, 1997, as cited in Whitehead, 2005: 221, my emphasis). Thus, "health education could usefully seek to help young people maximize their enjoyment" (2005: 222). It is possible to see in this research how secularism, ethics, and science are intertwined to argue the case for young people exercising educated choice in relation to pleasure and desire. For Whitehead, it is problematic when certain pleasures are characterized as immoral in sexuality education because this can have the unintended effect of inciting young people to rebel and can therefore reinforce harmful activities. In this logic, sexuality education that has an explicit moral agenda is constituted as unrealistic and unethical because it stands in the way of preparing young people to safely experiment.

At least some scientific and social scientific approaches are focused on preparing young people, as individuals, to become sexual actors who can minimize risk and maximize pleasure. This approach reinforces the discourse of individual pleasure and desire as well as affirming the importance of young people's autonomy in making educated choices about their own sexual behavior. Autonomy is seen as key to effective sexual education within this paradigm, but the politics of such an approach within different communities are not addressed. In his work, Whitehead (2005) uses science in such a way as to trump social, political, or cultural influences on sexuality education.

Reason and critical thinking in sexuality education curriculum are closely related to discussion of pleasure/desire and autonomy. To be autonomous subjects, the logic of the argument suggests that young people must first be taught how to make informed decisions about their sexual behavior. There is a focus on reason and education as central to helping young people develop as sexual subjects. While I am compelled by this argument, I am concerned that such an approach often fails to see value in other aspects of young people's lives that may influence their sexual decisions. Here I am thinking of kinship networks, culture and religion, spirituality and ethics and how these are integrated (or not) into young people's sexual decision making. I am also concerned that culture, religion, and morality are often constructed as somehow outside reason and therefore always something that diffuses rather than reinforces young people's capacity to act as agentic subjects.

The place of morality in relation to pleasure in sexuality education is certainly not straightforward. Nicholas Addison (2006), in his discussion of the gap between sexuality education and the lived experiences of young people in the UK, argues that young people's sexual autonomy and well-being are best served by engaging them in discussions about sexual desire. For Addison, "SRE is often framed by moral imperatives based on the prohibitions of Judaeo/Christian/Islamic teaching (Reiss and Abdul Mabud, 1998)" (2006: 352). Addison is not arguing for the removal of prohibitions; he wants sexuality education pedagogy to focus more on the way that these prohibitions operate to structure thought about sexuality. To clarify, Addison perceives the importance of admitting conversations about religion into sexuality education. But for him the focus of these conversations would appear to be on religion as prohibition.

Addison (2006) recognizes that secular and religious influences on the sexuality education curriculum are not stable, but that "tensions between these . . . imperatives have been further complicated by legislation that has oscillated between conservative and liberal perspectives" (2006: 352). Addison goes on to suggest his preference for an approach "where knowledge and responsibility are informed by the principles of freedom and choice (Bottery, 1998)" (Addison, 2006: 352). So Addison recognizes that morality is intrinsic to the production of SRE, but at the same time progressive sexuality education, as imagined by Addison, "refuses to satisfy or comfort . . . by providing a moral framework" (357). Here, moral frameworks become associated with intellectual laziness and a refusal of questioning; it is the antithesis of freedom and choice.

In Addison's imagining of a secular-progressive sexuality education, he has a preference for the ambiguous space that works of art can offer. He believes art

> provides a certain distance, [where] sexual norms can be questioned without either the prurient/censorial attitudes of the tabloid press or the clinical/moralising agendas of pedagogic discourse. In other words, within the discursive/hermeneutic space engendered by works of art, young people are able to bypass those instrumental discourses that are unhelpful in the formation of sexual well-being. (2006: 351)

For Addison, moralizing discourses (whether they are dressed up as religious or secular) are unhelpful because they are instrumental; they tell young people what to think rather than how to think. The progressive approach he favors promotes the questioning of sexual norms; this is a space of freedom and choice. Like Addison, I am keen to question moral frameworks, and in this examination I want to include frameworks that underpin my own scholarship in this area of research. Akin to Addison, this requires an approach to sexuality education that questions whether religion and morality are distinct. Unlike Addison, my imagining of progressivism refuses the constitution of religion as instrumental and therefore "unhelpful in the formation of sexual well-being" (Addison, 2006: 351).

The value of educating young people to be critical thinkers in relation to sexuality education is also apparent in an article by Lamb (1997) titled "Sex Education as Moral Education." Recognizing that there is no neutral position with regard to sexuality education, Lamb (1997) advocates the benefits of engaging young people in moral education that is focused on individual choices regarding sex and sexuality. She argues:

> The kinds of moral education curricula that emphasize individual decision-making seem readily applicable to issues of sex and sexuality . . . [T]he obvious problem or fear regarding their merger would be that sex education would become moralistic rather than morally related. . . . While some have argued effectively that even this "neutral" perspective contains hidden values . . . the overarching style that is aimed for in sex education is one of neutrality. To combine sex education and moral education would not have to mean teaching certain values relating to particular sexual acts but, instead, could mean a broadening of the entire enterprise of sex education to deal with . . . the role and construction of physical pleasure in our lives, aspects of sexual deviance and a focus on fantasy as well as sexual behaviour. (1997: 301, 302)

Lamb (1997) strives to articulate a vision for sexuality education that is morally related rather than moralizing, articulating the value of an approach that invites young people to think critically about pleasure, deviance, fantasy, and behavior. In this configuration of sexuality education, there are three important assumptions. First, there is agreement that a desirable sexuality education is one that is not moralistic. Second, it is claimed that a distinction can be drawn between morally related and moralistic sexuality education. Third, it is suggested that engaging young people in critical discussions of pleasure and desire represents a public good so long as these discussions locate pleasure and desire within specific cultural contexts and do not attempt to universalize these notions.

Akin to Lamb (1997), in my own research on sex and schooling, I have argued the value of "an ethics of pleasure [that] allows for the recognition of individual's agency in their own conduct and pursuit of pleasure" (Rasmussen, 2006: 217). In my discussion of pleasure in *Becoming Subjects* (2006), I draw on Foucault (1988) to make a similar distinction to Lamb between ethics that are moralizing and ethics that are focused on technologies of the self. Ethics that are focused on technologies of the self "permit individuals to effect by their own means or with the help of others a certain number of operations on their own souls, thoughts, conduct and ways of being" (Foucault, 1988, cited in Rasmussen, 2006: 216). In relation to Lamb's (1997) argument, such an approach might be constituted as more morally related than moralizing.

I am keen to implicate myself in this advocacy of a perspective that seeks to foster critical conversations about sexuality education—I am not a stranger to this argument. Yet I find myself increasingly unconvinced by the viability of drawing distinctions between morally related and moralizing sexuality education. I have come to conclude that much of the focus on autonomy and pleasure in sexuality education is best understood as a form of moralizing, which often works to exclude religious perspectives from the definition of good sexuality education, often for good political reasons. My aim in making this argument is not to privilege religion over science or vice versa but rather to consider how all sexuality education is moralizing and therefore to think more carefully about what type of moralizing we encourage in research and in practice. This also assumes an understanding that all moralizing is not given equal weight; certain political contexts will value secular sexuality education, while other contexts may be explicitly associated with a particular religious or cultural tradition.

I do assert that there is a strong faith within secular sexuality education. If we can pull together medically accurate information, scientific reason, and freedom from religion, then we can help young people to become more autonomous and liberated sexual subjects. For Scott (2009), this style of thought perpetuates a narrative "about the superiority of secularism to religion—as if the two categories were in internal opposition rather than discursively interdependent" (3). The problem of sexual pleasure in public and private discourse on religion is the subject of scrutiny in Kathleen Sands' (2000) text, *God Forbid: Religion and Sex in American Public Life*.

In discussing the place of pleasure in public debates on sexuality education in the US, Sands (2000) argues that

> if pleasure is given normative weight, then traditional religious criteria such as monogamy and procreation (which were not formulated to foster sexual pleasure!) cannot but be subject to examination . . . The conundrum . . . is that these and other values that can be advanced through sex just do not go together in any intrinsic way. Sexual pleasure is not automatically or easily confined to the bounds of interpersonal commitment; the exigencies of survival may defy those of self-actualization within one's sexual life . . . To affirm sexual diversity and dissent is to recognize that people have distinct and often incompatible views of what makes a sexual life good or bad (or at least good enough or too

bad). More than that, it recognizes that these disagreements are both profound and legitimate. (2000: 67)

This discussion of pleasure, desire, and autonomy highlights the complexity of "affirm[ing] sexual diversity" in an increasingly heterogeneous society. Sands's (2000) argument suggests that there can be little agreement about questions of pleasure and desire and their relationship to morality within the realm of sexuality education. She also underscores the complexities associated with the affirmation of pleasure as a normative good within sexuality education, given the conflicting opinions on the topic within public and private spheres. Sands's ideas are important in this discussion of pleasure, desire, and sexuality because she helps to underscore the problems of a critical sexuality education that is focused on autonomy, pleasure, and desire.

In our desire to affirm pleasure and desire, progressive researchers in sexuality education can fail to recognize the legitimate and profound differences within communities and relationships about how pleasure might be ethically constituted. Recognition that pleasure and desire are highly contested goods might provoke further interrogation of the role of these goods within sexuality education.

CONCLUSION

In this chapter, I have sought to undertake a close reading of a body of knowledge that I am most intimate with and have a great affection for. I have tried to trouble the ways in which pleasure and desire are configured within this body of knowledge to work against the assumption that sexual liberation is "the fruit of secularism" (Scott, 2009: 6). Inspired by Scott, I argue that discourses of pleasure and desire within sexuality education, as currently configured, are often (sometimes knowingly and sometimes un-reflexively) embedded in a secular framework. This observation is significant because it helps to account for the repetition of certain types of research within the field of sexuality education associated with discourses of pleasure and desire. It is recognised that in the field of sexuality education, a sustained call for more pleasure and desire has its own normalizing effects. I have sought to demonstrate that pleasure and desire in research on sexuality education must be understood as part of a broader politics of sexualism and that it is productive to consider how this research is shaped by "the terrain of its own political desire" (Weigman, 2006: 98). This is also a recognition that the field of sexuality education is performatively constructed. It is therefore worthwhile considering the chain of historicity that structures the intellectual boundaries of pleasure and desire in sexuality education because these boundaries continue to permeate future imaginings of research in sexuality education.

NOTE

1. In a later article, McClelland and Fine call for a "critical science of Adolescent sexualities... that suspends the 'givens' of adolescent sexualities" (2008: 67). The current research is sympathetic to this project, taking progressive sexuality education as one of the "givens" that needs interrogation.

REFERENCES

Addison, N. (2006). Acknowledging the Gap between Sex Education and the Lived Experiences of Young People: A Discussion of Paula Rego's *The Pillowman* (2004) and Other Cautionary Tales. *Sex Education: Sexuality, Society and Learning*, 6(4): 351–365.

Alagari, J.D., Collins, C., Morin S.F., & Summers, T. (2002). *Abstinence Only vs. Comprehensive Sex Education: What Are the Arguments? What Is the Evidence?* (Policy Monograph Series). San Francisco, CA: AIDS Research Institute.

Allen, L. (2001). Closing Sex Education's Knowledge/Practice Gap: The Reconceptualization of Young People's Sexual Knowledge. *Sex Education: Sexuality, Society and Learning*, 1(2): 109–122.

Appadurai, A. (2001). *New logics of violence*. Seminar, Number 503. Available from http://www.india-seminar.com/2001/503/503%20arjun%20apadurai.htm (Last accessed March 31, 2006).

———. (2004). The Capacity to Aspire: Culture and the Terms of Recognition. In V. Rao & M. Walton (Eds.), *Culture and Public Action* (pp. 59–84). New York: Russell Sage Foundation.

Asad, T. (2003). *Formations of the Secular: Christianity, Islam, Modernity*. Stanford, CA: Stanford University Press.

Connell, E. (2005). Desire as Interruption: Young Women and Sexuality Education in Ontario, Canada. *Sex Education*, 5(3), 253–268.

Elliot, K. (2003). The Hostile Vagina: Reading Vaginal Discourse in a School Health Text. *Sex Education: Sexuality, Society and Learning*, 3(2), 132–144.

Fine, M. (1988). Sexuality, Schooling, and Adolescent Females: The Missing Discourse of Desire. *Harvard Educational Review*, 58(1): 29–53.

Fine, M., & McClelland, D. (2006). Sexuality Education and Desire: Still Missing After All These Years. *Harvard Educational Review*, 76(3): 297–338.

———. (2007). The Politics of Teen Women's Sexuality: Public Policy and the Adolescent Female Body. *Emory Law Journal*, 56(4): 993–1038.

Foucault, M. (1988). Technologies of the Self. In L. Martin, H. Gutman, & P.H. Hutton (Eds.), *Technologies of the Self: A Seminar with Michel Foucault* (pp. 16–49). Amherst: University of Massachusetts Press.

Gibson, S. (2007). The Language of the Right: Sex Education Debates in South Australia. *Sex Education: Sexuality, Society and Learning*, 7(3): 239–250.

Halstead, J.M. (1999). Teaching about Homosexuality: A Response to John Beck. *Cambridge Journal of Education*, 29(1): 131–136.

Ingham, R. (2005). 'We Didn't Cover That at School': Education Against Pleasure or Education for Pleasure? *Sex Education*, 5(4): 375–388.

Irvine, J.M. (2002). *Talk about Sex: The Battles Over Sex Education in the United States*. California: University of California Press.

———. (2006). Emotional Scripts of Sex Panics. *Sexuality Research and Social Policy*, 3(3): 82–94.

———. (2007). Transient Feelings: Sex Panics and the Politics of Emotions. *GLQ*, 14(1): 1–40.

Kantor, L. M., Santelli, J., Teitler, J., & Balmer, R. (2008). Abstinence-only Policies and Programs: An Overview. *Sexuality Research and Social Policy*, 5(3): 6–27.

Lamb, S. (1997). Sex Education as Moral Education: Teaching for Pleasure, about Fantasy, and Against Abuse. *Journal of Moral Education*, 26(3): 301–315.

———. (2010a). Feminist Ideals for a Healthy Female Adolescent Sexuality: A Critique. *Sex Roles*, 62(5–6): 294–306.

———. (2010b). Toward a Sexual Ethics Curriculum: Bringing Philosophy and Society to Bear on Individual Development. *Harvard Educational Review*, 80(1): 81–105.

Lesko, N. (2010). Feeling Abstinent? Feeling Comprehensive? Touching the Affects of Sexuality Curricula. *Sex Education*, 10(3): 281–297.

Luker, K. (2006). *When Sex Goes to School: Warring Views on Sex—and Sex Education—Since the Sixties*. New York: Norton.

Mayo, C. (2008). Obscene Associations: Gay-Straight Alliances, the Equal Access Act, and Abstinence-Only Policy. *Sexuality Research and Social Policy*, 5(2): 45–55.

McClelland, S. I., & Fine, M. (2008). Embedded Science: Critical Analysis of Abstinence-Only Evaluation Research. *Cultural Studies—Critical Methodologies*, 8(1): 50–81.

Mepschen, P., Duyvendak, J. W., & Tonkens, E. H. (2010). Sexual Politics, Orientalism and Multicultural Citizenship in the Netherlands. *Sociology*, 44(5): 962–979.

Mills, J. (2012). I Should Get Married Early: Culturally Appropriate Comprehensive Sex Education and the Racialization of Somali Masculinity. *Spectrum: A Journal on Black Men*, 1(1): 5–30.

Morgan, S. (2013). Sex and Common-Sense: Maude Royden, Religion, and Modern Sexuality. *Journal of British Studies*, 52(1): 153–178.

Nussbaum, M. (2003). Women's Education: A Global Challenge. *Signs: Journal of Women in Culture and Society*, 29(2): 325–355.

Povinelli, E. A. (2006). *The Empire of Love: Toward a Theory of Intimacy, Genealogy and Carnality*. Durham, North Carolina: Duke University Press.

Puar, J. K. (2007). *Terrorist Assemblages: Homonationalism in Queer Times*. Durham: Duke University Press.

Rasmussen, M. L. (2004). Wounded Identities, Sex and Pleasure: "Doing It" at School. NOT! *Discourse: Studies in the Cultural Politics of Education*, 25(4): 445–458.

———. (2006). *Becoming Subjects: Sexualities and Secondary Schooling*. New York: Routledge.

Rasmussen, M. L., Rofes, E., & Talburt, S. (Eds.). (2004). *Youth and Sexualities: Pleasure, Subversion, and Insubordination In and Out of Schools*. New York: Palgrave.

Sands, K. (2000). *God Forbid: Religion and Sex in American Public Life*. New York: Oxford University Press.

Scott, J. W. (2009, April 23). *Sexularism*. Ursula Hirschman Annual Lecture on Gender and Europe, Florence, Italy.

Vergari, S. (2000). Morality Politics and Educational Policy: The Abstinence-Only Sex Education Grant. *Educational Policy*, 14(2): 290–310.

Weigman, R. (2006). Interchanges: Heteronormativity and the Desire for Gender. *Feminist Theory*, 7(1): 89–103.

Whitehead, D. (2005). In Pursuit of Pleasure: Health Education as a Means of Facilitating the "Health Journey" of Young People. *Health Education*, 105(3): 213–227.

6 On Not Feeling Homophobic

> To make the claim that there is not a universalized form of homophobia might strike some as strange. In fact, it might strike others as even stranger that what constitutes homophobia in one geopolitical space does not translate seamlessly to another geopolitical space. And if homophobia is in question, the what and the how of the idea of homosexuality are also in question.
>
> (Walcott, 2010: 315)

My focus in this chapter is on the topic of homophobia and its place in imaginings of progressive sexuality education in Australia and the US. I draw on research in anthropology, law, and studies of gender and sexuality in an attempt to complicate psychological understandings of homophobia that may underscore the popular use of scales to measure homophobic attitudes in preservice and in-service teachers. These interdisciplinary approaches to homophobia provide the basis for a critical reading of some contemporary pedagogical approaches to anti-homophobia education that may be read as progressive in diverse education contexts.

Clearly, Australia and the US provide different contexts in which to understand the place of homophobia in education. The concern of how to address problems related to homophobia and heterosexism in education has been more fraught in the US context than in the Australian context, where states have generally endorsed some form of CSE (Weaver, Smith, and Kippax, 2005). This is not to say that anti-homophobia education is not seen as a controversial issue in the Australian context, though attempts to address homophobia in teacher education and university education have not been confronted with as much organized resistance as in the US context (Gibson, 2007; Rasmussen, 2006). It is also true to say that in both the US and Australia, the question of how to deal with homophobia has not been uniform (Rasmussen, 2005, 2006).

In sexuality education it is often taken as assumed that homophobia is problematic, and the focus becomes ways in which to intervene against the reproduction of homophobic attitudes (Morrow and Gill, 2003; Ollis,

2010; Serdahely and Ziemba, 1984). For many, when they read about homophobia, they think of bullying or violence on the basis of sexuality. Homophobia is indeed problematic if it leads to any kind of discrimination in the classroom or wider society. As a consequence, strategies are devised and implemented to help students and teachers become less homophobic (Elia, 1993; Franck, 2002).

However, in devising these strategies, scales, and anti-homophobic education programs, religion is often disregarded. Monotheistic religions (Judaism, Christianity, and Islam), and adherents to these religions, are often characterized as holding conservative views pertaining to abstinence, sex before marriage, marriage, gender roles, and of course, homosexuality. On the other hand, secularism is frequently positioned as progressive, particularly on the question of gender and sexual diversity. Both of these characterizations obscure the diverse perspectives on gender and sexuality within and among people who identify as religious and nonreligious.

These beliefs about religion and secularism may underpin some attempts to construct education as the antidote to homophobia because they are informed by an understanding of people who avow to be religious and homophobic as uneducated about sexuality—a contention that I will explore further in this chapter. Within this framing, teachers and students who reject the lessons of anti-homophobia programs may be seen as ineffective or a problem in the battle against homophobia (Morrow and Gill, 2003). Those who stand up and confront homophobia are lauded (Blackburn, Clark, Kenney, and Smith, 2009; Ollis, 2010; Witthaus 2011; Zack, Mannheim, and Alfano 2010). However, if what we understand to be homophobia is in question, as Walcott suggests, what does this mean for some of the tools used in anti-homophobia education? How might pedagogies that problematize homophobia, including scales that measure homophobia (a tool deployed in anti-homophobia education in Australia and the US) be read against this proposition that what we understand homophobia to be is still in question? (For two examples of scales, see Clark, 2010; Rogers, McRee, and Arntz, 2009). In short, is it possible to measure something that is as difficult to classify as homophobia? Here I am arguing for a rethinking of the *concept* of homophobia. In this chapter, I will explore how this concept is increasingly antiquated and inapplicable.

I attempt to resist the co-option of anti-homophobia education within broader imaginings of education as a progressive project. The co-option of discourses about homophobic bullying within the frame of progressivism is discussed by Daniel Monk in his article "Challenging Homophobic Bullying in Schools: The Politics of Progress." Monk (2011) notes:

> The perception of education as the key tool for unlocking individual potential and for creating a fairer society remains an article of faith within liberal and progressive political paradigms . . . Research about homophobic bullying is inherently and inevitably a political project. Yet

while issues such as gay marriage and gays in the military are campaigns that have been exposed to lively critique within the LGBT community and academic literature, there has been very little similar debate about homophobic bullying, located as it is within the "benign" emancipatory liberal discourses of education and future-focused discourses of innocent and universal childhood. (2011: 191)

In analyzing attempts to combat homophobia through the use of scales, my attention is focused on the logic that underpins such interventions. I undertake this analysis because, like Monk, I think that there needs to be a lively critique of discourse (and research instruments) that may appear benign and that are conceived as part of an emancipatory or progressive project.

In the next section I consider Daniel Witthaus's adaptation of Betty Burzon's classification of homophobic types for use in workshops (in and outside of schools in rural and regional Australia); Ollis's pedagogical use of Riddle's Scale of Attitudes in a national sexuality education resource produced in Victoria, Australia; and Zack, Mannheim and Alfano's classification of archetypal responses to homophobic rhetoric for use in teacher education in the US. My study of these scales should not be read as a disavowal of the problem of homophobic bullying. I appreciate that for some young people, experiences of homophobia are profound, frequent, and devastating. The very real and continuing problem of homophobia in the Australian context has been played out nationally at the time of writing against the backdrop of Australian swimming star Ian Thorpe's coming out on national television. Thorpe, now in his early 30s, felt that he was unable to come out as a young man under the glare of an international spotlight. Thorpe has also been frank about how his decision to remain closeted took a significant toll on his mental health (ABC News, 2014).

Following on from an analysis of scales that have been developed to measure homophobia, I move to a consideration of the logics that underpin these scales. How is homophobia being interpreted in these scales? What is the relationship between anti-homophobia education and post-homophobic imaginings? How does homophobia intersect with cultural and religious difference in these scales, and what does this mean for the continued use of scales that purport to measure homophobia? Finally, I turn to some other ways of theorizing homophobia that might prompt educators and researchers to think differently about the question of homophobia and their use of scales to measure homophobia.

SCALING HOMOPHOBIA

Homophobia is commonly associated with psychological understandings of sexuality. There are hundreds of studies that use scales to measure homophobia; the following studies are just a few examples, which have been chosen particularly because of their focus on scales as useful in a pedagogical context (Clark, 2010; Elia, 1993; Franck, 2002; Morrow and Gill, 2003Pain and Disney, 1996; Rogers et al., 2009; Witthaus, 2011).

The scales generally originate in psychology, and their history in the measurement of homophobia goes back to at least 1980 (Hudson and Ricketts, 1980). It is beyond the scope of this chapter to provide a detailed analysis of the formation of these scales.[1] According to Monto and Supinski (2014), scales that measure homophobia or homonegativity (negative attitudes toward homosexuality) are important, because

> [h]omonegativity is associated with a range of negative qualities, including less openness to new experiences (Cullen, Wright, and Allesandri, 2002), greater general intolerance (Aosved and Long, 2006; Rogers, McRee, and Arntz, 2009), irrational beliefs (Plugge-Foust and Strickland, 2000), less tendency to form intimate relationships among men (Kassing, Beasley and Frey, 2005; Monroe, Baker and Roll, 1997), rape myth acceptance (Aoesved and Long, 2006; Kassing, Beesley and Frey, 2005; Nagoshi et al., 2008), and an inclination toward discriminatory behavior (Aberson, Swan and Emerson, 1999; Patel, Long, McCammon and Weunsch, 1995). Homonegativity has also been identified as a barrier to effective social work practice and effective psychological counseling (Barrett and McWhirter, 2002; Crisp, 2006a, 2006b; Raiz and Salzburg, 2007; Rees-Turyn, Doyle, Holland, and Root, 2008). On a darker note, homonegativity can be expressed as violence toward gay men and lesbians (Alden and Parker, 2005; Hamner, 1992). (2014: 900)

This long list of potential pathologies associated with homonegativity is instructive of the power of such scales to associate beliefs about sexuality with an array of negative behaviors, pathologies, social barriers, and "irrational beliefs" (900). Conservatism and religiosity are clearly related to greater homonegativity on this scale (906).

What are the possible consequences of the pedagogical use of such scales when they are utilized to educate people to assist them to become less homophobic? I situate such a rationale for the use of scales in educational contexts alongside contemporary research that is critical of how homophobia is conceptualized and sometimes utilized as part of "progressive" educational agendas.

Debbie Ollis, Lyn Harrison, and Claire Maharaj, working in teacher education in the Australian context, suggest sexuality educators may employ scales of homophobia as tools to support them in developing educational spaces that they perceive to be more affirming of sexual diversity. Ollis, Harrison, and Maharaj (2013) argue:

> The successful pre-service and in-service teacher education programs which do exist have demonstrated a number of elements that have been

seen to have promoted their success. These include a group-teaching model, seen as effective in developing the key skills of working together and communication (Thomas and Jones, 2005; Walker et al., 2003); and questionnaires and rating scales (including Riddle's scale of attitudes) on participants' own reactions, designed to provoke self-reflection amongst participants (Levenson-Gingiss and Hamilton, 1989; Ollis 2010; Thomas and Jones, 2005). (2013: 4)

For these authors, the scales are a means to provoke students to reflect on their own thinking about diverse sexualities. The scales are held to be particularly pedagogically persuasive because they enable preservice and in-service teachers to measure their own attitudes and to see how these measures might change in comparison to other points on the scale.

In their work with teachers, Ollis, Harrison, and Maharaj (2013) advocate the use of Riddle's scale (Riddle, 1994). Dorothy Riddle, the developer of Riddle's scale, was a psychologist and part of an American Psychological Association task force that effectively lobbied for the removal of homosexuality as a psychiatric disorder in the *Diagnostic and Statistical Manual*. The Riddle scale of attitudes was developed in the early 1970s when Riddle was based at the City University of New York (see Woodstock School website, 2013). The first published version of the scale did not appear until 1994. It is worth noting the context in which the Riddle scale was developed; it is now nearly 40 years old, but researchers and educators in Australia and the US still see the scale as having applicability within and outside the US (Hirschfield, 2001; Ollis, 2010; Ollis et al., 2013).

Let me be clear in stating that Ollis et al.'s decision to use the scale is in many ways unremarkable. For instance, Gay and Lesbian Health Victoria, the peak body for lobbying on issues related to enhancing the health and well-being of Victoria's gay, lesbian, bisexual, trans, and intersex communities also employs Riddle's scale in its professional development programs (see Gay & Lesbian Health Victoria, 2013).

Some researchers in counseling psychology have also questioned the value of such scales, arguing that

[t]he public discourse about sexual orientation is evolving, and it appears that there are a wide range of LGB-affirmative attitudes that may not be tapped by existing measures. Also, many LGB individuals have become more visible, causing many heterosexual individuals to experience ambivalent or uncertain attitudes (Worthington, Savoy et al., 2002). Finally, antigay violence reflects a level of attitude that encompasses hatred and violent behavior (Herek, 2000) that should certainly be conceptualized as extending beyond the level of "condemnation" reflected as the polar end of Herek's continuum of heterosexual attitudes. Attitudes reflecting "violent homonegativity" have not

been incorporated into existing measures. (Worthington, Dillon, and Becker-Schutte, 2005: 106)

Worthington et al. critique scales, such as Riddle's, which were developed in the 1970s because they don't reflect current climates regarding sexuality and gender. This is a concern in the context of the current chapter because those who devise the scales are themselves critical of the quality of the scales that are being deployed by some people in education. While Worthington et al.'s critique prompts them to develop more precise scales, I seek to question the drive to measure such attitudes, specifically when such scales are employed with a view to developing pedagogical strategies to eliminate homophobia.

Ollis (2010) has identified, and I would concur, that some teachers are reluctant to "recognise and affirm sexual diversity" in public schools, and she has developed a series of workshops to help teachers think about what might cause this reluctance (218). The workshops, which were part of a national Talking Sexual Health program, were also featured in a more recent resource, *Sexuality Education Matters* (Ollis et al., 2013) (an online resource for Australian teacher educators),[2] that aims

> . . . to present teachers with an examination of a range of discourses that have operated to position sexual diversity in a constraining and negative way . . . These include discourses of fear, illness, difference, and abnormality. The workshop also aimed to present teachers with others [discourses], which Johnson (1996) calls "a way forward" that can enable teachers to deconstruct heterosexuality, affirm diversity and position sexual diversity as the part of the normal spectrum of sexuality; in other words the positive subject positions. (Ollis, 2010: 220)

In Ollis's workshop, as discussed in her 2010 article, participants position themselves and their school in response to heterosexuality and homosexuality using Riddle's Scale of Attitudes (221). The following attitudes in relation to both heterosexuality and homosexuality appear on Riddle's scale:

Celebration

These people celebrate gay and lesbian people and assume that they are indispensable in our society. They are willing to be gay advocates.

Appreciation

These people appreciate and value the diversity of people and see gays as a valid part of that diversity. These people are willing to work to combat homophobic attitudes in others.

Admiration

This acknowledges that being gay/lesbian in our society takes strength.
Such people are willing to truly look at themselves and work on their own homophobic attitudes.

Support

These people support work to safeguard the rights of gays and lesbians.
Such people may be uncomfortable themselves, but they are aware of the implications of the negative climate homophobia creates and the irrational unfairness.

Acceptance

Still implies there is something to accept, characterised by such statements as "You're not a gay to me, you're a person." "What you do in bed is your own business." 'That's fine as long as you don't flaunt it." This attitude denies social and legal realities. It still sets up the person saying "I accept you" in a position of power to be the one to "accept" others. It ignores the pain, invisibility and stress of closet behaviour. "Flaunt" usually means say or do anything that makes people aware. This is where most of us find ourselves, even when we'd like to think that we are doing really well.

Tolerance

Homosexuality is seen as just a phase of adolescent development that many people go through and most people "grow out of." Thus, gays are less mature than straights and should be treated with the protectiveness and indulgence one will use with a child. Gays and lesbians should not be given positions of authority (because they are still working through adolescent behaviours), as they are seen as "security risks."

Pity

Heterosexual chauvinism. Heterosexuality is seen as more mature and certainly to be preferred. Any possibility of becoming straight should be reinforced and those who seem to be born "that way" should be pitied, as in "the poor dears."

Repulsion

Homosexuality is seen as a "crime against nature." People who identify as homosexual are sick, crazy, immoral, sinful, wicked etc., and anything is justified to change them (e.g. prison, hospitals). You might well hear this expressed as "Yuk! When I think about what they do in bed!" (Riddle, 1994 in Ollis et al., 2013: 92, 93).

The hierarchy at play in the scale is readily apparent; people who are repulsed by homosexuality appear at the bottom. In this structure it appears that the most desirable position a teacher might assume is that they come to celebrate homosexuality. The desirability of achieving celebration on Riddle's scale is discussed below:

> . . . [T]eachers also talked about the importance of Riddle's scale in challenging their notion of what the attitudes "tolerance" and "acceptance" really meant in relation to being inclusive. Kim was one of the three teachers prior to the professional development to feel that her program did not need changes to be inclusive. Yet even for her, the "Scale of Attitudes"' activity challenged her understanding and attitudes and made her reflect on the possibility that she too had some movement towards inclusiveness to make. She could remember thinking: "I was so liberated in my thinking but I'm probably not yet at celebration, you know, that's still one step on for me. So I guess that struck home because I thought, well, everybody's got somewhere to go as far as their thinking on homosexuality" (Kim, Phase 3). (Ollis, 2010: 224)

Kim's statement that "everybody's got somewhere to go as far as their thinking on homosexuality" demonstrates that she has absorbed the lesson of the scale, namely that many people's thinking about homophobia is in need of advancement. Ollis is, I think, pleased with this outcome because it points to the productivity of these scales in helping people diagnose their own shortcomings in regard to homophobic feelings.

What interests me, both in Ollis's and Kim's (the preservice teacher participant) use of the scale, is their investment in the logic employed by Riddle in developing the scale, namely, that celebration should be every teacher's ultimate destination. Later in this chapter, I critically consider this impulse to move teachers toward celebration. But first, I want to illustrate some other scales that are currently being used in anti-homophobia education in Australia and the US.

Daniel Witthaus is a prominent Australian anti-homophobia activist who has been doing advocacy related to gay and lesbian issues since the early 1990s. He spends a lot of time talking to school and community groups in rural and remote Australia. He is founder of the National Institute for Challenging Homophobia Education (NICHE).

On his Beyond That's So Gay website, in a resource titled "The Faces of Homophobia: Everyday Resistance Quantified . . ." (2011), Witthaus states that he has adapted Betty Burzon's (sic) model of homophobic types for the Australian context, as part of his Beyond That's So Gay Australia-wide training program. In her text *Setting Them Straight*, Berzon (1996), an author and psychotherapist, developed a series of homophobic types to help readers who encountered homophobic messages in everyday conversations. Other researchers have also drawn on Berzon's types in their anti-homophobia work (Rostosky, Riggle, Horne, and Miller, 2009; Van Wormer and McKinney, 2003).

In creating types that draw strongly on Australian stereotypes, Witthaus (2011) is no doubt using a form of language that he thinks will engage his audiences in regional and remote Australia. Witthaus has developed the following descriptors of different personality types that he relates in the following order.

The Romper Stomper[3]

Feel vulnerable and constantly under attack; Mobilised to counterattack those things and people that threaten their well-being; Typically male, their definition of reality is described as 'narrow' and their outlook "hateful."

The Frustrated Bogan[4]

Trouble coping with reality, and shows inflexibility in adapting within their environment; Frustration is primarily handled using aggression; Emotion is an important weapon, often shown by lashing out.

The Politician

Conservative individuals who jump onto the nearest "bandwagon" (e.g. polls); Desperate to fit in with the "in-group" and be seen to distance themselves from the "out-group"; Avoid taking responsibility for their attitudes and actions.

The Sheep

Thinkers who are dependent upon the opinion of others (i.e. the flock); Don't spend much time considering the consequences of discrimination; Their lack of a self-determined belief system paired with their apathy makes them dangerous in the hands of the wrong shepherd.

The Stirrer

Attempts to exploit the fears and frustrations of the other homophobic types; Exploits people's ignorance and fear of difference; Adept at stirring up anger in others and experts in uniting and building cohesion against a "common enemy."

The Almost Ally

Invariably well-educated and older people, often females, who pledge their LGBT allegiance; Often unaware of their own homophobia;

Unwilling to put themselves in situations where they, or others, could assess them as prejudiced. (Witthaus, 2011: 1, 2)

These portraits portray people who are homophobic as paranoid, hateful, conservative, socioeconomically disadvantaged, and unable to think for themselves. The type classified as the sheep, which appears to evoke religious metaphors (the shepherd) and their followers (sheep), are constituted as unthinking and non-agentic.

Akin to Ollis's (2010) use of Riddle's scale, Witthaus (2011) sees advancement of people along the scale as a clear goal of its use. This is apparent in the citation below:

> Experienced LGBT advocate and friend to religious communities, Anthony Venn-Brown, is clear that in any everyday conversation he has with homophobic opponents he only has one goal: to identify where they are on this very scale and to shift them one step forward. (Witthaus, 2011: 3)

Ollis and Witthaus are both committed to anti-homophobia education, and they share a belief that anti-homophobia education can help people become less homophobic. These scales are assembled within a liberatory framework that sees the value in progressing all people along a scale. In the logic of the scale, becoming less homophobic constitutes a more enlightened or liberated position.

Together with Harwood, I have previously argued that the expression of competing truths about homosexuality (including the expression of homophobia) is an important part of pedagogy about difference and inclusion. We believe that curtailing speech that is homophobic privileges particular understandings of inclusion (Harwood and Rasmussen, 2013). But we need to be cautious in making these contentions. Hateful speech toward other people—on the basis of their sexuality, gender, or race—is offensive. On the other hand, open debate about differing views and understandings can be progressive, even if they can be pigeonholed as regressive. I read these scales as pedagogically problematic because they assume in advance that homophobia is a uniformly understood and static concept that can be diagnosed according to personality type or scale. The use of personality types in Witthaus's (2011) work on homophobic bullying also reinforces the notion that homophobia is associated with pathology.

US education researchers Zack, Mannheim and Alfano (2010) have also designed a scale to measure "the varying levels of ability and willingness of the participants [111 student teachers] to address homophobia in their classroom. Ideally, we hoped that our participants would move from the lower levels of avoiders and hesitators to the higher levels of confronters and, ultimately, integrators" (102). Below are brief descriptors of each of the archetypal responses to homophobic rhetoric, classified by Zack et al. (2010):

Confronters

Many student teachers took it upon themselves to take time from the scheduled lesson plan to address homophobic slurs that were leveled against students. It was the consensus among these student teachers that homophobic rhetoric was widespread, considered socially acceptable, and posed a challenge to them as educators that was nearly impossible to conquer singlehandedly—but they were willing to give it a try. (103)

Integrators

A few student teachers sought to combat the issue of homophobia within the school by integrating homophobia reduction into the curriculum. These student teachers understood that queer culture is an important part of the multicultural repertoire and should not be excluded. (104)

Hesitators

By far the largest archetype, "hesitators" describes the largest group, those who felt a call to action to address the homophobia they witnessed, but lacked the set of skills necessary to create an atmosphere free of homophobic rhetoric or move students toward more accepting ideologies. The reasons for this lack of confidence varied among the student teachers, but were most commonly the result of 1) being accused of being gay by students, 2) encountering religious opposition in the students, and 3) feeling pressured to focus on content. (103)

Avoiders

While there was heated discussion regarding homophobic rhetoric, made evident by the numerous student teachers who volunteered the topic and confirmed how rampant the problem was, some student teachers chose to remain silent during the discussions. It is impossible to state with any certainty the reasons for these participants' withdrawal from the conversation. The silence may imply that they were on some level complicit with the level of homophobia being exhibited by students and unwilling to address these behaviors . . . Some of the avoiders may have been struggling with their own sexual identity. Or, we hypothesized, perhaps some were uncomfortable talking about anything dealing with sex in a public forum. While no student teacher freely admitted to doing nothing when encountering homophobic speech at their schools, their silence was telling. (102)

The archetypal responses developed by Zack et al. (2010) produce a hierarchy that measures people's capacity to address homophobia in a way that the researchers perceive as appropriate. The notion of progress is also apparent. The researchers, in talking about confronters, observe that "we were pleased that many felt confident enough to address homophobic speech when it presented itself and had the knowledge and skills to move students in a positive direction" (104). So participants who were characterized as most able and willing to address homophobia were the ones who conceptualized themselves as having the capacity to move students on from homophobic attitudes.

Avoiders, the archetype situated at the bottom of Zack et al.'s (2010) scale, are seen as potentially taking up this position for a multitude of reasons. Below they provide an account of the type of teacher education student who might take up the avoider position:

> Knowing that the discourse within our program favors pluralism and a regard for diversity, it is likely that some participants in the discussion remained silent because their personal views were in opposition to homosexual lifestyles. Perhaps they believed that the religiously, morally, and politically charged issue of homosexuality was outside the purview of public schooling. Or, maybe they were just too shy. Whatever the case, it seemed unlikely that these beginning teachers would be addressing the issues of homophobic hate-speech in any meaningful ways in the near future. (2010: 103)

This discussion allows that participants might have religious objections—this would account for their being labeled as avoiders. There is also recognition that the space of the university classroom featured in the research, which is described as one that "favors pluralism and a regard for diversity," meant that "some participants in the discussion remained silent" (Zack et al., 2010: 103).

This is a particularly salient observation because it indicates the ways in which religious objections to homosexuality have become unspeakable in some university classrooms. Avoiders read the classroom climate, know that homophobic utterances are unacceptable in this particular space, and thus know to keep silent. This shared understanding, on the part of professors and their teacher education students, that homophobia is unutterable, sets up a space that sets specific limits on pluralism and diversity, no doubt with the best of intentions.

Below, Zack et al. (2010) provide confronters with tips on how to deal with religious beliefs of students that are perceived as discriminatory:

> Student teachers should also be equipped with information that challenges the religious beliefs of students (when these beliefs are mired in discrimination) . . . Some organizations that can aid those entering

the teaching profession in solidifying their responses to religious and legal arguments against homosexuality include freedomtomarry.org, which provides advice on how to talk about marriage equality, and informedconscience.com, a group that explores homosexuality and the Catholic Church and provides alternative interpretations of scripture. (2010: 109)

I am concerned at what such directions might mean for teachers when they are working in schools and they encounter remarks that they perceive as homophobic from peers, parents, or students. Such an approach could set up teachers to conclude that certain students' beliefs are in need of correction or, at least, movement in a "positive direction." This prompts me to ask: When does saying no to homophobia become a means to discipline specific types of religious beliefs in the classroom?

The binaries at work in the production of scales utilized in anti-homophobic research and pedagogies are well summed up in a doctoral thesis titled *With Us or Against Us: Using Religiosity and Socio-Demographic Variables to Predict Homophobic Beliefs* (Schwartz, 2011). In this study, Erin Schwartz (a graduate of the Indiana State University doctoral program in counseling psychology) utilizes a psychological scale to measure the homophobic attitudes of people in the US who were, and were not, religiously affiliated. By employing a particular scale, Schwartz found that people who identified as fundamentalists in Christian traditions were more likely to be homophobic. One interpretation of Schwartz's findings might be that scales of homophobic beliefs are useful because they are helpful in determining who is "with us or against us." However, what is not so clear—who is the *us*?

Schwartz was surprised to note that level of education among people who were fundamentalist did not alter their level of homophobia—though age did.

> *The finding of no differences in homophobia based on level of education was surprising.* It had been expected that having more education and thus, more exposure to various points of view from sources other than family-of-origin and one's religious congregation, would play an important role in differences in homophobic beliefs. This unexpected finding indicates that education alone may not have an important impact on changing prejudicial beliefs.
>
> (Schwartz, 2011: 47, emphasis mine)

Such a finding may be unexpected to Schwartz because there is a firm belief that more education and exposure to gays and lesbians will have the effect of moderating people's homophobic tendencies. The strength of this belief, that people will become less homophobic when exposed to anti-homophobia education, is apparent in all the scales that I have discussed. In the context of this discussion of homophobia and progressive sexuality education, this belief is key because it reflects a repeated tendency to attribute homophobic beliefs to a lack of education in addition to religion.

RESEARCHING HOMOPHOBIC YOUTH

In their research on homophobia among adolescents in Canada and Belgium, Hooghe, Claes, Harell, Quintelier, and Dejaeghere (2010) also trouble the belief that there is a link between homophobia and educational attainment. They note:

> Despite arguments that hostility toward LGBT rights among Muslims can simply be attributed to their lower average education level or to a Mediterranean cultural factor, our study does not find support for these arguments. Our models included controls for educational background from two separate country samples with diverging immigration patterns. This allows us to isolate the religious factor quite unequivocally as an important element for the occurrence of negative feelings toward equal rights for LGBT groups. (2010: 396)

It is clear in this study that level of education does not correlate with level of homophobia. Hooghe et al. (2010) state that their finding, regarding the correlation between religion and homophobic beliefs in some people of Christian and Muslim faiths, is unremarkable. They go on to note that several research studies suggest "adherence to strict and fundamentalist forms of religion is positively associated to homophobia and anti-gay attitudes" (385). The correlations Hooghe et al. see between homophobia and religious fundamentalism lead them to question the assumptions that underpin scales that measure homophobia.

In an article by Hooghe, Dejaeghere, Claes, and Quintelier's subtitled "The Structure of Attitudes Toward Gay and Lesbian Rights Among Islamic Youth in Belgium" (2010), the researchers draw attention to the specific ways in which race, ethnicity, and religion are often highlighted as markers of increased homophobia in studies using homophobia scales. Hooghe, Claes et al. (2010) seek to problematize this type of research arguing that

> . . . the scales . . . all originate in a liberal, rights-oriented approach toward homosexuality, which is often at odds with a more religiously based understanding of homosexuality and homosexual behavior. Basically, this would imply that the measurement scales for homophobia that are conventionally used are not sufficiently cross-culturally valid to allow for unbiased understanding of the feelings toward homosexuality among various religious groups. These scales indeed originate from a secularized Western research setting and very little effort has been

devoted to the question [of] whether these scales can be used meaningfully in a more religious context. (2010: 50)

For the purpose of this discussion of scales and homophobia in the context of sexuality education, Hooghe, Dejaeghere et al.'s (2010) comments are particularly salient. While continuing to employ scales in their research, there is recognition by these researchers of the limitations of scales that measure homophobia.

Hooghe, Dejaeghere et al. (2010) illustrate the complexities of defining just what homophobia is in quantitative and qualitative research. Their own research using these scales has prompted them to question how scales that measure homophobia are rooted in systems of belief that almost ensure particular groups of people will be classified as homophobic. This prompts the question, how is it possible to understand religious reasoning on sex education using a frame that eschews the authority of secular reason (Rasmussen, 2010: 701)? To be clear, I perceive scales that measure or classify particular types of homophobia as embedded in the authority of a secular reasoning in which an anti-homophobic response is often conflated as a combination of ignorance, irrationality, religiosity, and miseducation.

What are the consequences then of employing these scales in anti-homophobia research and pedagogy to, once again, and, often not surprisingly, identify particular members of specific populations as homophobic? To my mind, the repeated use of homophobia scales is problematic because, in a Butlerian sense (Butler, 1999), the findings they produce are performative. Through the continued utilization and production of the scales, we come to know particular subjects as homophobic; in this respect the employment of scales can be seen as a liberal mechanism of exclusion.

THINKING DIFFERENTLY ABOUT HOMOPHOBIA IN TEACHING AND RESEARCH

As David Murray (2009) notes, "homophobia has gone global" and it is "increasingly attached to moral, political, and economic agendas around the globe" (viii). Homophobia has, indeed, gone global, but as the epigraph to this chapter suggests, this is not to say that homophobia can be easily translated across geopolitical sites. In countries like Australia and the US, which both have large communities of new immigrants, this is an important consideration because if imaginings of homophobia are not universal, then anti-homophobia education needs to be attuned to this. Significant differences in how people understand the question of homophobia are by no means confined to immigrant communities. For instance, people within Protestant religious communities across the US hold markedly different understandings of homophobia and heteronormativity.

Daniel Monk (2011), in his analysis of progressivism in discourses related to homophobic bullying, makes the point that anti-homophobic discourse is founded in "imaginations and representations of a post-homophobic time" (191). I construe scales that measure homophobia as part of broader constellation of discourses that seek to challenge homophobia, and as I have tried to illustrate, I do not perceive such scales as benign or emancipatory.

The progressive narratives implicit within scales that measure homophobia can be conceived as a technology explicitly designed to help students and teachers develop imaginings of post-homophobic time. Scales of homophobia very specifically construct responses to homophobia as something which might be improved, over time, by moving people along the scale from a position of *repulsion* to *celebration* (Ollis, 2010) or from *romper stomper* to *almost ally* (Witthaus). The scales simultaneously produce, and are embedded in, imaginings of post-homophobic time. Homophobia (so the logic of these scales suggests), we can all agree, is a problem. Consequently, it is also held to be true that individuals, who are identified as holding homophobic beliefs via technologies such as scales, can only benefit from exposure to anti-homophobia education. Part of my task here then is to elaborate why I think it is problematic to develop educational practices that are embedded in the reproduction of post-homophobic imaginings.

Imaginings of a post-homophobic time are problematic in part because such imaginings assume that some consensus has been derived on the subject of homophobia, yet anthropological studies of homophobia point to inconsistencies in the way that this concept is understood (Murray, 2009). For instance, Constance Sullivan-Blum (2009) in her study of contemporary American Christian homophobia notes that the evangelical Protestants she interviewed consistently denied that they were homophobic. Sullivan-Blum accounts for this reticence in part by drawing attention to the way in which her participants conceptualized people who are homophobic. They believed that "homophobes harbor an irrational fear of homosexuals" (51), and they did not perceive their attitude toward homosexuals as therefore homophobic. Rather, Sullivan-Blum notes, "most evangelical Protestants I spoke to are not afraid of homosexuals; rather they believe that homosexuality is sinful and must be rejected as morally wrong" (51). Such distinctions in the way that people understand the concept of homophobia, and the ways in which they imagine themselves and others as homophobic (or not), points to the challenges of anti-homophobia education and imaginings of a post-homophobic time.

Scales of homophobia might suggest that particular groups of people, such as evangelical Protestants, are more likely to be homophobic. However, if these people do not apprehend homophobia as something that is applicable to them, what does this mean for the application of the scale? Monk (2011) suggests:

> One might reasonably ask whether in highlighting the existence of homophobia in schools and developing strategies that enable it to be acknowledged by policy-makers it is necessary to engage with conflicting imaginations about an idealised post-homophobic world. The

argument here is that it is, for if homophobic bullying is made speakable through discourses of heteronormativity, then those outcomes become the form through which its success is evaluated. (2011: 194, 195)

Monk rightly points out that the success of anti-homophobia education is predicated on particular imaginings of homophobia that rarely admit conflicting perspectives. The scales can only be ruled a success if one can assume in advance that people who use the scales agree that heteronormativity is problematic. As Sullivan-Blum (2009) notes, evangelical Protestants perceive same-sex marriage as problematic for many reasons, one of which is that it disrupts the authority of scripture. Scales that fail to apprehend this will likely not have the desired pedagogic effect on people within this group. So effective education about homophobia may have to wrestle with the idea that there is not a shared learning outcome by which success can be evaluated.

Desirable outcomes associated with anti-homophobic education are also complicated by the fact that progressives share different notions of what success might look like in combating homophobia. For instance, I do not perceive scripture in the same way as evangelical Protestants, nor do I support same-sex marriage—but this is likely for very different reasons than evangelical Protestants.

My point here is that sometimes the tendency to construct particular events, people, places, ideas, or religions as homophobic may have the effect of constructing objections to post-homophobic imaginings as necessarily pathological, ignorant, and regressive. Foreseeably, people who don't agree with same-sex marriage, regardless of their motive, may come to be seen as in need of reeducation. Why people object is important and can be the stuff of a lively sexuality education classroom conversation.

It is also true that the necessity of conforming to post-homophobic imagining does not fall equally upon all people of different faiths. This is evident in Hooghe, Claes et al.'s (2010) quantitative studies of antigay sentiment among adolescents in Belgium and Canada. Discourses of homophobic bullying that are reproduced through the use of quantitative scales that measure homophobia may thus operate to reify binaries between Islamic fundamentalism and secular freedoms (Monk, 2011: 200). The problem of not conforming to particular readings of homophobia and post-homophobia is not limited to the sphere of religion; it may also become associated with homonationalism and terrorist assemblages (Puar, 2007). Particular groups of people who are marked as homophobic according to these scales can also be construed as a danger to secular sexuality education and to the safety of the imagined post-homophobic state.

CONCLUSION

Let me reiterate that I do recognize that discrimination related to gender and sexual identifications does exist. At the same time in this chapter, I have been attempting to complicate the pedagogical power that is associated with taking up the position of challenging, and measuring, homophobia. Scales of homophobia may be difficult to speak back to precisely because their righteousness is affirmed through images of the vulnerability of gay youth (Puar, 2012; Rasmussen, 2004). Though as Monk (2011) illustrates, the cost of such righteousness is "the extent to which it effectively silences other voices and reduces the experience of lesbian and gay young people to one of passive victimhood" (188).

I have situated scales that measure homophobia as part of a broader political project that is embedded in emancipatory imaginings of a post-homophobic world. To do this I have tried to consider some of the logics that underpin the use of such scales. By way of a conclusion, I have sought to make a list of provocations that illustrate what I perceive to be troubling logics that support the use of scales that measure homophobia of teachers and students. My hope is such a list might provoke ongoing debate about the ways that homophobia is taken up in education about gender and sexuality.

PROVOCATIONS

- *That we can agree on what homophobia is . . .*
- *That we can therefore measure homophobia . . .*
- *That there is a "right way" to respond to homophobia . . .*
- *That progressive teachers and students will challenge homophobia . . .*
- *That affirming homophobia is inadmissible in the bounds of liberal, secular, sexuality education . . .*
- *That people who are homophobic can benefit from anti-homophobic education . . .*

My hope is that taken together, these provocations might be used to open up conversations in which homophobia becomes less familiar. It is only by making homophobia strange in the context of anti-homophobic education that it may become possible to think differently about motivations and assumptions that underpin such pedagogical projects. Such provocations about homophobia are, as indicated in the epigraph to this chapter, also designed to provoke questions about the what and the how of homosexuality. If an aim of anti-homophobia education is to create spaces in which young people who are lesbian or gay identified may be safer, can we assume that taking homophobia's measure will necessarily have this outcome?

NOTES

1. For a history of the logic underpinning the development and validation of homophobia scales in the discipline of psychopathology, see Wright, Adams, and Bernat (1999).

2. See: http://www.deakin.edu.au/arts-ed/education/teach-research/health-pe/projects.php (accessed April 20, 2013).
3. The name Romper Stomper evokes the 1992 Australian film of the same name directed by Geoffrey Wright. The focus of the movie is racism enacted by a neo-Nazi skinhead group in a Melbourne working-class suburb.
4. *Bogan* is an Australian pejorative, which, according to the *Macquarie Dictionary*, is used to "describe a person, generally from an outer suburb of a city or town and from a lower socio-economic background, viewed as uncultured."

REFERENCES

ABC News. (2014). *Ian Thorpe to reveals he is gay, describes struggle with depression in tell-all interview with Sir Michael Parkinson*. Available from http://www.abc.net.au/news/2014–07–13/ian-thorpe-to-reveal-he-is-gay-in-michael-parkinson-interview/5592626(Last accessed August 6, 2014).

Berzon, B. (1996). *Setting Them Straight: You Can Do Something about Bigotry and Homophobia in Your life*. New York: Plume.

Blackburn, M., Clark, C. T., Kenney, L., & Smith, J. (2009). *Acting Out! Combating Homophobia through Teacher Activism* (Practitioner Inquiry Series). New York: Teachers College Press.

Butler, J. (1999). *Gender Trouble: Feminism and the Subversion of Identity*. New York: Routledge.

Clark, C. T. (2010). Preparing LGBTQ-allies and Combating Homophobia in a US Teacher Education Program. *Teaching and Teacher Education*, 26(3): 704–713.

Delbridge, A. (2003), The Macquarie Dictionary, Rev. 3rd edn, Macquarie Library, North Ryde, N.S.W.

Elia, J. P. (1993). Homophobia in the High School: A Problem in Need of a Resolution. *The High School Journal*, 77(1/2): 177–185.

Franck, K. C. (2002). Rethinking Homophobia: Interrogating Heteronormativity in an Urban School. *Theory & Research in Social Education*, 30(2): 274–286.

Gay & Lesbian Health Victoria. (2013). *Training Session Plan*. Available from http://www.glhv.org.au/files/Training_session_plan.pdf (Last accessed April 29, 2013).

Gibson, S. (2007). The Language of the Right: Sex Education Debates in South Australia. *Sex Education: Sexuality, Society and Learning*, 7(3): 239–250.

Harwood, V., & Rasmussen, M. L. (2013). Practising Critique, Attending to Truth: The Pedagogy of Discriminatory Speech. *Educational Philosophy and Theory [E]*, 45(8): 874–884.

Hirschfeld, S. (2001). Moving Beyond the Safety Zone: A Staff Development Approach to Anti-heterosexist Education. *Fordham Urban Law Journal*, 29(2): 611–640.

Hooghe, M., Claes, E., Harell, A., Quintelier, E., & Dejaeghere, Y. (2010). Anti-Gay Sentiment among Adolescents in Belgium and Canada: A Comparative Investigation into the Role of Gender and Religion. *Journal of Homosexuality*, 57(3): 384–400.

Hooghe, M., Dejaeghere, Y., Claes, E., & Quintelier, E. (2010). "Yes, But Suppose Everyone Turned Gay?": The Structure of Attitudes Toward Gay and Lesbian Rights among Islamic Youth in Belgium. *Journal of LGBT Youth*, 7(1): 49–71.

Hudson, W. W., & Ricketts, W. A. (1980). A Strategy for the Measurement of Homophobia. *Journal of Homosexuality*, 5(4): 357–372.

Monk, D. (2011). Challenging Homophobic Bullying in Schools: The Politics of Progress. *International Journal of Law in Context*, 7(2): 181–207.

Monto, M. A., & Supinski, J. (2014). Discomfort with Homosexuality: A New Measure Captures Differences in Attitudes Toward Gay Men and Lesbians. *Journal of Homosexuality*, 61(6): 899–916.
Morrow, R., & Gill, D. (2003). Perceptions of Homophobia and Heterosexism in Physical Education. *Research Quarterly for Exercise and Sport*, 74(2): 205–214.
Murray, D. (Ed.). (2009). *Homophobias: Lust and Loathing Across Time and Space*. Durham, North Carolina: Duke University Press.
Ollis, D. (2010). 'I Haven't Changed Bigots But. . .': Reflections on the Impact of Teacher Professional Learning in Sexuality Education. *Sex Education*, 10(2): 217–230.
Ollis, D., Harrison, L., & Maharaj, C. (2013). *Sexuality Education Matters: Preparing pre-service Teachers to Teach Sexuality Education*. Burwood, Vic: Deakin University.
Pain, M., & Disney, M. (1996). Testing the Reliability and Validity of the Index of Attitudes Toward Homosexuals (IAH) in Australia. *Journal of Homosexuality*, 30(2): 99–110.
Puar, J. K. (2007). *Terrorist Assemblages: Homonationalism in Queer Times*. Durham: Duke University Press.
———. (2012). Coda: The Cost of Getting Better: Suicide, Sensation, Switchpoints. *GLQ: A Journal of Lesbian and Gay Studies*, 18(1): 149–158.
Rasmussen, M. L. (2004). Wounded Identities, Sex and Pleasure: "Doing It" at School. NOT! *Discourse: Studies in the Cultural Politics of Education*, 25(4): 445–458.
———. (2005). Sexualities and Education in Australia: Which Way Forward? *Curriculum Perspectives*, 25(3): 51–53.
———. (2006). *Becoming Subjects: Sexualities and Secondary Schooling*. New York: Routledge.
———. (2010). Secularism, Religion and 'Progressive' Sex Education. *Sexualities*, 13(6): 699–712.
Riddle, D. (1994). *The Riddle Scale. Alone No More: Developing a School Support System for Gay, Lesbian and Bisexual Youth*. St Paul, Minnesota: Minnesota State Department.
Rogers, A., McRee, N., & Arntz, D. (2009). Using a College Human Sexuality Course to Combat Homophobia. *Sex Education: Sexuality, Society and Learning*, 9(3): 211–225.
Rostosky, S., Riggle, E., Horne, S., & Miller, A. (2009). Marriage Amendments and Psychological Distress in Lesbian, Gay, and Bisexual (LGB) Adults. *Journal of Counseling Psychology*, 56(1): 56–66.
Schwartz, E. C. (2011). *With Us or Against Us: Using Religiosity and Socio-demographic Variables to Predict Homophobic Beliefs*. Unpublished Doctoral Dissertation. Indiana State University, College of Education. Available from http://scholars.indstate.edu/handle/10484/1820 (Last accessed May 7, 2015).
Serdahely, W., & Ziemba, G. (1984). Changing Homophobic Attitudes through College Sexuality Education. *Journal of Homosexuality*, 10(1–2): 109–116.
Sullivan-Blum, C. (2009). 'It's Adam and Eve, Not Adam and Steve': What's at Stake in the Construction of Contemporary American Christian Homophobia. In D. Murray (Ed.), *Homophobias: Lust and Loathing Across Time and Space* (pp. 48–63). Durham, North Carolina: Duke University Press.
Van Wormer, K., & McKinney, R. (2003). What Schools Can Do to Help Gay/Lesbian/Bisexual Youth: A Harm Reduction Approach. *Adolescence*, 38(151): 409–420.
Walcott, R. (2010). 'Not Simple Homophobia': African Same-Sex Desires, Politics, and the Limit of Homosexual Rights. *GLQ*, 16(1–2): 315–317.

Weaver, H., Smith, G., & Kippax, S. (2005). School-based Sex Education Policies and Indicators of Sexual Health among Young People: A Comparison of the Netherlands, France, Australia and the United States. *Sex Education: Sexuality, Society and Learning*, 5(2): 171–188.

Witthaus, D. (2011). *The Faces of Homophobia: Everyday Resistance Quantified. . .* Available from http://thatssogay.com.au/wp-content/uploads/2011/08/For_the_hand_BTSG.pdf (Last accessed October 10 2012).

Woodstock School website. (2013). *Dorothy Irene Riddle.* Available from http://newsarchive.woodstockschool.in/Alumni/DistAlum/riddle.htm (Last accessed April 20 2013).

Worthington, R., Dillon, F., & Becker-Schutte, A. (2005). Development, Reliability, and Validity of the Lesbian, Gay, and Bisexual Knowledge and Attitudes Scale for Heterosexuals (LGB-KASH). *Journal of Counseling Psychology*, 52(1): 104–118.

Wright L., Jr, Adams, H., & Bernat, J. (1999). Development and Validation of the Homophobia Scale. *Journal of Psychopathology and Behavioral Assessment*, 21(4): 337–347.

Zack, J., Mannheim, A., & Alfano, M. (2010). "I Didn't Know What to Say. . .": Four Archetypal Responses to Homophobic Rhetoric in the Classroom. *High School Journal*, 93(3): 98–110.

7 Progressive Public Pedagogies of Pregnancy and Choice

In this chapter, I interrogate public pedagogies of sexual education that may be constituted as progressive and secular. A woman's right to choose is a key theme in progressive sexuality education, and here I consider how competing secular perspectives are positioned in public debates around pregnancy, abortion, and choice. Others have turned their attention to the different ways teen mothers' choices are calibrated by distinctions of race, class, and ability in filmic representations (Jarman, 2012; Lutterell, 2011). Lutterell, in her discussion of *Juno* (Reitman, 2007) and *Precious* (Daniels, 2009), perceives these films as public pedagogies that orient young women to their bodies, sexuality, and maternal subjectivities in ways that continue to cultivate class and race inequality (Lutterell, 2011: 295). Akin to Lutterell, I see these films as public pedagogies of sexuality education. My focus is on how these films, and associated popular and scholarly commentaries, orient readers toward pedagogical assemblages that are regulated by particular attachments among liberalism, feminism, and secularism. These public pedagogies have ramifications for progressive sexuality education because they are powerful devices for teaching about choice and pregnancy and their intersections with race and class.

The popular power of these discourses is evident in four films that were produced about choice and pregnancy in 2007. I refer to—*Juno*[1] (Reitman, 2007), *Knocked Up*[2] (Apatow, 2007), and *Waitress*[3] (2007), all produced in the US, and *4 months, 3 Weeks, and 2 Days*[4] from Romania (Mungiu, 2007). *Precious*,[5] directed by Lee Daniels, is also frequently cited in commentaries about these films (Capiello and Froman, 2011; Lutterell, 2011).[6] In this chapter my focus is not primarily these films but rather feminist scholarship and commentary related to the films.

I perceive these commentaries as a powerful form of pedagogy within the field of progressive sexuality education. Taken together these films can illustrate different varieties of secularism and sexuality that circulate in the writings of feminists on the subjects of choice, abortion, and pregnancy. Rather than focusing on how progressive discourses related to secularism are constituted vis-à-vis religion on the subject choice, my focus in this chapter is on identifying distinctions made between secular discourses on the subject of abortion. Following Risøy and Simes, I am also interested in exploring how secular debates about abortion echo "Schmitt's argument that most of the important political concepts are secularised religious concepts, including that of the Sovereign" (2014: 22). Discussions about abortion, even when they are avowedly secular, are often embedded in different forms of moral authority that may be informed by religious motifs.

"THE GOOD ABORTER," CHOICE, AND STATES OF EXCEPTION

Penelope Deutscher's (2008) analysis of states of exception attends to how legal and political apparatuses assume authority over women's bodies. Deutscher argues that abortion is, increasingly, only constituted as permissible in particular "exceptional" cases (i.e., in the US this might relate to how a woman fell pregnant; how long she has been pregnant; whether or not she has seen a fetal ultrasound of her unborn child; or whether she has obtained parental consent). Feminist discourses explored in this chapter are sometimes inseparable from the legal and moral discourses Deutscher identifies that continuously reinforce abortion as a state of exception.

Solve Marie Risøy and Thorvald Sirnes (2014) also explore the terrain of abortion and notions of exception—specifically looking at the field of selective abortion—when pregnant women are advised that their fetus is compromised. They argue that in the terrain of selective abortion, particular subject positions manifest:

> The good aborting mother, the good aborter and the responsible woman are subject positions that are related to, and depend on, the self-sacrifice. Therefore it represents a privileged meaning dimension, and a core element in the narratives. (2014: 20, 21)

Particular subject positions related to notions of exception and the good aborter also manifest in films about choice. In later sections I explore some of the subject positions that emerge in debates about these films and the different ways that they evoke differing states of exception. By analyzing progressive discourses about abortion, I underscore the complicated threads of progressivism that can make it difficult to apprehend. Such analysis also makes it plain that progressive sexuality education is by no means univocal.

Hadley Freeman, a feminist columnist for the progressive newspaper *The Guardian*, in an article titled "A Choice That Films Ignore" (Freeman, 2008) ponders the messages about abortion conveyed in the films *4 Months, 3 Weeks, and 2 Days; Juno; Knocked Up;* and *Waitress*. In her analysis it is possible to see how competing notions of "the good aborter" have also come to infuse progressive commentaries on abortion. Freeman sees these films as a

> ... product of a generation that has had the luxury of legal and relatively easy access to abortion. The danger is that one forgets what the

alternative really meant, and as a result sentimentalises it. It is surely no coincidence that these films are emerging from a country that has had eight years of ultra-conservative Republican rule. (Freeman, 2008)

Freeman constitutes these films as regressive texts because they don't give the topic of abortion the serious consideration she feels it deserves. It appears that these films are also problematic for Freeman insofar as they emphasize ease of access, which Freeman argues is not an accurate depiction of the availability of abortion, especially in recent times. Freeman's reading of abortion might also be read as part of what Deutscher perceives as

> the repeated creation of abortion as a state of permanent exceptionality ... [and therefore as] one of the essential workings of twentieth- and early-twenty-first-century biopolitics concerning women's reproductivity. (2008: 65)

In my reading of Deutscher, Freeman is likely to apprehend abortion as something that is constituted by exceptionality because it has always been thus. Bringing this back to notions of progressivism in sexuality education—progressive stances such as Freeman's can be seen as somewhat paradoxical because they simultaneously seek to preserve abortion as a right (something that should be legal and accessible) while upholding abortion as an exception—*abortions as a luxury that should not be abused.*

In her response to *Juno*, Shelby Knox[7] writing in *The Huffington Post* focuses her attention on the challenges women face in accessing abortion in the US. She writes:

> Already pregnant, Juno decides to, in her words, "procure a hasty abortion." She makes an appointment, choosing the clinic that does not require a parent's signature ... Juno is presumably lucky enough to live in one of the 17 states that does not require parental notification or consent and one of the 13% of counties that has a provider, many young women are stopped at this point in the process. Political maneuvering to chip away at the right to abortion has left many young women without options, which has contributed not only to the rise in the teen birth rate but also driven some desperate young women and their partners to turn to dangerous "black market" abortions or to attempt to end the pregnancy themselves, often with tragic results. (Knox, 2007: para. 8)

Knox's (2007) analysis draws readers' attention to how states of exception literally compromise women's (especially poor, young women's) access to abortion in many states and counties in the US. Knox, like Freeman, clearly sees abortion rights as under attack. Knox's analysis is focused on the state's role in curtailing women's access to abortion, especially younger women like Juno.

For Knox and Freeman, *Juno* is problematic because it doesn't depict any of the difficulties of abortion access "because the plot hinges on getting to the adoption option, the viewer is never asked to consider what it means to be frightened away from receiving medical care" (Knox, 2007: para. 9). She also argues teen birth rates will continue to rise if "young people [are denied] responsible, medically accurate sex education and young women continue to be denied and frightened away from reproductive health care" (Knox, 2007: para. 11). Conceivably, Juno could be read as a film that introduces abortion as a possibility for young women, therefore partially fulfilling Knox's pedagogical desire for sex education about choice that is not frightening. But for Knox, the failure of *Juno* to address structural inequalities associated with access to abortion (which are arguably incredibly frightening in the US context—as Knox well demonstrates) means that the pedagogy of abortion access in *Juno* fails the feminist progressive test.

By way of contrast to *Juno*, Hadley Freeman (2008) points to the Romanian film

> *Four Months, Three Weeks and Two Days*—[which] depicts the horrors women in Romania had to go through to get an abortion when it was still illegal 20 years ago. Its message is stark: choice is not about giving silly young women a lazy form of contraception that destroys families; it is about giving women control over their lives. (Freeman, 2008: para. 4)

For Freeman, the Romanian film teaches the right lessons about abortion—that is, abortion is not to be used at will by the young and lazy, but rather its use is appropriate when it is used by mature women in a sovereign fashion. So abortion in Freeman's analysis is related to choice, but choice has its limits. For Knox, it is crucial that viewers get the lesson that states of exception apply to abortion. *Juno* is compromised, she believes, because of its failure to convey to viewers just how insidious exceptions are.

Like the legal frameworks that determine what conditions enable a woman to exercise self-sovereignty on the subject of abortion, Freeman's analysis appears to set out particular conditions under which abortion might be rendered as related to sovereignty and control and other circumstances in which it is associated with a woman who is clearly not exercising sovereignty (but is, rather, lazy and destructive). Freeman's impetus here is no doubt to preserve choice. By arguing against the belittlement of choice—Freeman anticipates that women's right to choose is precarious. But by setting out the conditions under which choice is appropriate, Freeman's comments mimic and potentially reinforce the logic underpinning political and legislative states of exception, exceptions that can be seen to curtail women's sovereignty (Deutscher, 2008).

Concerns about the precarity of access to abortion in Britain are also apparent in Kay Wither's (2008) review of *4 Months, 3 Weeks, 2 Days*:

> Mungui's film reminds us of the importance of giving women the control over their lives *and to not take such rights for granted*. With predictions that the abortion time limit in Britain could be cut under a Conservative Government, this message is a salient one. (102, my emphasis)

Withers believes that abortion rights in Britain may be potentially compromised by the election of a conservative government.[8] She underscores the necessity of not assuming that abortion rights are stable and enduring, and she perceives the harrowing abortion narrative in Mungui's film as a salutary reminder of this precarity.

I concur with Withers, Knox, and Freeman —abortion rights are tenuous, and this is a serious problem. *4 Months, 3 Weeks, 2 Days* is constituted as a necessary pedagogical device in relation to abortion; a filmic reminder of the consequences that can ensue when abortion rights are removed.

My overall argument here is that there is a tendency to situate *4 Months, 3 Weeks, 2 Days* as a morally superior form of progressive pedagogy compared to that provided by *Juno*—in part because *Juno* is not sufficiently weighty on the subject of abortion. My preference would be to resist the temptation to determine which film is the most progressive but rather to utilize these films to inquire into how exceptions operate and are sustained *in conservative and progressive political discourses* relating to choice and abortion.

In an article titled "Blind Spots and Failed Performances: Abortion, Feminism and Queer Theory," Jennifer Doyle (2009) draws on the work of Penelope Deutscher and Jeannie Ludlow to argue

> ... there is a hierarchy within feminist discourse about abortion with a premium placed on "traumatized" abortion stories—in which the ordinariness of abortion is eclipsed by politically expedient narratives about unwanted pregnancies brought on by sexual violence and abuse. The implicit demand that "abortion be an exception, and not a normal part of 'women's lives'" (Ludlow, p. 32) pushes the extreme suffering of victims of rape and abuse into the public sphere and throws a blanket of silence, shame and anxiety over nearly every other kind of unwanted pregnancy as they become stigmatized as personal failures ... One of the many nasty effects of this form of narrative policing is the stigmatization of the agency of the vast majority of women who choose to have abortions—because their choice becomes a disorder of will and desire (Doyle, 2009: 26)

Doyle speaks to the importance of stories about abortion being sufficiently traumatic and distinct from the everyday choices people make in their lives. Good feminist subjects make the decision to abort or to keep their child based on a well-reasoned decision; they don't take abortion for granted, using it like contraception;[9] and they display sufficient remorse and trauma when relinquishing their child. When unplanned pregnancies are portrayed by progressive commentators as ill conceived, insufficiently painful to the psyche, or as a luxury, these critiques reinforce the logic of exception.

I recognize that this argument implicates me as a progressive within abortion debates, and this is a position that I am happy to adopt in the context of this book. As I note in my introduction, I am not above the fray of progressivism in this analysis. I am deeply embedded in the production of discourses that are, have been, and no doubt will be, constituted as progressive. I don't see this as problematic, as my aim is not to reject progressive sexuality education, or to distance myself from it, but rather to inquire closely into a field in which I am deeply embedded. This also means being willing to articulate my own positions in relation to progressive discourses. I also acknowledge that thinking about abortion as unproblematic may be offensive to some people, religious and nonreligious.

LIBERALISM, FEMINISM, AND PEDAGOGIES OF CHOICE

With the exception of *4 Months, 3 Weeks and 2 Days*, these films all deal with an unplanned pregnancy where women decide to keep the baby. Reitman and Apatow (directors of *Juno* and *Knocked Up*) refuse the constitution of these films as political interventions into the abortion debate. Notwithstanding these protestations, commentators and researchers have read these movies in this context, wondering about the relationship between the films and the cultural politics of the abortion debate in the US (Freeman, 2008; Hornaday, 2007; Latimer, 2009; Lutterell, 2011; Tilman, 2008). Simon During (2007) suggests the abortion debate is a site in which determining what is and what isn't secular has become increasingly complex:

> The division between the secular and non-secular is less hard-edged than it seems. To offer a well-trodden example from the U.S. abortion debate: Is "the right to life" a secular or religious principle? Even "the right to choose" can be regarded as religiously sanctioned, were we to pursue Harold Laski's supposition that "the affirmation of the right of each human being to fulfill his individuality" constitutes Christianity's best contribution to world civilization. Indeed the political cogency of the abortion debate sound-bites depends on their grounds being indeterminable in regard to secularism . . . (para. 3)

During draws attention to the point that it is not only possible but also important to use secular justifications in the abortion debate to be persuasive on the subject. He is arguing, and I agree, that secular justifications generally hold more sway in political debate. Consequently, secular justifications are equally important, whether one is pro-life or pro-choice or avowedly neutral. This is because secularisms, in the present moment, are very powerful and persuasive in countries like Australia, Canada, England, and the US.

Below I identify and examine competing secular claims utilized in research and commentaries on *Juno* and *Knocked Up*. This analysis demonstrates how different participants in these debates rely upon differing secular justifications. Such analysis enables me to demonstrate some of the complexities that adhere to labeling something as a secular maneuver. Following During (2007), just because a claim is secular, it is not necessarily apparent what position it is advancing.

In commentaries, *Juno* and *Knocked Up* have often been cited in unison. This is probably because they were released in the same year, and their subject matter is not dissimilar; both deal with unplanned pregnancy; both women decide to keep the baby; both protagonists are white, cool, and highly agentic; and both could access an abortion but choose not to. In a review of these movies in the *Brownsville Herald*, titled "*Knocked Up*, but Looking for More," Laura Tillman echoes other critics (Clarke, 2007; Freeman, 2008; Hornaday, 2007) when she writes about the representation of characters in these films. This excerpt from Tillman's commentary begins with a quote from Mia Mask, a professor of film at Vassar College:

> "In film, white people get to be individuals because they exist independent of their race. For a Hispanic or African American character [see *Precious*], that pregnancy is tied up in the 'problem' of those ethnic groups having too many children or getting pregnant too young. For the white character it isn't seen as indicative of anything other than her specific situation." Part of the hilarity in 'Knocked Up' and 'Juno' comes from the notion that their unplanned pregnancies are exceptional, and therefore fodder for unlikely comedic scenarios. (Tillman, 2008)

Tillman is particularly critical of *Juno* and *Knocked Up*, as opposed to *Precious*, because she reads these films as failing to deal with the ways in which racial and class politics mediate choice in the US. She goes on to note both directors' hope that the films engage with "human experiences that transcend the politics of pregnancy" (Tillman, 2008).

In terms of revenue these films did appear to transcend the politics of pregnancy; they were both hugely successful, rating 14 and 15 in 2007[10] in terms of box office returns. It seems that these films also want to transcend the politics of abortion. In a press conference about *Knocked Up*, a journalist says to Judd Apatow, "I don't think the word abortion ever comes up in this [film]," and Apatow responds by saying that the movie is about the story of what happens when you decide not to get an abortion (Duran, 2008). Judd Apatow is on record as being pro-choice.[11] In an interview with Margaret Pomerantz, an Australian film critic, Apatow expresses surprise at people's dismay over his portrayal of the main character's decision not to get an abortion.

> Judd Apatow: ... But I think it's really interesting, as somebody who is pro-choice, is that it's so shocking that she doesn't get an abortion.
> Seth Rogen: Yeah.
> Judd Apatow: I mean I'm not trying to make any kind of statement about what anyone should do, but it's really interesting that people act like it's such a weird choice not to get an abortion. I didn't realise that it was such a common way to go.
>
> I mean, I think, you know, some people do, some people don't. What's, you know, what is the, you know what is the shock of either choice? Because choices are available to people and people make both choices. But it does seem to have set off a flurry of discussion about it, which is probably healthy in some way, I guess, or completely pointless. (ABC, 2014)

Apatow is making a case that choice is something that shouldn't be shocking either way. Clearly, many feminist commentators disagree on this point. Apatow's discussion of choice suggests choice isn't constrained, either way, and is therefore a purely individual decision; thus the movie is perfectly in alignment with his pro-choice politics.

Kay Withers (2008) discusses *Juno* in a review in the journal *Public Policy Research*. She writes that the film is clearly not pro-life, but she does perceive it as symptomatic of those who too easily assume abortion's availability:

> Despite an early scene in which a pregnant Juno is congratulated by a pro-life campaigner for cancelling her abortion at the last minute, the film can hardly be taken as anti-abortion in stance. Instead, it has been argued that rather than stem from an anti-abortion culture the film takes abortion for granted, perhaps mistakenly, as a choice that will always be available. (101)

For Withers, the decision not to articulate a stance on abortion is symptomatic of US anti-abortion culture (see also Freeman, 2008; Latimer, 2009). *Knocked Up* has received critiques similar to this. Both films are seen by some feminist commentators as failing not because of what they have done but because of what they fail to do (Clarke, 2007; Hornaday, 2007). Both films appear tailor-made to carry progressive public pedagogical interventions on the subject of abortion, but both refuse to address the issue of abortion in any depth. Apatow counters that the film is pedagogical precisely because it has provoked public discussion about choice.

In an online interview about the film *Knocked Up*, Apatow justifies his decision to guide the film away from a political stance on abortion:

> I am pro choice and I don't think anyone should tell anyone else what to do with their bodies or their points of view. I think those decisions are very personal and no one has the answer, so I am pretty solid in that position. But I also think it's a very interesting story when you decide not to get an abortion.
>
> (Crave Online Australia, 2007)

Apatow justifies the film's narrative because he believes the decision whether to have an abortion is personal. The director of *Juno*, Jason Reitman, adopts a far more libertarian stance in comparison to Apatow when questioned about how this film addresses the subject of choice. This is from an interview with an unnamed representative from the website Coming Soon:

> **CS (Coming Soon):** I'm amazed the abortion issue keeps being brought up even though it literally takes up like two minutes of the movie . . . Knowing that you, Diablo, and Ellen are all Pro-Choice, are you worried about your movie being taken to heart by the pro-life movement?
>
> **Jason Reitman:** I want everyone to see this movie. . . . I'm not really pro-choice, I'm not really pro-life, I think either of those infer that I want other people to be pro-choice or pro-life. I'm libertarian and I think people should make decisions for themselves. If you want to be pro-life god bless you. If the pro-lifers think it's theirs and the pro-choicers think it's theirs I think that's fantastic. I'd much rather want that. (Douglas, 2007a)

The secular justification mobilized by Reitman has a long history, as Wendy Brown (2006) points out in her book *Regulating Aversion*.

> The Lockean argument for religious tolerance involves situating moral and theological truth at the individual, private, non-political level and divesting the state—the formal site of political community in liberalism—of matters of collective belief beyond the most abstract constitution principles . . . (39, 47)

In situating abortion and associated bodies and stances as personal, Apatow (2007) is thus associating himself with a long liberal and progressive tradition in which morality and religion is privatized. Other researchers have made this link between liberalism and the privatization and marketization of choice in these films (see Thoma, 2009; Lutterell, 2011; Hoerl and Ryan Kelly, 2010). In this liberal tradition, abortion movies like *Juno* and *Knocked Up* refuse to cast judgment on the subject because "no one has the answer" (Apatow in Crave Online Australia, 2007). This formation of liberalism, as Brown (2006) points out, partially appeals to universal human rights (because it assumes that liberal values are protective rather than universalizing).

For reasons not dissimilar to those expounded by Brown, progressive critics (mainly feminist progressives) have questioned the liberal stance on abortion in *Juno, Knocked Up*, and *Waitress*. They argue that choice is precarious in the US, a precarity that is linked to the gender, race, religious, and class politics that relates to how abortion is accessed (Lutterell, 2011). Lutterell sums up this objection when she argues that pedagogically these films "orient viewers to miscomprehend the relationship between social forces and inner lives" (2011: 297). For Lutterell, the issue of choice is mischaracterized when it is constructed as personal. In her critique of *Juno, Knocked Up*, and *Waitress*, Pamela Thoma (2009), writes "[d]espite their levity, these films do serious cultural work in the construction of national identity and participate in the depoliticizing processes of a US postfeminist culture that negotiates the power of female consumers in a post-9/11, neoliberal global marketplace" (410). These feminist critics see these movies as depoliticizing choice, while the directors of *Knocked Up* and *Juno* see these films as an affirmation of women's right to choose.

In the context this book, I am interested in how these films, and the responses they have evoked, surface specific types of progressive discourses on sexuality education—two being liberal progressivism and feminist progressivism, their associations with "the good aborter," and debates about choice and sovereignty. In some of these commentaries, liberal and feminist perspectives are seen as distinct and even at odds. Liberal progressivism, it is argued, privatizes choice, while feminists reject this move—drawing attention to the structural determinants that hinder abortion access.

Tracking progressive discourses that circulate in relation to these films about choice and abortion enables me to demonstrate how secular justifications shift according to subject, time, and place. In apprehending how progressive sexuality education manifests, it is important to understand some of the different currents of thought within progressivism. In promotional interviews, Diablo Cody (the screenwriter for *Juno*) and Ellen Page (the actor who played Juno) defend their progressive credentials—speaking back to some of the critiques of the film I have outlined:

> **Diablo Cody:** You know what? Anybody can embrace the film that wants to embrace the film, but I will say on the record that *it's not pro-life propaganda and it's not a political movie*. . . . I thought it was kind of a lefty, edgy movie that would like piss people off, because she was joking about abortion. I thought it was irreverent. I had no idea

that anybody would ever perceive it as this right wing Valentine, which I'm not saying that everybody has, but I think some people have perceived it as such . . . I'm sure Jason [Reitman] has said this, but we think as the movie as personal, not political, and I think Juno's decision to not have an abortion is very personal. . . . As the person who wrote it, to me, it was fear-based, as opposed to this moral conundrum. Obviously, that's going to happen, and I've been concerned about it from the beginning. I was concerned about how that would come across. (Douglas, 2007b, my emphasis)

Ellen Page: When I get all these questions about abortion and choice I just think, "Give me a break. It's a damn movie. Is this really what we're here to talk about?" I feel like people just bring that up because they want a damn story or something . . . It's frustrating. *I'm obviously completely pro-choice, and I feel like older white men with money should definitely not be able to decide what happens with a women's uterus, unless we want to go back to clothes hangers, you know what I'm saying?*

(Douglas, 2007c, my emphasis)

Cody and Page are aghast at the idea that people would think they are anything but progressive—after all how could you be pro-choice, a feminist, and lefty and not be progressive? This version of progressivism, as articulated here by Cody and Page, is one that has proven to have incredibly broad popular appeal within the US and beyond. This isn't to say that I agree with Cody and Page's insistence that these films are progressive. Rather, their readings interest me for what say about the familiarity and acceptability of particularly popular notions of progressivism, notions that I believe also permeate sexuality education. In this variation, progressivism on abortion is constituted as a simple equation—it's about choice and women's self-sovereignty. Like Cody and Diablo, those who perceive themselves as affiliated with comprehensive sexuality education may equate this with progressivism without ever feeling the need to really interrogate or justify this progressivism. But, as the feminist critiques of *Juno* and *Knocked Up* suggest, what constitutes a progressive discourse in relation to choice debates is hardly settled.

In Chapter 3 I underscored how young people that I interviewed in a school in Melbourne equated progressive sexuality education with the absence of religious influence. Diablo Cody makes a somewhat similar distinction when defending Juno's progressive credentials, stating, "As the person who wrote it, to me, it was fear-based, as opposed to this moral conundrum" (Douglas, 2007b). For Cody, Juno's treatment of abortion as about fear, not morality, is part of what distinguishes this film as lefty and progressive.

Students I interviewed about sexuality education seemed to instinctively draw a similar line. They knew that questions of religion and morality were inappropriate in the context of sexuality education, but they thought that discussions of an issue like arranged marriage was permissible in the English classroom. The subtext here was that sexuality education is about the facts, whereas in the English classroom, opinions (morals) are admissible. This has some affiliations with Lesko's (2010) notion of "feeling scientific" (288). Lesko argues that CSE should direct "learners to be confident in their scientifically-grounded knowledge, to release 'old' feelings of shame or repression, and to take an empowered approach to managing risks" (292). Predominantly White inner-suburban students of CSE that I interviewed in Melbourne have received a similar education about sexuality that is offered in films such as *Juno*. These agentic pedagogies affirm students and viewers in their progressive outlooks, drawing together feminist and liberal discourses of progressivism where religion is privatized.

PROGRESSIVE SEXUALITY EDUCATION, REASON, AND CREDIBLE ABORTION PEDAGOGIES

Some feminist critiques of *Juno*, *Waitress*, and *Knocked Up* are critical of the way these films dealt with (or failed to deal with) the issue of abortion; these films are therefore constructed by critics as ultimately injurious to feminism. Ann Hornaday, in a commentary in the *Washington Post* on *Knocked Up* and *Waitress* (Shelley, 2007), argues that *Knocked Up* lacks courage because it fails to deal with abortion in a credible way:

> Both films are predicated on unplanned pregnancies and both confect, through all manner of narrative conceits and messy logic, reasons for their female protagonists to carry their unwanted babies to term (and, in the case of "Knocked Up," wind up with so the wrong guy) . . .
> (Hornaday, 2007: para. 2)

In Hornaday's commentary, the main character (Katherine Heigl as Alison Scott) is seen as lacking credibility because she decides not to abort. This argument situates certain types of women as ideally exercising the right to choose to have an abortion. Implicit in Hornaday's critique is a rendering of the abortion narrative in *Knocked Up* as illogical and the protagonist's actions as irrational.

In a review of *Juno* in the journal *Off Our Backs*, the authors read *Juno* in the context of US debates, about AOUM sexuality education. The authors write:

> The antiquated "morality" of neo-conservative Puritanism keeps us from seeking rational solutions that have been proven effective in other countries and goes on to ask "why are so many school systems offering

abstinence as the only option to these sexually active teens? And why does this film not comment on this dangerous situation?"

(Haines, Ruby, McCaslin, Mantilla, and Rodgers, 2007: 73).

In part, the characters in *Juno* and *Knocked Up* are particularly irksome for commentators such as Hornaday and Haines et al. because their protagonists are constructed as hyper agentic yet irrational. Explicit in Haines et al.'s critique is the separation of reason and morality. In the bounds of this logic, a proper treatment of abortion would be informed by reason, a reason freed from the bonds of "neo-conservative Puritanism" (Haines et al., 2007: 73).

I want to push back against Haines et al.'s reading because of its characterization of pro-life politics as an antiquated form of morality. This critique addresses people who agree with the authors, those *"seeking rational solutions"* to choice (Haines et al., 2007: 73, emphasis in original). The form of pedagogical address I am arguing for throughout this text in regard to sexuality education recognizes people might be pro-life and pro-choice depending on the day, time of life, context, and historical moment; they might be irrational and pro-choice; they might be morally pro-choice. They might also be pro-choice and have no access to an abortion.

In an article on *Juno*, *Knocked Up*, and reproductive politics in popular culture, Heather Latimer (2009) also challenges these films progressive bona fides:

> For instance, Jason Reitman, the director of *Juno*, and Judd Apatow, the director of *Knocked Up*, each claim that they are 'pro-choice' even though they avoid abortion in their films. This can be seen as symptomatic of how insidious the terms of anti-abortion politics have become; it is completely routine now to be both pro-choice and to embrace foetal personhood, or to argue for a woman's reproductive freedom, but be uncomfortable with the 'A' word (as abortion is referred to in *Knocked Up*). (214)

Reitman and Apatow fall short in Latimer's eyes because of the inconsistency between their own perceived politics, their embrace of "foetal personhood," and also because of their discomfort with the "A" word. For Latimer, this chain of signification does not ring true—it is inconsistent. In Latimer's reading of progressive discourses related to sexuality and reproductive politics, pro-choice does not equate with the "embrace of foetal personhood."

For Latimer, popular films about pregnancy such as *Juno* and *Knocked Up* would be enhanced if they "presented the politics of choice *in a more honest manner* because it would have acknowledged, at base, that all reproductive politics are political" (Latimer, 2009: 223, my emphasis). This reading surfaces the well-trodden boundaries of the debate on abortion. An honest appraisal of abortion is one where the politics are consistently pro-choice or pro-life. Positions that muddy the water between pro-life and choice debates are constituted as problematic, disingenuous, and dishonest.

I concur with Latimer's analysis insofar as I think these films can be read as pro-choice and that they embrace fetal personhood. People adopting this combination of positions are not uncommon. In a survey of attitudes toward science and religion in the US, Timothy O'Brien and Shiri Noy identified what they termed a post-secular perspective, "a distinctive worldview that reconciles science and religion in all but a few ways" (2015: 94). Latimer's critique of *Juno* and *Knocked Up* relies on particular alignments of values toward abortion, alignments that may not be borne out in people's everyday experiences of choice and abortion. Arguably, it might be difficult to determine whether *Juno*, *Waitress*, and *Knocked Up* offer more comfort to anti-abortion or pro-choice perspectives. Maybe in this respect these films can play an important pedagogical role precisely because they refuse to be didactic on the subject of abortion.

A recently released film in the US, *Obvious Child* (2014), directed by Jillian Robespierre, is described by Karley Sciortino (2014) in *The Guardian* as "a movie about a girl who gets an abortion and lives happily ever after. In the real world, this is a familiar story—an obvious story, even" (para. 1). Presumably, this same observation could be made about *Juno*, *Waitress*, or *Knocked Up*. Sciortino goes on to describe this film as preferable to *Juno* because *Juno* sends the message that it is better to have the child than to have an abortion, contra the protestations of Cody and Page. In making this judgment Sciortino cites the restrictions being placed on abortion access in the US:

> In light of the many abortion restrictions and new anti-abortion laws being passed across America, which are jeopardizing women's reproductive rights, and in some states setting back the situation of women by decades, the movie's release feels timely. One of its best scenes is a conversation between Donna [Jenny Slate] and her friend Nellie (Gaby Hoffmann), who has previously had an abortion herself. When Donna asks Nellie about her experience, she answers matter-of-factly: "I never regret it." Later, when Donna is debating whether to tell her one-night-stand about the pregnancy, Nellie is adamant that it's Donna's body, and therefore Donna's decision to make. She adds, in what may be the film's strongest line, "We already live in a patriarchal society where a group of weird old white men in robes get to legislate our cunts."
>
> (Sciortino, 2014: para. 5)

Obvious Child (2014) and Sciortino's (2014) article affirm secular-progressive audiences—as well as echoing Ellen Page's comments in response to feminist critiques of *Juno*. This progressive stance ardently reinforces abortion as a woman's right. Unlike *Juno*, where the abortion is avoided, in *Obvious Child* the abortion is portrayed in such a way that viewers understand it will not undo the protagonist. The audience learns that it is not up to the courts to decide what women should do with their bodies. Sciortino's (2014) review calls on a combination of liberal and feminist perspectives (it's Donna's body; it's her private choice—not for courts to decide). I share Sciortino's affiliation with these ideas, and I am all for popular cultural pedagogies of sexuality that make the case for abortion not being a state of exception. But I don't think that *Obvious Child* is superior to *Juno* because of the argument it makes, even though it is one with which I strongly identify. The scenarios in *Juno*, *Waitress*, and *Knocked-Up* also have important roles to play in provoking debate about choice, access to abortion, ambivalence, rationality, relationality, sexual freedom, feminism, and reproductive politics. It is too early to tell if *Obvious Child* can do that same work or if it will have as wide appeal.

CONCLUSION

In countries like the US, Australia, Canada, and England, movies about abortion, choice, and unplanned pregnancy are evaluated in relation to a constellation of often competing secular-progressive imaginaries. This analysis of commentaries on popular films related to choice and pregnancy has illustrated how states of exception are operationalized in these progressive narratives. I have also sought to tease out competing liberal narratives related to choice and feminism. Some of these pedagogies work to privatize religion and morality in pedagogies of abortion—while others remain steadfastly mute on the question of abortion. To my mind both approaches are problematic insofar as they work to sustain separations between religion and progressivism in debates about abortion. I have also highlighted the tendency of progressive abortion pedagogies to impress upon their audiences their own holy trinity: the truth that feminism, reason, and a clearly articulated pro-choice stance belong together.

In progressive discourses of public sexuality education, safeguarding abortion rights has a number of dimensions: affirming the separation of church and state; prioritizing reason over morality; refusing to take a moral position; upholding an individual's right to choose (more liberal than feminist); upholding women's right to choose (more feminist than liberal). The layers of progressivism are apparent in the debates I have traced in this chapter, debates that mean movies by writers and directors who purport to be liberal and pro-choice may also be construed as liberal and antichoice. Good feminist subjects, namely White, female, professionals such as Alison Scott in *Knocked Up* are expected to follow a certain script in the case of an unplanned pregnancy (see *Obvious Child*). Together these films and their

140   *Progressive Public Pedagogies of Pregnancy and Choice*

associated commentaries illustrate how liberalism, secularism, and feminism construct overlapping and competing progressive pedagogical assemblages of unplanned pregnancy.

NOTES

1. *Juno* stars Ellen Page as the title character, a whip-smart teen confronting an unplanned pregnancy by her classmate Bleeker (Michael Cera). With the help of her hot best friend Leah (Olivia Thirlby), Juno finds her unborn child a "perfect" set of parents: an affluent suburban couple, Mark and Vanessa (Jason Bateman and Jennifer Garner), longing to adopt. Luckily, Juno has the total support of her parents (J. K. Simmons and Allison Janney) as she faces some tough decisions, flirts with adulthood, and ultimately figures out where she belongs. See http://www.foxsearchlight.com/juno/.
2. Alison Scott is an up-and-coming entertainment journalist whose 24-year-old life is on the fast track. But it gets seriously derailed when a drunken one-night stand with slacker Ben Stone results in an unwanted pregnancy. Faced with the prospect of going it alone or getting to know the baby's father, Alison decides to give the lovable doofus a chance. An overgrown kid who has no desire to settle down, Ben learns that he has a big decision to make with his kid's mom to be: will he hit the road or stay in the picture? Courting a woman you've just knocked up, however, proves to be a little difficult when the two try their hands at dating. As they discover more about one another, it becomes painfully obvious that they're not the soul mates they'd hoped they might be. With Alison's harried sister Debbie and henpecked brother-in-law Pete the only parenting role models the young lovers have, things get even more confusing. Should they raise the baby together? What makes a happy lifetime partnership after all? A couple of drinks and a wild night later, and they've got nine confusing months to figure it out. See https://www.yahoo.com/movies/film/knocked-up.
3. This is the story of one woman trapped in a life from which she dreams of escape. Jenna's (Russell) secret ambition is to save enough money from her waitressing job to leave her overbearing and controlling husband (Sisto). Jenna is a sharp, sassy woman with a gift for making unusual pies whose recipes are inspired by the trials, tribulations, and circumstances of her life. An unwanted pregnancy changes the course of events, giving her an unexpected confidence via letters to her unborn baby. See http://www.foxsearchlight.com/waitress/.
4. During the final days of communism in Romania, two college roommates Otilia (Anamaria Marinca) and Gabita (Laura Vasiliu) are busy preparing for a night away. But rather than planning for a holiday, they are making arrangements for Gabita's illegal abortion, and unwittingly, both find themselves burrowing deep down a rabbit hole of unexpected revelations. Transpiring over the course of a single day, Mungiu's film is a masterwork of modern filmmaking, by parts poignant and shocking. Nominated for four European Film Awards including Best Picture and one of the standout hits of the Telluride, Toronto, and New York Film Festivals, *4 Months, 3 Weeks, and 2 Days* is a modern classic that will stay with you long after you've left the theater. See http://trailers.apple.com/trailers/independent/4months3weeks2days/.
5. Precious Jones (Gabourey "Gabby" Sidibe) is a high school girl with nothing working in her favor. She is pregnant with her father's child—for the second time. She can't read or write, and her schoolmates tease her for being

fat. Her home life is a horror, ruled by a mother (Mo'Nique) who keeps her imprisoned both emotionally and physically. Precious's instincts tell her one thing: if she's ever going to break from the chains of ignorance, she will have to dig deeply into her own resources. See https://itunes.apple.com/us/movie/precious-based-on-novel-push/id354657251,
6. It is the only film that has an African American protagonist, the eponymous Precious. Her story and struggles are distinctly different to those portrayed in the other US films. Precious is depicted as more precarious in terms of class, familiar relations, dis/ability, and education (Jarman, 2012). *Juno, Waitress, Knocked Up*, and *Precious* all involve unplanned pregnancies, in Precious's (Gabourey Sidibe) case, she is pregnant as a result of incest, while in *Waitress* the pregnancy is situated in the context an abusive heterosexual relationship.
7. The byline of Knox's article reads, "Itinerant Feminist Organizer. Writer. Speaker. Revolutionary."
8. At time of writing, the conservative government has not altered abortion law.
9. In contemplating different representations of abortion, Doyle (2009) discusses the controversy surrounding "Yale University fine arts student, Aliza Schvarts's art project where she artificially inseminated herself once a month over the course of nine months, and took abortifacients near the date when her period was due . . . because she never took a pregnancy test, there is no record of her having successfully fertilized an egg, of having been pregnant, or of having aborted an embryo" (36, 37).
10. See http://www.imdb.com/list/ls003293723/.
11. Apatow makes this clear in a 2009 interview with Hadley Freeman, "As for the accusation from some quarters that Knocked Up was anti-abortion, Apatow shrugs easily: 'I'm as pro-choice as you can get, but the movie would have been 10 minutes long if she had an abortion.'" See: http://www.theguardian.com/film/2009/aug/27/interview-judd-apatow.

REFERENCES

ABC. (2014). *At the movies: Knocked up interview*. Available from http://www.abc.net.au/atthemovies/txt/s1950263.htm (Last accessed August 14, 2014).

Apatow, J. (2007). *Knocked up*. Directed by Judd Apatow, Released by Universal Pictures. Available from http://www.knockedupmovie.com/ (Last accessed 18 November, 2008).

Brown, W. (2006). *Regulating Aversion: Tolerance in the Age of Identity and Empire*. Princeton, New Jersey: Princeton University Press.

Cappiello, J.D., & Vroman, K. (2011). Bring the Popcorn: Using Film to Teach Sexual and Reproductive Health. *International Journal of Nursing Education Scholarship*, 8(1). Available from http://www.degruyter.com.ezproxy.lib.monash.edu.au/view/j/ijnes.2011.8.issue-1/1548–923X.2133/1548–923X.2133.xml?rskey=u8rvfY&result=1

Clarke, C. (2007). Just Don't Say the A-word. *The Guardian*. Available from http://www.theguardian.com/film/2007/nov/23/1 (Last accessed August 20, 2014)

Crave Online Australia. (2007). *Judd Apatow may have killed Jerry Falwell*. Available from http://www.craveonline.com.au/lifestyle/interviews/157136-judd-apatow-may-have-killed-jerry-falwell (Last accessed August 14, 2014).

Daniels, L. (2009). *Precious*. Directed by Lee Daniels and screenplay by Geoffrey S. Fletcher. Distributed by Lionsgate.

Deutscher, P. (2008). The Inversion of Exceptionality: Foucault, Agamben, and "Reproductive Rights". *South Atlantic Quarterly*, 107(1), 55–70.

Douglas, E. (2007a). Jason Reitman Tackles Teen Pregnancy in Juno, Posted December 7. *Crave Online Australia*. Available from http://www.comingsoon.net/news/movienews.php?id=40048 (Last accessed November 25, 2008).

———. (2007b). The Inimitable Ellen Page on Juno Posted December 3. *Crave Online Australia*. Available from http://www.comingsoon.net/news/movienews.php?id=39821 (Last accessed November 25, 2008).

———. (2007c). Juno Screenwriter Diablo Cody, Posted December 13. *Crave Online Australia*. Available from http://www.comingsoon.net/news/movienews.php?id=40048 (Last accessed November 25, 2008).

Doyle, J. (2009). Blind Spots and Failed Performance: Abortion, Feminism, and Queer Theory. *Qui Parle: Critical Humanities and Social Sciences*, 18(1), 25–52.

Duran, R. (2008). *Frat-Pack tribute interview: Knocked up's Judd Apatow*. Available from http://www.the-frat-pack.com/reviews/knockedup-judd.html (Last accessed August 21, 2014).

During, S. (2007). *The Mundane against the secular*. The Immanent Frame website. Available from http://blogs.ssrc.org/tif/2007/11/10/the-mundane-against-the-secular (Last accessed March 15th, 2015).

Freeman, H. (2008). A choice that films ignore (posted January 28). *The Guardian*. Available from http://www.guardian.co.uk/commentisfree/2008/jan/28/healthand wellbeing.film (Last accessed August 21, 2014).

Haines, M., Ruby, J., McCaslin, D., Mantilla, K., & Rodgers, M. (2007). Juno: Feminist or Not? *Off Our Backs*, 37(4): 70–73.

Hoerl, K., & Ryan Kelly, C. (2010). The Post-nuclear Family and the Depoliticization of Unplanned Pregnancy in Knocked Up, Juno, and Waitress. *Communication and Critical/Cultural Studies*, 7(4): 360–380.

Hornaday, A. (2007, July 15). Pregnant with Meaning? Alas, We Were Expecting More. *WashingtonPost.com*. Available from http://www.washingtonpost.com/wp-dyn/content/article/2007/07/13/AR2007071300370.html (Last accessed August 21, 2014).

Jarman, M. (2012). Cultural Consumption and Rejection of Precious Jones: Pushing Disability into the Discussion of Sapphire's *Push* and Lee Daniels's *Precious*. *Feminist Formations*, 24(2): 163–185.

Knox, S. (2007). Hollywood Bests Washington on Teen Sex, *The Huffington Post*, 17 December 2007. Available from http://www.huffingtonpost.com/shelby-knox/hollywood-bests-washingto_b_77155.html. (Last accessed August 17, 2014).

Latimer, H. (2009). Popular Culture and Reproductive Politics: Juno, Knocked Up and the Enduring Legacy of the Handmaid's Tale. *Feminist Theory*, 10(2): 211–226.

Lesko, N. (2010). Feeling Abstinent? Feeling Comprehensive? Touching the Affects of Sexuality Curricula. *Sex Education*, 10(3): 281–297.

Luttrell, W. (2011). Where Inequality Lives in the Body: Teenage Pregnancy, Public Pedagogies and Individual Lives. *Sport, Education and Society*, 16(3): 295–308.

Mungui, C. (2007). *4 Months, 3 Weeks and 2 Days*, Mobra Films.

O'Brien, T., & Noy, S. (2015). Traditional, Modern, and Post-Secular Perspectives on Science and Religion in the United States. *American Sociological Review*, 80(1): 92–115.

Reitman, J. (2007). *Juno*. Directed by Jason Reitman and written by Diablo Cody. Distributed by Fox Searchlight Pictures. Available from http://www.foxsearchlight.com/juno/ (Last accessed August 21, 2014).

Risøy, S.M., & Sirnes, T. (2014). The Decision: Relations to Oneself, Authority and Vulnerability in the Field of Selective Abortion. *BioSocieties*, 39. Available from http://www.palgrave-journals.com/biosoc/journal/vaop/ncurrent/full/biosoc 201439a.html (Last accessed March 15, 2015).

Robespierre, J. (2014). *Obvious Child*. Directed by Gillian Robespierre and screenplay by Gillian Robespierre. Distributed by A24 and The Exchange.

Sciortiono, K. (2014). 'Abortion rom-com' Obvious Child Is Important—Because It's So Ordinary. *The Guardian*, June, 13, 2007. Available from http://www.theguardian.com/film/2014/jun/12/obvious-child-rom-com-jenny-slate-ordinary (Last accessed August 14, 2014).

Shelly, A. (2007). *Waitress*. Written and Directed by Adrienne Shelly. Distributed by Fox Searchlight pictures.

Thoma, P. (2009). Buying Up Baby: Modern Feminine Subjectivity, Assertions of "Choice," and the Repudiation of Reproductive Justice in Postfeminist Unwanted Pregnancy Films. *Feminist Media Studies*, 9(4): 409–425.

Tillman, L. (2008). *'Knocked Up,' but looking for more: Re-casting pregnancy in pop-culture.* Available from http://www.brownsvilleherald.com/news/local/article_f470729a-a076-525b-a3a5-4ba6d2f41003.html?TNNoMobile (Last accessed August 21, 2014).

Withers, K. (2008). Reviews: Juno and 4 Months, 3 Weeks and 2 Days. *Public Policy Research*, 15(2): 101–102.

8 Ireland, Canada, and Australia
Tracing Progressive Sexuality Education Across Borders

The relationships among religion, progressivism, and secularism, and how they have played out via sexuality education in Ireland, Canada, and Australia is the focus of this chapter. There is a strong emphasis on Catholicism and the ways in which public control and funding of Catholic schools interweave with the production of progressive discourses of sexuality education. By attending to how progressive-secular imaginaries of sexuality education manifest across these sites, I also hope to capture some of what is distinct and common in their production; this might increase understanding of how these imaginaries are assembled and how they travel across borders. What does progressive sexuality education look like in places such as Ireland, which have long histories of intensive church involvement in schooling? Do visions for progressive sexuality education differ much in places like Canada, Australia, and Ireland, given their different histories of secularism?

Canadian debates about sexuality education were part of the genesis of this book. Research for this manuscript began while I was on sabbatical at the University of British Columbia in Vancouver, Canada, in 2008; I also visited Toronto in 2012.[1] On both visits I was struck by the differences and similarities in debates about sexuality education in Australia and Canada. One immediate difference I noted was that issues related to secularism, sexuality, and education appeared to be a part of ongoing public debates in a way that is rarely the case in Australia. Debates about the public funding of religious schools and how that relates to questions of homophobia are not things that are as contentious in Australia as they are in Canada. Maybe this is partially because the Australian education system is significantly more privatized than its Canadian counterpart and because public funding of religious education is not directed exclusively to Catholic schools, as is the case in some Canadian provinces. Issues regarding funding of school chaplains in schools and the place of special religious instruction in public schools are often in the news in Australia, but debates that specifically reference schooling, sexuality, and education felt much more prominent in Canada than was my experience in Australia.

I spent several years living in Idaho in the US in the 1990s. The discourse of progressivism in Canada sometimes felt a world away from my own experiences of combatting an anti-lesbian and gay ballot while in Idaho.

Though David Rayside and Clyde Wilcox warn against a tendency to construct Canada as the more progressive neighbor to the US, noting the US is generally constructed as

> ... resistant to LGBT claims, while Canada has undergone a political and legal revolution and now embraces them fully. They are all misleading. These two countries are distinct, to be sure, but there are also more parallels than is widely appreciated. (2011a: xvi)

Part of my interest in pursuing a sabbatical at a Canadian university was linked to this perception (in which I was clearly implicated) that Canada was a place where progressives in sexuality education in Australia might look to see what was possible in terms of reform in this field.

The selection of Ireland as a case study was influenced by conversations with Pam Alldred, while I was visiting England in 2012. Alldred suggested that incorporating a case study of a country such as Ireland might help deepen my understanding of progressivism in sexuality education. An invitation by Aoife Neary to participate in a symposium on sexuality and schooling in Ireland in 2013 also prompted me to think about what it meant to navigate questions of progressive sexuality education in a country context where the Catholic Church continued to have a dominant influence in education. Ireland's education landscape is dominated by Catholicism, but Ireland has legalized marriage equality prior to Australia (an event that is often held up as a mark of a country's progressive bonafides). Ireland would appear to be a place that is quite quickly shifting ground on questions of sexuality—and therefore an interesting site in which to investigate progressive-secular imaginaries of sexuality education.

Below I provide some more detail on sexuality education in these three countries, but first it is necessary to sketch some basic information about how each of their education systems is arranged. A principal focus of my comments is on the place of Catholicism and religious education in each of these school contexts. This analysis is not offered in the spirit of a methodical comparative analysis. I am keenly aware that the descriptions I offer are tentative—this is partially because of the limitations of space. Primarily my observations are trying to grasp some fundamental differences in how education and religiosity are interwoven in these three contexts, with a view to considering how these differences and similarities might shape progressive discourses of sexuality education. A book could easily be dedicated to the nuances of this interrelationship in each country context.

CATHOLIC AND SECULAR ENTANGLEMENTS IN IRISH EDUCATION

Catholicism has shaped Ireland's history and cultural identity and maintains a strong influence on many parts of political and civil life. This history shapes current debates about secularism in ways that are distinct from cultural associations and understandings of secularism in places such as Canada and Australia. While Catholicism continues to have a strong influence on debates about education and sexuality in Ireland, this is also a country that has taken a secular turn on questions of sexual diversity.

Public education is still very much dominated by the Catholic Church in Ireland. Breda Gray (2013) notes "92% of primary schools and 49% of second-level schools continue under Catholic patronage" (2).[2] In Ireland, the educational philosophy of the body responsible for the patronage (or management) of a school is reflected in the school ethos (mission). The Irish state provides for free primary education, but patron bodies that define the ethos of the school and appoint the board of management run the school on a day-to-day basis. The situation in Ireland is "unique among European countries: since the foundation of the state, almost all schools have been religious" (Rougier and Honohan, 2014: 3). Even though the Catholic Church is withdrawing from schools in some areas, the influence of the Catholic Church continues to be strong within the Irish system (Gray, 2013; Rougier and Honohan, 2014).

Given this configuration of schooling in Ireland, conversations about secularism and sexuality education in the Irish context can clearly not be separated from the Catholic Church's cultural significance and its historical and contemporary influence in education debates. The Catholic Church continues to be a significant player in education debates in Australia and Canada, but the significance of the Church in Ireland is much more pronounced. Conversations about secularism and sexuality education in the Irish context thus need to include "an internal accounting of how this historical privilege [accorded to Catholicism] structures the possibility of communication across differences" (Mahmood, 2010: 298).

In an analysis of religion and the public square in Ireland, Siobhan, Mullally, and Darren O'Donovan (2011) argue that in countries such as Canada, Australia, and Aotearoa-New Zealand, religious ties have steadily lapsed. They see Ireland as distinct because

> [t]he lapse in religious ties has come much later . . . hastened by revelations of systematic child abuse within the Catholic Church, economic liberalisation and immigration. Despite this lapse, the relevance of religion has not waned. While greater pluralism in public discourse is evident, it is not clear that Ireland could be defined as secular, given the continuing entanglement of Church and State, particularly on matters relating to education and family law reform. (11)

Ireland's ambiguous relationship to secularism is underscored by Mullally and O'Donovan's analysis. This ambiguity is productive because it provides a means of interrogating how progressivism, sexuality education, and secularism are linked and put under pressure in a place that is still strongly entangled with Catholicism.

Tensions about the production and conceptualization of sexuality education in the Irish context may, Leslie Sherlock suggests, be further complicated by the fraught reception of "European" human rights discourses in Ireland and resistance to discourses that construct all Europeans as homo-inclusive and liberal or homophobic and not liberal enough (Kulpa, 2014; Sherlock, 2012). European and international organizations such as The Council of Europe and the Committee on the Elimination of Racial Discrimination have both called on Ireland to increase the diversity offerings available to better reflect changes in Ireland's cultural and religious and diversity (Rougier and Honohan, 2014: 9). These observations illustrate how debates about sexuality, secularism, and schooling within specific country contexts are shaped not only by religion but also by national and transnational perceptions of rights discourses.

PUBLIC SCHOOLING, RELIGION, AND EDUCATION IN CANADA AND AUSTRALIA

In the Canadian context there are ongoing debates about provincial government funding for religious education. Debates about sexual freedom have also tended to trump arguments related to religious freedom in public schools (see the following sections); this trend has not been the same in Australia, where the place of religion in public and private schooling has been strengthened under successive conservative and progressive federal governments (see Maddox, 2014).

In grasping secularism and sexuality education in the Canadian context, it is also important to recognize that there are significant differences within and between provinces regarding the history of religious education, the history of sexuality, and the history of secularism. The Canadian Secular Alliance illustrates some of these differences regarding funding of religious education in the Canadian context:

(1) Ontario, Alberta, and Saskatchewan still offer full public funding to Catholic schools—a historical artifact originating from "denominational privileges" enshrined in section 93 of the Constitution Act, 1867. All other provinces do not have (or have since eliminated) this constitutional obligation.
(2) British Columbia, Alberta, Saskatchewan, Manitoba, and Quebec offer partial funding (typically 40–60 percent) to religious schools of any faith that meet some provincial criteria (typically agreeing to teach the provincial curriculum, submit to standardized testing, and employ certified teachers). All other provinces do not support private religious schools with public money.

> The combination of these policies means that: (a) New Brunswick, Nova Scotia, Prince Edward Island, and Newfoundland offer zero funding to religious schools of any kind; and (b) *Ontario is the only province with the especially unjust combination of 100 percent funding for Catholic schools and zero funding for all other religious schools.* (Canadian Secular Alliance, 2009: Section 1.1 Public Funding of Religious Schools in Canada, my emphasis)

For the Canadian Secular Alliance, the state funding of religious education is problematic, but Ontario's ongoing funding of Catholic schools, and the exclusion of funding to all other religious denominations, is especially egregious.[3]

Government funding of private religious schools is also debated in Australia, but unlike Canada, Australian governments fund religious schools of many denominations as well as nonreligious private schools (Campbell and Proctor, 2014: 261). Many Australians who are not religious send their children to these private schools (religious and nonreligious)—which has caused some religious schools to insist that parents demonstrate their faith commitments before accepting enrolments (Campbell and Proctor, 2014: 264). Public schools continue to be responsible for educating the majority of Australian school students,[4] though this majority is slowly eroding—especially at the senior secondary level. Public schools have been the site of secular controversies related to the appointment of school chaplains who, at time of writing,[5] must be religious. There has also been heated political, judicial, and popular debate about whether or not states should continue to fund special religious instruction of students attending public primary schools (Maddox, 2014).

> As Craig Campbell and Helen Proctor note in *A History of Australian Schooling*, it is clear that the numbers of children receiving a religiously influenced schooling have increased since the 1980s, and this trend shows every indication of continuing . . . [N]ot all parents who enrolled their children in religiously affiliated schools were happy with the religious teaching . . . [S]ome of them liked other aspects of the school and were prepared to tolerate the religious teaching in order to access them (Campbell and Proctor, 2014: 263, 264; Campbell, Proctor, and Sherington, 2009).

Paradoxically, as the number of young people enrolled in schools with religious affiliations increases, the number of young people in Australia who identify as religious continues in a steady decline. More than half of the 22 percent of Australians who reported no religious affiliation in the last national census are less than 30 years old (Bouma and Hughes, 2014). Therefore, Australia has increasing numbers of young people identifying as nonreligious, but at the same time it has more young people than ever before attending religiously affiliated schools.

Ireland, Canada, and Australia 149

This fleeting introduction to the place of religion in schooling in each of these country contexts hopefully demonstrates that relationships among secularism, religion, and education are by no means straightforward. Ireland achieved marriage equality prior to Australia, yet one might argue that the Irish population has received little in the way of messages in support of marriage equality within the context of a Catholic education, which is the school experience of the majority of Irish students. Australia, home of Sydney's Gay and Lesbian Mardi Gras, one of the world's largest gay and lesbian festivals, has so far failed to win support in the federal parliament for a vote on marriage equality. Does the Australian education system, with young people increasingly experiencing education in religiously affiliated schools, play a part in an ongoing reticence to bring this issue to a vote? In short, how do school systems influence the production of progressive-secular imaginaries?

SEXUALITY EDUCATION IN THE CURRICULA IN IRELAND, AUSTRALIA, AND ONTARIO, CANADA

When it comes to secondary[6] sexuality education curriculum in Ireland, Australia, and Canada, there are many similarities. I found this surprising given the different structures of schooling in these countries. In Ireland, relationships and sexuality education (RSE) curricula is strongly informed by the principles of CSE. RSE is located within the curriculum area of social, personal, and health education (SPHE). In Australia, sexuality education is taught within the curriculum area of personal development, health, and physical education (PDHPE). In Ontario, Canada, sexuality education curriculum is delivered as part of health and physical education (HPE).

Next I juxtapose three extracts from sexuality education curricula in Ireland, Ontario in Canada, Victoria, Australia, as well as a draft of the Australian National curriculum. These excerpts are taken from curriculum documents that are aimed at secondary students. Australia has no compulsory sexuality education in the senior years (11 and 12). Compulsory sexuality education in Australian public schools generally ends at the end of year 10. In Ontario, the recently revised secondary health and physical education curriculum comprises four compulsory healthy active living education (HALE) courses, one in each of Grades 9 through 12. Ireland also offers sexuality education through to the end of schooling—mirroring the Canadian context. One similarity of these curricula is in their location of sexuality education within broader curriculum frameworks within the domain of health.

Table 8.1 below includes examples of statements about what should be incorporated in sexuality education in the Irish curriculum, the Australian draft curriculum, the curriculum in the state of Victoria, Australia, and the curriculum in the province of Ontario, Canada. I have chosen to juxtapose some of the statements physically to underscore some of the similarities in language use. I have also, where possible, juxtaposed statements intended for students of the same age.

Table 8.1

Irish RSE Curriculum (Senior Cycle) (ages 15–18) (2011)	Australian draft PDHPE Draft Curriculum (ages 14–15) (2015)	Catching on Later, Victoria,[7] Australia (AUSVELS 9 and 10) (ages 14–15) (2013)	Ontario, Canada: HPE Curriculum (ages 14–15) (revised 2015)
– Distinguish among sexual activity, sexuality, and sexual orientation. – Demonstrate genuineness, empathy, and respect in different types of relationship scenarios. – Design an awareness campaign highlighting different ways to negotiate sexual relationships to avoid unwanted sexual activities and/or unprotected sexual intercourse. – Clarify understanding of and comfort with different sexual orientations. – Demonstrate how to relate respectfully to others of a different sexual orientation.	– Explore the nature and benefits of meaningful and respectful relationships to develop skills to manage a range of relationships as they change over time. – Critically examine how a range of sociocultural and personal factors influence sexuality, gender identity, sexual attitudes, and behavior. – Develop an understanding of the roles that empathy, ethical decision making, and personal safety play in maintaining respectful relationships.	– Examine roles and responsibilities in sexual relationships. – Look at factors influencing the development of identity. – Study variations in relationships over time. – Discuss sexuality and sexual health. – Examine assumptions, community attitudes, and stereotypes about young people and sexuality. – Identify support strategies for young people experiencing difficulties in relationships or with their sexuality. – Review policies and practices related to sexual harassment, homophobia, and discrimination.	– Think ahead about sexual health, consent, and personal limits. – Respond to bullying and harassment (including sexual harassment, gender-based violence, homophobia, and racism). – Review relationships—skills and strategies. – Prevent pregnancy and STIs. – Look at factors affecting gender identity and sexual orientation and related supports. – Demonstrate an understanding of factors that contribute to health development. – Demonstrate the ability to apply health knowledge and living skills to make reasoned decisions and take appropriate actions relating to personal health and well-being.

Irish RSE Curriculum (Senior Cycle) (ages 15–18) (2011)	Australian draft PDHPE Draft Curriculum (ages 14–15) (2015)	Catching on Later, Victoria,[7] Australia (AUSVELS 9 and 10) (ages 14–15) (2013)	Ontario, Canada: HPE Curriculum (ages 14–15) (revised 2015)
–Learn how to demonstrate genuineness, empathy, and respect in different types of relationship scenarios.			– Demonstrate the ability to make connections that relate to health and well-being—how their choices and behaviors affect both themselves and others.

Given the country contexts in which these curricula have been formulated, I anticipated they might have been more distinct. The curricula overlap in their focus on empathy, inclusion, and respect for others within and outside relationships. With the exception of the Australian draft curriculum, they all explicitly mention sexual orientation and/or homophobia. They are all nominally inclusive of sexual diversity. I recognize that the capacity of teachers to incorporate such content in practice may be constrained in all three contexts due to teachers' concerns about the consequences of teaching topics they perceive as controversial. There appears to be an assumption in all the curricula that young people may be sexually active when at school.

In writing about the RSE curriculum in postprimary schools in the Irish context, Paula Mayock, Karl Kitching, and Mark Morgan draw on Inglis (1998) and Kiely (2005) to argue that

> ... the programme does not deal with a number of sensitive topics, such as masturbation. It is also claimed that the definition of sex proposed in the RSE resource materials privileges a heterosexual identity and that the programme promotes a limited kind of sexual subjectivity, which obscures sexual pleasure and desire. (Mayock et al., 2007: 10)

This critique of the Irish context, which is arguably still relevant for the 2011 Irish curriculum, would also hold true in the Australian context where sexuality education, at least within the context of PDHPE in the national curriculum, is highly constrained in policy, curriculum, and practice. Although the Victorian curriculum document, Catching on Later (2013), is much more explicit on these topics—explicitly mentioning masturbation, sexual pleasure, homophobia, gay, lesbian, bisexual, transgender, and intersex.

Currently a revised draft of the Australian PDHPE curriculum is awaiting approval.[8] This revised draft makes no explicit mention of gay, lesbian, bisexual, transgender, or intersex issues, though it does have one paragraph on the importance of addressing student diversity.

Same-sex attracted and gender-diverse young people are becoming increasingly visible in Australian schools. The Australian Curriculum: HPE is designed to allow schools flexibility to meet the needs of these young people, particularly in the health context of

> relationships and sexuality. As students facing these issues exist in all school communities, it is expected that opportunities will be taken when implementing the Health and Physical Education curriculum to ensure teaching is inclusive and relevant to their lived experiences.
> (ACARA, 2012: 18)

The draft Australian curriculum could be constituted as less progressive (if inclusion of LGBTI issues is a measure of progressivism) than the Victorian curriculum. The two documents were prepared contemporaneously, which illustrates the variations regarding the influence of progressive sexuality education within country contexts.

At time of writing, Ontario, Canada, has just published a revised sexuality education curriculum. In the glossary for this new curriculum, there is a clear association between sexuality and pleasure (this is also true for the Victorian curriculum):

> sexuality. A term that encompasses sex, gender identities and roles, sexual orientation, eroticism, pleasure, intimacy, and reproduction. Sexuality is experienced and expressed in thoughts, fantasies, desires, beliefs, attitudes, values, behaviors, practices, roles, and relationships.
> (Ontario Ministry of Education, 2015b: 216)

The glossary also incorporates definitions of *bisexual, gay, gay straight alliance, gender, gender-based violence, gender expression, homophobia, intersex, lesbian, transgender, transsexual*, and *two-spirited*. The Irish curriculum and the Australian draft curricula both avoid any mention of these terms.

A focus on sexual pleasure is also reiterated in a discussion of human development and sexual health in the Ontario curriculum:

> Sexual health, understood in its broadest sense, can include a wide range of topics and concepts, from sexual development, reproductive health, choice and sexual readiness, consent, abstinence, and protection, to interpersonal relationships, sexual orientation, gender identity and gender expression, affection and pleasure, body image, and gender roles and expectations.
> (Ontario Ministry of Education, 2015b: 42)

Ontario's revised curriculum has been seen as worthy of comment in the news. Media commentators portray the revision as marking significant progress—no longer leaving students "in the dark" about sexuality:

> Come September, teachers across Ontario can sit down with their students with a revamped sexual-education curriculum that finally brings the province up to date with the rest of the country and no longer leaves them "in the dark."
> (Do, 2015).

This revised curriculum is also being reported as enabling teachers to specifically address sexting, homophobia, and masturbation (in the context of puberty).[9] While the curriculum is yet to be implemented at time of writing, it would appear to have the potential to address some of the concerns identified by Inglis (2008) and Kiely (2005) in their critiques of the Irish curriculum. The current Irish curriculum also explicitly makes mention of pleasure by analyzing

> the concepts of love, being in love and the importance of love in its various aspects, including closeness, intimacy, distance, pleasure and commitment.
> (National Council for Curriculum and Assessment, 2011: 27)

Pleasure here is clearly associated with "being in love" and "commitment." The draft Australian national curriculum makes no mention of sexual pleasure, masturbation, HIV or acquired immunodeficiency syndrome (AIDS). Catching on Later, the Victorian curriculum, also provides explicit mention of sexual pleasure, utilizing a definition taken from the International Sexuality and HIV Curriculum Working Group:

> Sexuality can be a source of great pleasure and meaning in life. Sexual activity is only one aspect of sexuality. People experience sexuality through their physical feelings, emotions, thoughts, identity, and relationships. Cultural norms, individual experiences, and hormones all influence the way we understand and experience sexuality.
> (Department of Education and Early Childhood Development, 2013: 70)

Unlike the Irish curriculum, sexual pleasure in the curricula of Ontario and Victoria is not explicitly linked to love and commitment.

Australia and Ireland have quite distinct schooling contexts, but their national curriculum frameworks relating to sexuality education are not dissimilar. If progressivism were associated with the level of religiosity within the governance of a school system, one might anticipate that the Australian curriculum would be more progressive than its Irish counterpart. This is demonstrably not the case, at least not at the national level.

The revised Canadian curriculum and the Victorian curriculum arguably represent the future of progressive sexuality education insofar as they are explicit in their inclusion of LGBTI issues, homophobia, sexual pleasure, and masturbation. The revised sexuality education curriculum is the subject of some controversy in Ontario. Members of Ontario's Progressive Conservative Party have been outspoken in their opposition to this new curriculum.

However, the sharp distinctions being drawn between the new Ontario curriculum and its predecessor may also be overblown:

> Jen Gilbert, an associate professor in the faculty of education at York University, says the 1998 curriculum has suffered a bad rap in the wake of the release of the new syllabus. Granted, "sexuality went online" since then and family norms shifted. But in its day, the 1998 version was more than adequate. "At a time when everyone else in North America was talking about abstinence, Ontario came out with this very comprehensive sex education program," Gilbert says. "So I see this curriculum as picking up and inheriting that progressive legacy."
>
> (Wells, 2015).

Gilbert's comments suggest progressivism is a hallmark of contemporary sexuality education curricula—and that Ontario was perceived as particularly progressive relative to the North American context, even prior to the new curriculum being introduced. In terms of curricula standards, Ireland and Australia appear to lag behind in the progressive stakes, at least at the national level.

The state of Victoria in Australia sees itself very much at the forefront of progressive sexuality education (Jones and Hillier, 2012). They note that

> Victoria (VIC) is the most extreme ideological battleground in published Australian school education policy texts. It features the most explicit pro-diversity policies in the public sector; principally the eight-page Supporting Sexual Diversity in Schools (VIC Government 2008) and large sections on gender identity and sexuality in other policies (VIC Government 2007, 2010a). Yet, it also has the most blatantly conservative Catholic policy (Catholic Education Office Melbourne) that prohibits teaching around premarital sex, safe sex, body functions and individualism (2001, 7–8).
>
> (Jones and Hillier, 2012: 440)

In tracing the place of pleasure, sexual diversity, and masturbation across these curricula within these diverse contexts, my point is not to determine which of these places might be constituted as the most progressive in terms of sexuality education.

Principally, my argument is that degrees of progressivism in sexuality education may be difficult to predict when looking at broader educational structures, such as Catholic ethos (Ireland) or growth of religious schools (Australia). This is apparent when comparing Irish and Australian national curricula. The disconnect among national, state, and provincial discourses on sexuality education in differing Australian and Canadian sexuality education curricula documents also underscores that progressivism is not linear or uniform within different country contexts. This point is echoed in the research of David Rayside (2014) in that he observes the uneven nature of reform on issues related to sexuality and sexual diversity in Canadian, British, and US schools.

SEXUAL DIVERSITY, RELIGION, AND PROGRESSIVE-SECULAR IMAGINARIES

In the Australian context, research suggests schools often overlook this curriculum area because of competing curriculum demands, teacher discomfort, and lack of preservice teacher education (Mitchell et al., 2011). Tiffany Jones and Anne Mitchell acknowledge problems with delivery of sexuality education but also trace what they perceive as significant shifts in sexuality education provision in the Australian context, following the release of the first national HIV/AIDS strategy in 1989. They argue the strategy was utilized

> [m]any times . . . to broker a useful partnership between health and education authorities and, in government schools at least, *it was the final step to taking the teaching of sexuality education out of the hands of moralists who had previously promoted a conservative Sexual Morality focus*, ensuring a more liberal Sexual Risk/Harm Reduction focus for the foreseeable future.
> (Jones, 2011b; Jones and Mitchell, 2014: 226, my emphasis)

This observation from Jones and Mitchell (2014) highlights a perceived binary in the Australia context between those who would conceptualize sexuality education as about promotion of sexual morality versus those who principally conceptualize sexuality education in a more liberal secular frame.

Jones and Mitchell's comments also speak to the fundamental importance of struggles related to HIV/AIDS in shaping international discourses related to sexuality education. The public health emergency associated with the onset of HIV/AIDS was perceived as a lever that could be used to argue for an explicit focus on health over morality. In a time of national emergency (represented by HIV/AIDS) supporters of a progressive approach, in the Australian context, successfully constituted concerns about morality as, at last, out of place. For this reason, at least in the Australian context, discourses related to progressive sexuality education are also inextricably linked to discourses related to gender and sexual diversity in sexuality education.

In Ireland, where the Catholic Church appears to continue to play a dominant role in education, progressive discourses of secularization are by no means absent. This is apparent in research and activism related to the implementation of RSE in all schools, which is inclusive of teachers' and students' diverse genders and sexualities.

The prominence of discourses related to sexual diversity in schooling in Ireland is apparent in the formation of groups such as the Gay and Lesbian Equality Network (GLEN), founded in 1988, which has a strong commitment to issues related to young people and education. The LGB teachers' group within the Irish National Teachers' Organisation (INTO) (Neary, 2012, 2014), founded in 2004, is also lobbying for reform of the Employment Equality Act, which allows religious schools to discriminate against teachers on the basis of their sexual orientation. Similar religious exemptions are in place in some Australian states at time of writing.

In her study of sexuality education in Ireland and Sweden, Leslie Sherlock (2012) notes the tensions and dilemmas that the religion or secular division evokes for "outside facilitators" of sexuality education. This includes "youth sexual health service providers, civil servants, and researchers" (384). Sherlock's study reflects on common perceptions about sexuality education in each context and how this has influenced the participants' understandings of their differing sociopolitical contexts. Sherlock writes that in Ireland

> ... narratives frequently linked late [in comparison to other countries in the European Union] sexuality education introduction and challenges with implementation to the Catholic Church's continued official and unofficial role in society. (2012: 388)

Sherlock notes the tensions that this caused for participants with some feeling that Catholicism was an impediment to their (health promotion) job with several participants directly relating the "complex" challenges they faced with the continued dominance of Catholic schooling in this context (388–389). Sherlock also observes that other participants, while accepting of Catholic school's choice to prioritize a Catholic ethos, still perceived conflicts between a Catholic ethos and the task of health promotion (388–389). Sherlock's research suggests that it not possible to assume in advance how teachers will deal with the presence of Catholicism in the school.

Research also indicates that teachers demonstrate constraint in teaching sexuality education in publically funded secular and Catholic schools in Ottawa.[10] Analyzing the provision of sexuality education in this context, Karen Phillips and Andrea Martinez (2010) observe that provision at both secular and Catholic schools was sufficient in terms of education about risk but note that teachers in both school systems heavily emphasized the value of abstinence. Catholic schools in urban (but not rural areas) were reluctant to engage with secular health partners.

Phillips and Martinez further describe the differences between urban and rural areas in terms of how teachers teach sexuality education. In urban areas,

> former Catholic students identified many barriers to open discussions of sexuality and condom demonstrations in their schools. The rural Catholic school teachers, however, promoted Social, Personal and Health Education services in spite of the Catholic doctrine, perhaps cognizant of the limited services, privacy and other SRH [Sexual and Reproductive Health] barriers represented in rural communities" (2010: 378).

In the Canadian and Australian contexts, it appears that teachers are often reluctant to embrace sexuality education. In the Canadian context it is suggested that this may partially be because "the curricula of most Bachelor of Education programmes for students majoring in either elementary or secondary education do not include required or elective [sexual health education] SHE courses (McKay and Barrett 1999)" (Cohen, Byers, and Sears, 2012: 300). This is also true in Ireland and Australia.

Cohen, Byers, and Sears further argue that Canadian teachers they surveyed

> . . . were even less willing to teach about more sensitive topics (e.g. sexual pleasure and orgasm, masturbation, sexual behaviour). This may be because only about one-third had received any training to teach sexual health. Clearly, and consistent with past research conducted in Canada, the USA, and Australia (Levenson-Gingiss and Basen-Engquist 1994; Milton 2003; Ninomiya 2010), many Canadian teachers are being asked to teach sexual health without adequate preparation. *Even if they are using a curriculum that has empirical support, these teachers are unlikely to provide SHE that has positive effects on students' sexual decision-making and sexual health outcomes.* (2012: 311, my emphasis)

This Canadian research echoes Australian research, where more than half of the teachers in a study by Smith et al. (2011) cited time constraints and exclusion from the curriculum as reasons for not covering a sexuality education topic (see also Mitchell et al., 2011). About a fifth of the teachers also named a lack of support in either training, resources or by management or policy as a reason for not teaching a topic. Just under 50 percent of teachers said that they were careful about the topics they taught because of possible adverse community reactions, while 40 percent of teachers said that cultural religious values in the community influenced their teaching of sexuality education (Mitchell et al., 2011). In Australia, students attending Catholic schools continue to report institutional homophobia and the erasure of nonheterosexual identities in sexuality education curricula (Gahan,

158 Ireland, Canada, and Australia

Jones and Hiller, 2014), though such reports are surely not exclusive to students attending Catholic schools.

In the Irish context the Catholic ethos is reported to contribute to teachers feeling constrained in teaching sexuality education. Aoife Neary draws on a number of contemporary studies to argue

> ... the Irish education system has played a central role in policing and reproducing norms of (hetero) sexuality through practices of silence, non-recognition and misrepresentation that impact on both students and teachers (O'Carroll and Szalacha, 2000; Lodge and Lynch, 2004; O'Higgins-Norman, 2004, 2009; O'Higgins-Norman, Galvin and McNamara, 2006; Minton et al., 2008) ... The Catholic church is central in considering sexuality in Irish schools (Inglis, 1998) given its powerful "zone of influence" in education (Lynch, 1989, 131). (Neary, 2012: 2, 3)

Elizabeth Kiely (2005) has also attributed the shaping of the curriculum in Ireland to the Catholic ethos. Kiely is influenced by the work of Michelle Fine (1988) and argues for a greater emphasis on pleasure and desire in the Irish context. Kiely notes a departure from the strict Catholic moral teaching on right and wrong, which dominated the Irish sex education discourse in times past; the RSE program does not aggressively impose moral precepts on students. It seeks instead to make up subjects capable of exercising responsibility and self-care broadly in keeping with the kind of liberal, individualist, lifestyle project advocated in RSE (2005: 261).

In Kiely's analysis it is possible to see the production of a particular narrative within sexuality education, whereby secular discourses are constructed as temporally in advance of religious discourse. Within such a narrative, strict Catholic teaching is something that belongs in the past. In the conclusion to her paper, Kiely endorses the World Health Organization's definition of sexuality, a definition that is informed by religious, spiritual, and historical influences, presumably recognizing the role they play in the present.

The relationship between Catholic ethos and teachers who identify as LGBTI in Ireland is the subject of Lodge, Gowran, and O'Shea's research project "Valuing Visibility" (2011). Anne Lodge, reflecting on this research, writes:

> Teachers and other school personnel as well as a variety of education stakeholders sensed that school ethos operated as a key blocking mechanism inhibiting change with regard to policy and practice vis-à-vis the recognition of diverse sexualities in Irish post primary schools. (2013: 18)

Lodge argues a Catholic ethos not only acts as a reason not to act but that it is also used to avoid embarrassment and confusion associated with what she perceives as a lack of expertise regarding contradictory church teachings about diverse sexualities.

The impact of a religious school ethos on LGBTI teachers has also been the subject of research by Aoife Neary. Like Lodge, Neary is critical of the workings of Catholic ethos in schools, but she also underscores the complicated attachments of teachers to religious ethos within and outside schools. She notes that the removal of religious exemptions and the implementation of

> ... a secular education system will not ensure that the workings of religious "ethos" will suddenly disappear ... Despite negative, delegitimizing experiences of religiosity, the majority of teachers had religious attachments and many sought religious involvement in the celebration of their [civil partnerships] CPs in line with the cultural weight of religiosity in Ireland ... [At the same time] religious "ethos" worked through overt and subtle means to reproduce fear and isolation in LGBTQ teachers and maintain schools as heterosexually privileged spaces. (2012: 2)

In concluding her analysis, Neary warns against "quick fix secular solutions" in the Irish context, arguing that such an approach fails to apprehend the tensions between sexuality and religion that permeate teachers' lives (2014: 13). It is apparent from Neary's analysis that there are cultural ties with religion, and despite the dilemmas that it may provoke and the subtle types of exclusion that this continues to cause, teachers and individuals continue to express attachments toward religion. Secularism won't quickly erase these attachments. Rejecting Catholic ethos as entirely out of place and out of date in contemporary sexuality education may have the effect of creating stronger divisions between morality, faith, and religion and evidence, reason, and secularism—divisions that don't necessarily reflect the complex ways in which sexuality and faith are interwoven in schools and in people's everyday experiences.

I do not doubt that the Catholic ethos impacts on the production of sexuality education in the Irish context. I also think that there is a need for more rigorous international comparative research that attempts to grasp the significance of this impact. In my reading of research on sexuality education provision across Australia, Canada and Ireland, my impression is that teachers' reluctance to tackle sexuality education is widespread and can be attributed to an array of factors.

Determining the relationship between this reluctance and the take-up of sexuality education, from religious and secular standpoints, is far from straightforward in diverse educational settings. *This isn't to say that religious ethos is not a significant factor*. Both Catholic and secular systems can be stifling, homophobic, and, I would assume, progressive. This may be an argument for studies of school climate that can measure students' and teachers' experiences of homophobia—alongside studies that refuse the notion that progressivism in sexuality education can only thrive in the absence of religion. In the next section I consider the interrelationship between gay politics and secular progressive imaginaries of sexuality education.

PUBLIC FUNDING OF CATHOLIC SCHOOLS, LGBTI RIGHTS, AND HOMOPHOBIA IN ONTARIO

The Canadian Secular Alliance has been vocal in its support of issues related to sexuality and schools in Toronto, Ontario.[11] Consequently, affiliations have been forged between organizations that promote secularism and those that advocate for LGBTI rights issues. In this section I trace different ways in which secular progressive imaginaries have shaped activism in relation to LGBTI rights, both within teacher education and in allegiances formed between organizations like the Canadian Secular Alliance and queer activism.

The reporting of a rally held by the Canadian Secular Alliance supporting defunding of Ontario's Catholic schools captures some of the affiliations between these two groups. In a column reporting on the rally for *The Torontoist*, Kelli Korducki states:

> "Ontario Can't Afford Religious Discrimination" read the banner behind the speaker's podium at Sunday afternoon's Canadian Secular Alliance rally to protest public funding of Catholic schools . . . Maybe pragmatic arguments weren't necessary to sway this small crowd of roughly 100 attendees, many of whom stood toting signs demanding the cessation of faith-based bigotry (and wearing T-shirts gently reminding the world that "Some chicks marry other chicks. Get over it.").
> (Korducki, 2011: para. 1)[12]

Here an economic rationalist imperative neatly aligns with same-sex marriage in a rally against state funding of Catholic schools.[13] It is noteworthy that the fit among secularism, sexuality, and schooling is observed but unremarkable in Korducki's report. In the sociopolitical space of this rally, secular feelings were at one with LGBTI rights.

At least in this instance, protesting public funding of Catholic schools and LGBTI rights is seen to neatly align—such alliances are helpful in grasping the reach of secular progressive imaginaries. In this framing, LGBTI rights are considered under threat by Catholic schools; therefore, protesting public funding of Catholic schools becomes an obvious strategy for LGBTI activists. Such an alliance also serves the secular alliance, broadening their constituency to incorporate LGBTI activists.

This assumed relationship between secularism and LGBTI rights is also apparent in the framing of educational research on teachers' acceptance of LGBTI sexualities. In a study of how teachers' conduct anti-homophobia education in Toronto public schools, Tara Goldstein, Anthony Collins, and Michael Halder (2008) argue for more resources to support educators who are negotiating boundaries between "professional and personal commitments to equity and human rights education and their own and others' personal and community religious beliefs about homosexuality" (47). This study is premised on the understanding that homophobia needs to be eliminated from public schools—an issue addressed in more detail in Chapter 6. My focus here is on how being a responsible Canadian teacher in relation to homophobia has come to be shaped in particular ways through progressive secular imaginaries in educational research.

Goldstein et al. write in their study about one preservice teacher candidate, Aneeta, who

> . . . described her religious beliefs as somewhat orthodox and, as such, she did not fully condone homosexuality. Despite her strong religious beliefs, Aneeta was open to discussing homophobia and presenting it as a part of equity or human rights education to her students. However, ". . . if people [students] want some sort of support on that [coming out as LGBTQ]," she said, "I don't think that I would be the person to give support on it. Yet, despite these religious reservations, Aneeta "would definitely be willing to direct them in . . . whatever . . . they might need." Working through how to negotiate one's personal and community religious beliefs that do not condone homosexuality with one's public and professional role to implement the Board's anti-homophobia policy is a complex task. It points to the kind of teacher development opportunities boards of education and teacher education institutions need to address. In Aneeta's case, this negotiation work began in her pre-service teacher education course, "Working Towards Equity in Education," and by participating in our research study. *However, without further opportunities to continue this work, Aneeta's skill in implementing anti-homophobia school policy will not likely advance.*
>
> (Goldstein, Collins, and Halder, 2008: 57, 58, my emphasis)

The description of Aneeta's skills as not likely to advance suggests Goldstein et al. perceive her as having some way to go in developing her capacity in implementing anti-homophobia policies. It is possible that Aneeta's skill in implementing anti-homophobia policy is perceived to be lacking because her preference would be to provide a referral to a student who was dealing with issues such as coming out rather than provide the support herself. The implication is that Torontonian teachers, if they were properly able to implement the anti-homophobia policy, would feel confident in supporting students on their own and would probably not need to provide them with a referral to seek such support.

Aneeta's willingness to participate in the research study, to incorporate anti-homophobia education into her teaching, together with her capacity to acknowledge that others might be better placed to offer support to students who are personally dealing with issues related to coming out, suggests to me that she is well advanced in her capacity to implement anti-homophobia education. This analysis makes me wonder what advanced capacity to implement anti-homophobia education might ideally entail, especially for teachers like Aneeta (secular or religious), who don't fully condone homosexuality and likely have little personal experience of issues related to non-normative gender and sexual identities.

The assumption underpinning Goldstein et al.'s analysis appears to be that teachers will advance in implementing the anti-homophobia policy only when they can overcome their own homophobia and provide personal support to all students. On this reading, teachers like Aneeta "who do not fully condone homosexuality" must always be read as failing to grapple appropriately with the anti-homophobia school policy. Sexual freedoms appear to have trumped religious freedoms in this analysis of the implementation of a teacher's role in implementing anti-homophobia education policy.

Does progressive sexuality education that endeavors to buttress the rights of LGBTI students also need to construct teachers like Aneeta as needing to advance? To my mind Aneeta is already a useful ally. This is underscored by her willingness to admit to conflicts between her own beliefs and the provision of support for students—and by her willingness to redirect students to staff who are willing to provide support. More education for teachers like Aneeta suggests all teachers need to be on the same page about homophobia in all circumstances. Such a position appears to fail to take seriously any conflicts teachers might experience between sexual and religious freedoms. It could also potentially send students into the arms of teachers who may be ill equipped to provide the support they need because teachers find themselves in a climate in which they are no longer willing to publicly admit such misgivings—because doing so could situate them as in need of advancement.

SEXUAL FREEDOM, GAY–STRAIGHT ALLIANCES, AND CHILD FUNDAMENTALISM

In this section I trace some of the politics of gay–straight Alliances (GSAs) in Ontario, the debates that preceded their emergence in publicly funded Roman Catholic Schools, and the legislation surrounding this. The Accepting Schools Act, Bill 13, which passed in the Ontario legislature in July 2012, allows for GSAs to be formed in schools across Ontario (including Catholic and public schools) with a view to creating school cultures that are accepting of gender and sexual difference. Studying transcripts of submissions to the Legislative Assembly of Ontario regarding the "Accepting Schools Act" and "Anti-Bullying Act" (Bills 13 & 14, May, 2012), it is possible to see how sexual freedom and religious freedom are often (not always) constructed as oppositional within these debates. I place these transcripts at the intersection of gay politics and what Barbara Baird has termed "child fundamentalism" (2008)—where saving the children discourses take on particular types of moral force within gay identity politics.

The tendency to see sexual freedom and religious freedom in oppositional terms is explored in the work of Janet Jakobsen (2005), where she notes "gay politics has all too often bought into the idea that because the problem of sexual regulation seems based in religion, the answer is to defend secular freedom" (288). The blending of gay rights discourses and protests against public funding of Roman Catholic Schools in Toronto (see previous section) is one example where sexual freedom is sought via the abolition of funding for Roman Catholic schools. Such an approach clearly situates the problem of sexual regulation in public funding of Roman Catholic schools.

Jakobsen and Pelligrini (2009) also note the tendency among activists arguing identity-based claims[14] to focus on religion as oppositional. They argue ". . . focusing on religion alone not only occludes the many religious people who are themselves gay or supporters of gay rights, it also perpetuates the idea that religion is 'the' problem blocking gay rights and sexual freedom more generally" (2009: para. 4). They argue further that

> a shift in framework—from gay rights to the basic ground of freedom and equality—would do much not only for gay people . . . it could significantly alter how controversial issues are approached . . . We might move beyond the identity politics of rights-based movements, even as we preserve the ability to act on identity—and rights-based claims. Who knows, but we might even create the basis for . . . the possibility of creating a "new majority" that goes beyond individual issues to larger questions and practices of liberty and justice for all. Achieving this new majority cannot happen if we trade off some people's sexual freedom for some other people's religious freedom (or vice versa) . . . (Jakobsen & Pellegrini, 2009: para. 10)

Debates about the place of GSAs in Ontario's Catholic schools bring some of these issues regarding the relationship between gay identity-based claims and opposition to religion to the surface.

Douglas Elliot, a lawyer for the Ontario GSA Coalition, states in his submission to the Assembly Standing Committee that

> . . . there can be no religious or cultural justification for refusing these rights [the right to establish GSAs in Catholic schools] . . . Even if the existence of these clubs did somehow interfere with the religious beliefs or cultural traditions of others, how could that trivial interference possibly out-weigh the safety of children in our schools? *Is religious sensitivity more important than a black eye? Is cultural tradition more*

important than suicide? The UN says no and Canada says no. There is no religious exemption in our law for assault and no cultural free pass for psychological harassments. Our schools should be safe for everyone. (Elliot, 2012, my emphasis)

The extract is noteworthy for a number of reasons. First, Elliot seeks to create the perception of an international consensus on rights related to sexuality by invoking the authority of the United Nations. Yet countries that share strong political, cultural, and historic ties with Canada, such as Australia, Ireland, and England all have varying levels of religious exemption regarding issues related to gender and sexual identification in education contexts. Elliot also constructs cultural and religious objections to GSAs as trivial when counterbalanced with children's safety. The argument that children's safety renders all objections to the Accepting School's Act trivial is a political maneuver that might be characterized as a form of what Barbara Baird terms "child fundamentalism."

In her article, "Child Politics: Feminist Analyses," Baird uses this notion of "child fundamentalism" to

> . . . describe both formal and informal secular and religious discourse that mobilises the figure of "the child" in such ways that constitute this figure as a fixed and absolute category. Political scientists define fundamentalism as "a style of thought in which certain principles are recognised as essential 'truths' that have unchallengeable and overriding authority, regardless of their content."
> (Baird, 2008: 291; Heywood, 2002: 63)

The principal focus of Baird's article is conservative politicians in Australia and their production of child fundamentalism. More recently, critiques of the It Gets Better project (Puar, 2012) have attempted to trouble more progressive formations of child fundamentalism. It Gets Better, as Puar points out, is part of a broader politics that is "continually reproducing the exceptionalism of human bodies and the aggrieved agential subject, [a] politics typically enacted through 'wounded attachments'" (2012: 157). Debates about GSAs in Ontario occur in a cultural climate where speaking back to discourses that invoke the child (Baird, 2008; Edelman, 1998) as at-risk and "suicidal" is increasingly difficult. In such a context those who object to the legislative support of the GSA on cultural and religious grounds are, through the mechanism of a secular child fundamentalism, constructed as effectively putting all LGBTI children at risk.

One organization that has been quite active in the GSA debates in Ontario is the Centre for Inquiry (CFI). According to its website, "The Centre for Inquiry promotes and advances reason, science, secularism and freedom of inquiry in all areas of human endeavor."[15] In addition to making a submission to the Legislative Assembly of Ontario on Bills 13 and 14, this organization has also undertaken investigations and made a series of videos posted on YouTube about this debate.[16] In his submission to the assembly, Justin Trottier, the national communications director of the CFI makes the following argument:

> The evidence is clear and compelling: Three quarters of LGBT students feel unsafe at school; 42% of LGBT youth have had thoughts of suicide at some time. I think we're all familiar with those and other statistics at this point, and no one disputes those or the need to fight bullying ... The Centre for Inquiry stands for secularism; that is, church-state separation. As the Ontario GSA Coalition paper compellingly argues, the acceptance of public funds by an institution entails that that institution will not discriminate.
>
> (Trottier, 2012)

As in many other submissions to the assembly, Trottier emphasizes the subjection of LGBTI youth. Essential truths about the victimization of gay children thus became the basis for a broader argument that advances "church–state" separation. Arguably, a subtext of Trottier's discussion of statistics relating to discrimination experienced by LGBTI youth is that public funding of Catholic schools compounds such discrimination. Or, conversely, more secularity equals less suicide.

In his article, "Young, Gay, and Suicidal: Dynamic Nominalism and the Process of Defining a Social Problem with Statistics," Tom Waidzunas identifies the development of an

> ... increasingly universal discourse found in many scientific documents and media reporting, all gay youth are equally at increased risk for suicide, regardless of level of family acceptance, school climate, sex, race, class, nation, region, or any other imaginable variable. The erasure of difference in the attribution of risk leads to the depiction of youth in very different circumstances as equally at risk, effectively "homogenizing" the category "gay youth." (Waidzunas, 2012: 213)

Waidzunas's analysis of the ways in which LGBTI young people are homogenized as "at-risk" focuses on how particular statistics are repeatedly deployed that give the impression of a clear correlation between LGBTI young people and suicidality. For Waidzunas, such discussions are misleading because of the way they homogenize the category "gay youth."

The reinforcement of statistics that homogenize "gay youth" as "at-risk" here serves a broader purpose dear to the CFI, namely the cessation of public funding to Roman Catholic schools in Ontario. For organizations such as the CFI, GSA debates in Ontario provide an opportunity to construct religious freedom and sexual freedom as diametrically opposed. This is not to say that Roman Catholic schools and teachers do not discriminate against LGBTI students and their parents and teachers. It is also important to note here that all schools have homophobic elements. The elimination of religious funding and the right to name GSAs can be no guarantor that homophobia will cease.

In considering how secularism is linked with sexual freedom in debates about GSAs in Ontario, it is also important to acknowledge the role of the Ontario English Catholic Teachers' Association (OECTA) in supporting the passage of Bills 13 and 14. An editorial in *The Globe and Mail* on June 6, 2012, notes:

> The 43,000 members of the Ontario English Catholic Teachers' Association (OECTA), like so many others, recognize that the Vatican's position contradicts Canadians' constitutional right to be free from discrimination based on sexual orientation. They embrace the part of the law that allows students to use the name "gay-straight alliance" in Catholic schools because they are the adults who walk the halls and see the bullying that takes place in high school. They are the ones who know how bullying can damage and even destroy a child's education. And they seem to understand better than their employer that banning the term "gay-straight alliance," as one Toronto-area Catholic high school did, is an official endorsement of intolerance and a direct contradiction of the Assembly of Catholic Bishops of Ontario's recent statement that bullying in any form is unacceptable (any form except theirs?). (*Globe* Editorial, 2012: para. 2)

The OECTA is on the record as supporting the Ontario governments Bill 13 and 14, though officials of the Catholic Church did not support the bills' passage. I agree that in Catholic schools, people are discriminated against on the basis of their gender and sexual identification as a result of Catholic doctrine. Though, I also want to be clear in arguing that discrimination based on sexual and gender identification has many causes, religiosity being just one of those causes.

SCIENCE, CANADIAN PROGRESSIVISM, AND DEMOCRATIC IMAGININGS OF SEXUALITY EDUCATION

This study of Canadian progressive secular imaginaries has principally focused on the province of Ontario. I shift now to a more recent incident regarding religion and sexuality education in Edmonton, in the province of Alberta. Here I consider how progressive sexuality education is seamlessly interwoven with debates about democracy in Canada and the US.

In 2014, a controversy erupted over the teaching of a compulsory sexuality education unit at McNally High, a public high school in Edmonton. Emily Dawson, a former student of McNally High, and her mother, Kathy Dawson, filed a complaint about the compulsory unit with the Alberta Human Rights Commission.[17] The unit was administered by the Pregnancy

Care Centre (PCC), which is affiliated "with Care-Net, a U.S. based Christian group that opposes abortion."[18]

As a result of the complaint and the associated media coverage the Edmonton Public School Board (EPSB) decided in July 2014 that the PCC would no longer be able to administer programs in their public schools. The Dawsons objected to the program because it was religiously based and degrading to women and single parent families; promoted fear and shame around sex; and shut down conversations about same-sex relationships in the context of discussions about abstinence—they also alleged the program was unscientific and antidemocratic.

In an interview with the Canadian Broadcasting Commission titled "Teen, Mother Launch Complaint Against Abstinence-Based Sex Ed," Kathy Dawson expanded on her objections, stating she

> ... was also upset the class appeared to focus on values instead of science. "I don't want them in the secular school," she said. "They may have a spot in the Catholic school ... because they are faith-based ... My issue isn't with them ... because it's such a wide variety of families going to these (public) schools, let's leave the science to the school and the values to the parents." (CBC News, 2014a)

The Dawsons' objection rests in part on a perception that public schools, if they are to be truly secular, need to respect the division of values and science in the provision of sexuality education. School-based sexuality education, Kathy Dawson argues, is something that should be discussed in a scientific fashion. Education about values and sexuality is seen as a parental prerogative and not appropriate for discussion in a secular public school. The progressive impulse here is to remove all mention of values in sexuality education from the public school, which is portrayed as a space that should be neutral (scientific) on the subject of sex.

The PCC, in defending the program, argued that the information that they provided was scientific and supportive of an abstinence-based approach.

> The Calgary Pregnancy Care Centre, which is part of the same network as the Edmonton organization, says the group's workshops are based on scientific principles and statistics from Statistics Canada and Alberta Health Services. Both organizations are affiliated with Care-Net, a U.S.-based Christian group that opposes abortion. "While we have a faith background, the religious part does not come up in the public school or education," said Jutta Wittmeier, director of the Calgary centre. "*That's just not part of the program, it's science- and research-based.*" (CBC News, 2014b, my emphasis)

For the Dawsons, the PCC program is problematic in part because it refuses to admit that its program is not only scientific but also crafted to affirm the Christian values that underpin the PCC. Members of the PCC are no doubt aware that if they were explicit about what underpinned their reading of the science, then they may compromise their place within public schools. Therefore, both the Dawsons and the PCC agree that sexuality education must be scientific. Both are also taking particular value positions on sexuality education—though arguably, neither position is transparent. Both rely on the recourse to science to defend their positions. Echoing Simon During's (2007) comment on the abortion debate in the US (see Chapter 7)—the sound bites all depend on their stances being indeterminable in regard to secularism.

In the case of the Dawson's objections to the PCC program, in the first instance the EPSB was inclined to support the continuation of the program, variations of which had been running in different schools in Alberta for more than a decade. A school nurse was asked to evaluate the program for the EPSB, and according to a board official, it was found that the program met the standards set by Alberta Education. So the sexuality education was not seen by the EPSB as in contravention of the official curriculum. The PCC also administers programs in other parts of Alberta. Notwithstanding the PCC's affirmation that the program was curriculum compliant, a view affirmed by the EPSB-appointed nurse evaluator—the EPSB ultimately decided that the PCC would be indefinitely barred from future delivery of CSE programs.

A student and parent insist that the program is value laden and therefore has no place. The staff from the PCC evoke secular justifications for its continuation, underscoring its scientific credentials and therefore the legitimacy of its place in the official curriculum. Public school officials in Edmonton affirm the program is compliant with the official curriculum of Alberta but perceive, after some attempts to argue for the preservation of the program, that politically it is no longer defensible. Just what a secular sexuality program looks like in Alberta is clearly not straightforward, at least to EPSB officials.

In the public discourses surrounding this debate, scientific sexuality education is constructed as admissible within secular schooling. In this manner the gold standard for sexuality education within a progressive secular imaginary becomes a scientifically based sexuality education. This approach is constituted as the most fitting within a secular frame precisely because it does not impose a value system but rather allows students to weigh the evidence on sexuality, risk, and promiscuity. Perceptions about what is admissible in sexuality education are consequently shaped by the perception that Canadian secularism is fundamentally scientific.

Alex McKay, research coordinator at the Sex Information and Education Council of Canada (SIECC), expresses surprise that the PCC is teaching in Canadian schools. He is quoted stating that Canada "has been far ahead of the U.S. when it comes to teaching about sexual health free of ideology or religion" (CBC News, 2014b). While McKay expresses surprise at the

PCC's presence in Edmonton schools, in his academic work he has advocated for a place for religion in a democratic sexuality education.

McKay has made this argument drawing on liberal political theory to distinguish ideological sexuality education from democratic sexuality education—preferring the latter. McKay's vision for a democratic sexuality education does

> . . . not mean that the fundamentalist Christian needs to give up her belief that homosexuality is morally wrong . . . any more that it means the secular psychologist needs to give up his belief that gays, lesbians and bisexuals are as psychologically healthy as heterosexuals . . . but simply that we accord them the opportunity for expression within the context of a democratic culture and this also occurs in education. (1998: 133, 134)

Following McKay's argument, one might anticipate that the PCC do indeed have a place in Canadian schools, but McKay's preference may be that the Dawsons and the PCC are explicit about their conflicting beliefs—*rather than relying on scientific justifications for the implementation and critique of a program that is inevitably values based.*

Writing in the US context, partially inspired by McKay, Nancy Kendall states that sex education should be replaced with citizenship education. She argues public schools should provide

> . . . opportunities for students to express their beliefs and opinions to discuss the reasons for their beliefs, [thus] classrooms could meet *some* of the needs of *diverse* constituents . . . They would provide more conservative parents with assurances that their students would understand these issues are fundamentally linked to morals and values . . . It would provide more liberal parents with assurances that their students are learning to critically engage in scientific research and debate. (2013: 249, emphasis in original)

Kendall and McKay want morals and values to be debated as part of sexuality education in a fashion that "emphasiz[es] the necessity in a democracy to tolerate, and perhaps even recognize and respect, others' perspectives" (Kendall, 2013: 251). McKay and Kendall's positions may be read as somewhat distinct from that advocated by Goldstein et al. in relation to anti-homophobia education for teachers in Toronto. That is, they believe that education about sexuality can and should countenance conflicting perspectives.

McKay and Kendall's democratic solutions to the provision of sexuality education are also moral and ideological because they affirm their particular vision of the progressive-secular imaginary. In short, I don't think they adequately deal with religious objections that might foreground tradition, faith, and custom above "young people's inalienable right to freedom of belief and the opportunity to critically deliberate between competing ideological perspectives" (McKay, 1998: 135). People who prefer this settlement are likely those who perceive religion and democracy as clearly distinct and sexuality education as first and foremost about autonomy of the individual.

Wendy Brown seeks to underscore some of the shortcomings of such liberal democratic framings because of the calculations they make about individual rights:

> Out of this equation, liberalism emerges as the only potential rationality that can produce the individual, societal and governmental practice of tolerance, and, at the same time, liberal societies become the broker of what is tolerable and intolerable . . . [T]he intolerance associated with fundamentalism is equated with the valorization of culture and religion at the expense of the individual, an expense that makes such orders intolerable from a liberal vantage point. (Brown, 2006: 166)

For Brown, liberalism sets out the rules of what is tolerable—anything that contravenes that rationality of tolerance is judged illiberal and intolerable. Democratic sexuality education (McKay) and sexuality education as citizenship education (Kendall) both rely on liberalism as the arbiter of what is tolerable. In this respect, both positions are the product of a progressive secular imaginary in which it is possible to conceptualize a space in which sexuality education might be democratic *within a liberal and critical frame.*

Brown prompts me to wonder whether progressive secularism is working toward a time in which the PCC is constituted as intolerable because it valorizes culture and religion at the expense of the individual. PCC does not do this explicitly. If it did, it may be acceptable as one of many diverse beliefs and opinions advocated in the approaches taken by McKay and Kendall. But, like Brown, I wonder about what protections democratic sexuality education offers organizations (not individuals) like the PCC that are constituted as ideological rather than democratic or secular.

This discussion should not be read as a defense of the PCC or the Dawsons. Rather, it is an attempt to craft out a space in which it is possible to see that both the PCC and the Dawsons are mobilizing particular frames of secularism to shape sexuality education. At present, it would appear that the Dawsons' framing has more political currency within the political scene in Alberta.

CONCLUSION

In tracing sexuality education across Ireland, Canada, and Australia, my aim has been to consider how progressive discourses of sexuality education travel across borders. I have observed that discourses that reflect a progressive approach to sexuality education are evident in the written curriculum across all three countries, despite their having quite different structural relations to religion. I have also briefly considered how progressivism is mediated by the absence and presence of religious influences upon the curriculum and within the broader culture. Relationships among religion, progressivism, secular and religious schooling, and sexuality education are uneven, and the advance of progressivism is not uniform. I am not the first to make the observation that reform that is constituted as progressive is uneven in sexuality education within and across country contexts (Rayside, 2014). Rayside also points out that Canadian Catholic educators (like their secular counterparts) "vary widely in attitudes towards sexual diversity" (2014: 210).

My aim has not been to judge which system is the most progressive, and for this reason this comparative analysis is somewhat distinct from some other research in this field that is focused on demonstrating the conservative nature of US sexuality education relative to education in Scandinavian countries (Rose, 2005; Weaver et al., 2005). Rather, I have attempted to grasp how progressive-secular imaginaries shape contemporary curricula. But I have also sought to demonstrate that these imaginaries have a larger orbit, influencing public debates about funding of religious schools, the role of GSAs, and teachers' conduct. I have argued that attitudes toward sexual and gender diversity are increasingly a key marker of the progressive status sexuality curriculum, and this is also true of how teachers are being judged in relation to expressions of homophobia. I have also attempted to trace some of the political tactics that are used to advance progressive causes and speculated on how these tactics sometimes entrench religious–secular binaries. They can also produce discourses of child fundamentalism that reinforce the notion of LGBTI youth as always at risk. Secular progressivism might also work to ensure that religious discourses take particular forms and shapes to be tolerable within the discourses of liberalism. Progressive sexuality education is a powerful assemblage across all three country contexts.

NOTES

1. Thanks to Professor Bill Pinar and the University of British Columbia for hosting me during this sabbatical in 2008. Thanks also to Associate Professor Jen Gilbert at York University and Professor Wayne Martino at Western Ontario for providing me with an opportunity to present on this work during my 2012 visit.
2. In secondary education voluntary secondary schools (which are largely Catholic) educate approximately 50 percent of second-level students in the Irish context. Vocational and community colleges educate approximately 30.4 percent, and community and comprehensive schools educate approximately 15.6 percent of all pupils. The 77 community schools in Ireland comprise less than 10 percent of the total number and are the nearest to what would be deemed public schools in secondary education in Canada, Australia, and the US. See: http://www.education.ie/en/Schools-Colleges/Information/Diversity-of-Patronage/ (accessed May 15, 2013).

3. In Ontario, from 2012 to 2013 there were a total of 2,031,195 students enrolled. Of those, 643,089 (approximately 31 percent) were enrolled in state-funded Roman Catholic schools, while 1,388,106 (68 percent) were enrolled in state-funded public schools (see Ontario Ministry of Education, 2015a). In personal correspondence, Statistics Canada informed me that while they do have enrolment numbers of students enrolled in different types of education systems across Canada, these are not broken down by religious classification (as an Australian researcher this seemed like a curious anomaly because statistics based on education and religious affiliation are part of standard reporting in the Australian Bureau of Statistics data on education).
4. For instance, in Victoria, Australia, in 2013 63 percent of students were enrolled in government schools, 23 percent were enrolled in Catholic schools, and 14 percent were enrolled in independent schools. Australian Bureau of Statistics Data from 2012 suggests that across Australia, Catholic (20.5 percent) and independent schools (14.2 percent) accounted for 34.7 percent of all students, while public schools enrolled 65.2 percent of students.
5. Successive conservative and progressive federal governments have supported funding for chaplains. Conservative governments have insisted that chaplains must be religious, while governments that are styled more progressively determined chaplains in schools required specific qualifications, which meant chaplains could identify as religious or nonreligious.
6. Referred to as *second level* in Ireland and *high school* in Canada.
7. Catching on Later (Department of Education and Early Childhood Development, 2013) came into being under a Liberal/National Party government. The Liberal/National Party is generally associated with more conservative politics in the Australian context. The party also reformed laws on religious exemptions, reasserting religious schools' right to discriminate against staff on the basis of belief.
8. The curriculum was drafted in 2012 and was still awaiting approval in 2015.
9. See http://news.nationalpost.com/2015/02/20/ontarios-new-sex-ed-will-cover-homosexuality-masturbation-and-consent-not-everyones-saying-yes/.
10. Public and religious schools in Ottawa use the Ontario curriculum.
11. The Secular Party of Australia also advocates for the removal of religion from state schools and has explicit policies on sex education provision—see Secular Party of Australia (2013).
12. See http://torontoist.com/2011/09/gsa-rally-rouses-hope-and-faith/.
13. State funding of secular and religious education is depicted as economically inefficient by secularists and their supporters because having parallel systems leads to duplication of functions and personnel.
14. I see advocacy of GSAs as an example of an identity-based claim.
15. See http://www.cficanada.ca/.
16. See http://www.youtube.com/watch?v=nvJ9M1TkJyQ.
17. See http://www.cbc.ca/news/canada/edmonton/teen-mother-launch-complaint-against-abstinence-based-sex-ed-1.2703535.
18. See http://www.cbc.ca/news/canada/edmonton/edmonton-school-board-drops-abstinence-based-sex-ed-after-complaint-1.2704291 (accessed July, 11, 2014).

REFERENCES

ACARA (Australian Curriculum, Assessment and Reporting Authority). (2012). *Australian curriculum health and physical education: Foundation to year 10.* Available from http://consultation.australiancurriculum.edu.au/Static/docs/HPE/F-10Curriculum.pdf (Last accessed May 7, 2015).

Baird, B. (2008). Child Politics, Feminist Analyses. *Australian Feminist Studies*, 23(57): 291–305.
Bouma, G. D., & Hughes, P. J. (2014). Using Census Data in the Management of Religious Diversity: An Australian Case Study. *Religion*, 44(3): 434–452.
Brown, W. (2006) *Regulating Aversion: Tolerance in the Age of Identity and Empire*. Princeton, New Jersey: Princeton University Press.
Campbell, C., & Proctor, H. (2014). *A History of Australian Schooling*. Sydney: Allen & Unwin.
Canadian Secular Alliance. (2009). *Public financing of religious schools*. Available from http://secularalliance.ca/about/policies/public-financing-of-religious-schools/ (Last accessed July 17, 2014).
CBC News. (2014a). *Teen, mother launch complaint against abstinence-based sex ed*. Available from http://www.cbc.ca/news/canada/edmonton/teen-mother-launch-complaint-against-abstinence-based-sex-ed-1.2703535 (Last accessed August 20, 2014).
———. (2014b). *Edmonton school board drops abstinence-based sex ed after complaint*. Available from http://www.cbc.ca/news/canada/edmonton/edmonton-school-board-drops-abstinence-based-sex-ed-after-complaint-1.2704291 (Last accessed August 20, 2014).
Cohen, J. N., Byers, E. S., & Sears, H. A. (2012). Factors Affecting Canadian Teachers' Willingness to Teach Sexual Health Education. *Sex Education*, 12(3): 299–316.
Department of Education and Early Childhood Development. (2013). *Catching on later: Sexuality Education for Victorian Secondary Schools*. The Department of Education and Early Childhood Development, Melbourne, July 2013. Available from https://fuse.education.vic.gov.au/content/407ed837–2c8b-4842–9a22-fe7f8bb07b99/catchingonlater.pdf (Last accessed May 7, 2015).
Do, T. T. (2015). Ontario's New Sex ed Curriculum 'The Most Up-to-date' in the Country: Grades 1 to 12 Curriculum Addresses Sexual Orientation, Sexting and Consent. *CBC News*, February 25, 2015. Available from http://www.cbc.ca/m/touch/news/story/1.2969654 (Last accessed May 7th, 2015).
During, S. (2007). *The Mundane against the secular*. The Immanent Frame website. Available from http://blogs.ssrc.org/tif/2007/11/10/the-mundane-against-the-secular (Last accessed March 15, 2015).
Edelman, L. (1998). Future Is Kid Stuff: Queer Theory, Disidentification and the Death Drive. *Narrative*, 6(1): 18–30.
Elliott, D. (2012). *Committee Transcripts: Standing Committee on Social Policy—2012-May-14 — Bill 14, Anti-Bullying Act, 2012*. Available from http://www.ontla.on.ca/web/committee-proceedings/committee_transcripts_details.do?locale=en&BillID=2550&ParlCommID=8963&Business=&Date=2012–05–14&DocumentID=26335#P597_167377 (Last accessed August 20, 2014).
Fine, M. (1988). Sexuality, Schooling, and Adolescent Females: The Missing Discourse of Desire. *Harvard Educational Review*, 58(1): 29–53.
Gahan, L., Jones, T., Hillier, L. (2014). An Unresolved Journey: Religious Discourse and Same-Sex Attracted and Gender Questioning Young People. *Research in the Social Scientific Study of Religion*, 25: 202–229.
Globe Editorial. (2012). Catholic Teachers Right to Back Ontario's 'Gay-straight Alliance' Rule. *The Globe and Mail*. Available from http://www.theglobeandmail.com/commentary/editorials/catholic-teachers-right-to-back-ontarios-gay-straight-alliance-rule/article4237217/ (Last accessed August 21, 2014).
Goldstein, T., Collins, A., & Halder, M. (2008). Anti-Homophobia Education in Public Schooling: A Canadian Case Study of Policy Implementation. *Journal of Gay & Lesbian Social Services*, 19(3–4): 47–66.
Gray, B. (2013). *New Foundation: School "Ethos" and LGBT Sexualities*, paper presented at *New Foundation: School "Ethos" and LGBT Sexualities* meeting

(funded by the Irish Research Council and in association with the British Educational Research Association, Sexualities Special Interest Group, May 17, 2013). University of Limerick, Limerick, Ireland. Available from http://www3.ul.ie/gcs/wp-content/uploads/2013/03/Final-Publication-New-Foundations-Conference-Summary-Report3.pdf (Last accessed May 7, 2015).

Inglis, T. (1998). *Lessons in Irish Sexuality*. Dublin: University College Dublin Press.

Jakobsen, J. R. (2005). Sex + Freedom = Regulation: WHY? *Social Text*, 23(3–4): 84–85: 285–308.

Jakobsen, J.R., & Pellegrini, A. (2009). Religious and Sexual Freedoms Are Not Opposed. *The Immanent Frame: Secularism, Religion, and the Public Sphere*. Available from http://blogs.ssrc.org/tif/2009/07/22/religious-and-sexual-freedoms-are-not-opposed/ (Last accessed August 21, 2014).

Jones, T.M., & Hillier, L. (2012). Sexuality Education School Policy for Australian GLBTIQ students. *Sex Education*, 12(4): 437–454.

Jones, T. M., & Mitchell, A. (2014). Young People and HIV Prevention in Australian Schools. *AIDS Education and Prevention*, 26(3): 224–233.

Kendall, N. (2013). *The Sex Education Debates*. Chicago: University of Chicago Press.

Kiely, E. (2005). Where Is the Discourse of Desire? Deconstructing the Irish Relationships and Sexuality Education (RSE) resource materials. *Irish Educational Studies*, 24(2): 253–266.

Korducki, K. (2011). Canadian Secular Alliance Rally Rouses Hope and Faith. *Torontoist*. Available from http://torontoist.com/2011/09/gsa-rally-rouses-hope-and-faith/ (Last accessed July 16, 2014).

Kulpa, R. (2014). Western Leveraged Pedagogy of Central and Eastern Europe: Discourses of Homophobia, Tolerance, and Nationhood. *Gender, Place & Culture: A Journal of Feminist Geography*, 21(4): 431–448.

Lodge, A. (2013). Valuing Visibility? An Exploration of the Construction of School Ethos to Enable or Prevent Recognition of Sexual Identities. In A. Neary, B. Gray & M. Sullivan (Eds.), *New Foundations: School 'Ethos' and LGBT Sexualities* (pp. 12–19). Limerick, Ireland: University of Limerick.

Lodge, A., Gowran, S., & O' Shea, K. (2011). *Valuing Visibility: An Exploration of How Sexual Orientation Issues Arise and Are Addressed in Irish Post-Primary Schools*. Report submitted to R& D committee, Department of Education and Skills.

Maddox, M. (2014). *Taking God to School: The End of Australia's Egalitarian Education?* Crows Nest, N.S.W: Allen & Unwin.

Mahmood, S. (2010). Can Secularism Be Otherwise? In M. Warner, J. Van Antwerpen, & C. Calhoun (Eds.), *Varieties of Secularism in a Secular Age* (pp. 282–299). Cambridge: Harvard University Press.

Mayock, P., Kitching, K., & Morgan, M. (2007). *RSE in the Context of SPHE: An Assessment of the Challenges to Full Implementation of the Programme in Post-primary Schools*. Dublin, Ireland: Crisis Pregnancy Agency/Department of Education and Science. Available from http://www.education.ie/en/Publications/Education-Reports/Relationships-and-Sexuality-Education-RSE-in-the-Context-of-SPHE-An-Assessment-of-the-Challenges-to-Full-Implementation-of-the-Programme-in-Post-primary-Schools-Summary-Report.pdf (Last accessed August 21, 2014).

McKay, A. (1998). *Sexual Ideology and Schooling: Towards Democratic Sexuality Education*. Albany: State University of New York Press.

Mitchell, A., Smith, A. M. A., Carman, M., Schlichthorst, M., Walsh, J., & Pitts, M. K. (2011). *Sexuality Education in Australia in 2011*. Monograph Series Number 81. Melbourne, Australia: Australian Research Centre in Sex, Health and Society, La Trobe University. ARCSHS Monograph. Available from http://www.latrobe.

edu.au/data/assets/pdf_file/0019/148060/Sexual-Education-in-Australia-2011.pdf (Last accessed August 21, 2014).
Mullally, S., & O'Donovan, D. (2011). Religion in Ireland's 'Public Squares': Education and the Family and Expanding Equality Claims. *Public Law*, April 2011: 284–307.
National Council for Curriculum and Assessment. (2011). *Social, Personal and Health Education Curriculum: National Council for Curriculum and Assessment*. Dublin: NCCA. Available from http://www.ncca.ie/en/Curriculum_and_Assessment/Post-Primary_Education/Senior_Cycle/SPHE_framework/SPHE_Framework.pdf (Last accessed May 7, 2015).
Neary, A. (2012). Lesbian and Gay Teachers' Experiences of 'Coming out' in Irish Schools. *British Journal of Sociology of Education*, 34(4): 583–602.
———. (2014). *Unravelling 'Ethos' and Section 37(1): The Experiences of LGBTQ Teachers*. Limerick, Ireland: University of Limerick.
Ontario Ministry of Education. (2015a). *Quick facts: Ontario schools 2012–13*. Available from http://www.edu.gov.on.ca/eng/general/elemsec/quickfacts/2012–13/quickFacts12_13.pdf (Last accessed January 29, 2015).
———. (2015b). *The Ontario curriculum grades 9–12: Health and physical education (Revised)*. Available from http://www.edu.gov.on.ca/eng/curriculum/secondary/health9to12.pdf (Last accessed May 7, 2015).
Phillips, K. P., & Martinez, A. (2010). Sexual and Reproductive Health Education: Contrasting Teachers', Health Partners' and Former Students' Perspectives. *Qualitative Research*, 101(5): 374–379.
Puar, J. K. (2012). Coda: The Cost of Getting Better: Suicide, Sensation, Switchpoints. *GLQ: A Journal of Lesbian and Gay Studies*, 18(1): 149–158.
Rayside, D. (2014). The Inadequate Recognition of Sexual Diversity by Canadian Scholars: LGBT Advocacy and Its Impact. *Journal of Canadian Studies*, 48(1): 190–225.
Rayside, D., & Wilcox, C. (2011a). Preface. In D. Rayside & C. Wilcox (Eds.), *Faith, Politics, and Sexual Diversity in Canada and the United States* (pp. xv–xvii). Vancouver, California: UBC Press.
———. (2011b). The Difference that a Border Makes: The Political Intersection of Sexuality and Religion in Canada and the United States. In D. Rayside & C. Wilcox (Eds.), *Faith, Politics, and Sexual Diversity in Canada and the United States* (pp. 1–26). Vancouver, California: UBC Press.
Rose, S. (2005). Going Too Far? Sex, Sin and Social Policy. *Social Forces*, 84(2): 1207–1232.
Rougier, N., & Honohan, I. (2014). Religion and Education in Ireland: Growing Diversity—or Losing Faith in the System? *Comparative Education*, 51(1): 71–86.
Secular Party of Australia. (2013). *Policies*. Available from http://www.secular.org.au/policies/#sexEducation (Last accessed July 17, 2014).
Sherlock, L. (2012). Sociopolitical Influences on Sexuality Education in Sweden and Ireland. *Sex Education*, 12(4): 383–396.
Smith, A., Schlichthorst, M., Mitchell, A., Walsh, J., Lyons, A., Blackman P., & Pitts M. (2011). *Sexuality Education in Australian Secondary Schools 2010*. Monograph Series No. 80, Melbourne: La Trobe University, the Australian Research Centre in Sex, Health & Society.
Trottier, J. (2012). *Hansard Debate, Standing Committee on Social Policy, Legislative Assembly of Ontario*, May 15, p. 156. Available from http://www.ontla.on.ca/committee-proceedings/transcripts/files_html/15-MAY-2012_SP008.htm (Last accessed August 20, 2014).
Waidzunas, T. (2012). Young, Gay, and Suicidal: Dynamic Nominalism and the Process of Defining a Social Problem with Statistics. *Science Technology Human Values*, 37(2): 199–225.

Weaver, H., Smith, G., & Kippax, S. (2005). School-based Sex Education Policies and Indicators of Sexual Health among Young People: A Comparison of the Netherlands, France, Australia and the United States. *Sex Education: Sexuality, Society and Learning*, 5(2): 171–188.

Wells, J. (2015). Changing Ontario's Sex ed Curriculum only a 'Starting point'. *The Star*, February 28, 2015. Available from http://www.thestar.com/news/insight/2015/02/28/changing-ontarios-sex-ed-curriculum-only-a-starting-point.html (Last accessed April 13, 2015).

Conclusion
The Conceits of Secularism in Sexuality Education

In the introduction to this book, I stated what I thought were some of the conceits of secularism; in concluding the book I want to return to each of these conceits and unpack them further:

- Sexuality education is optimal when it is underpinned by rigorous scientific research and rational debate.
- Sexuality education needs to promote sexual autonomy to ensure that young people are able to act as autonomous sexual subjects.
- Sexuality education is responsible for the cultivation of tolerance of sexual and gender diversity.
- Sexuality education in public education precludes discussion of the intersections among faith, religion, and morality (such conversations should happen in private settings, e.g., family, church, mosque, or temple).

Threaded throughout these conceits is a specific rendering of the relationships among sex, religion and secularism where the "problem is as much secular freedom as it is religious regulation" (Jakobsen, 2005: 286). Progressive sexuality education is often preoccupied with apprehending the problems inherent in religious regulation. While there is no denying that there are problems associated with religious regulation within the field of sexuality education, less is known about the problems associated with secular freedom and its relationship to sexuality education. One of the challenges of this task is that secularism is not easy to pin down, and it is not something that researchers in sexuality education have generally explicitly engaged in detail—though this is certainly changing (for some examples of recent scholarly work in this area, see Baker, Smith, and Stoss, 2015; Reiss, 2014, Shipley, 2014; Svendsen, 2012).

Together, these conceits identify some of the problems of secular freedom I perceive within sexuality education. Next I attempt to grasp how these conceits operate. This is followed by a short analysis of some of the structures of thought and feeling that sustain attachments to "the traditional view of secularism" in which "freedom from religion brings about human liberation" (Jakobsen, 2005: 286).

SEXUALITY EDUCATION IS OPTIMAL WHEN IT IS UNDERPINNED BY RIGOROUS SCIENTIFIC RESEARCH AND RATIONAL DEBATE

> Recently, many states have implemented requirements for scientific or medical accuracy in sexuality education and HIV prevention programs. Although seemingly uncontroversial, these requirements respond to the increasing injection of ideology into sexuality education, as represented by abstinence-only programs.
>
> (Santelli, 2008: 1786)

John Santelli, a prominent advocate of evidence-based sexuality education sets up a neat dichotomy between ideology and science. AO programs are ideological; science, presumably, is not. There is a further assumption that those who support AO approaches to sexuality education are the only ones driven by ideology in debates about sexuality education. In this respect, scientists stand above the fray and are therefore capable of providing medically accurate, evidence-based sexuality education. The power of this oft-repeated belief in the value of evidence in sexuality education provision is reiterated by UNESCO (2009); such thinking continues to be widespread and highly persuasive in sexuality education. *I do not want to argue against the value of medicine in the production of sexuality education.* However, I do believe that sexuality education is about much more than the provision of scientific information about the efficacy of condoms or the ways in which STIs are transmitted—good sexuality education is therefore steeped in ideology. I also recognize this is certainly not a new insight.

Stranger-Hall and Hall (2011, see Introduction) suggest a way around this might be to divide sexuality education explicitly into social studies components that focus on ethics, behavior, and decision making and science components that focus on pregnancy, STI prevention, and reproductive biology. Such an approach assumes that science and social science can be divided in a straightforward fashion. I do not believe that this is the case in sexuality education; for instance which elements of family planning are scientific, and which are social?

It is possible to see these assumptions about science and sexuality education are being played out in our conversations with participants about what can be discussed in sexuality education within the confines of public schools. As discussed in Chapter 3, Dirk, like Santelli, sees no place for discussions of abstinence in sexuality education that are not evidence based. In Chapter 5, I consider how Whitehead weaves together discourses of health and science to argue for a version of sexuality education that embraces young people's desire for pleasures and risk taking. This argument is utilized by Whitehead as a counter to approaches that involve explicit moral agendas, which are characterized by Whitehead as potentially harmful and unethical. And, in Chapter 8 I consider public discourses about science, secularity, and abstinence, in which religious and nonreligious organizations brand themselves as secular in the hope of staking a valid claim to educate about sexuality.

What these discussions of sexuality education, science, and public schooling have in common is an attachment to the idea that sexuality education can be rational when wedded to rigor and science. The flipside of this argument is that sexuality education that is explicitly about morality is ideological, lacks rigor, and is likely unscientific. While these beliefs about rigor and science in sexuality education continue to flourish, sexuality education curricula in Ireland, Australia, and Canada explicitly engage young people in conversations about different types of relationships, what it means for relationships to be meaningful, homophobia, and consent. As was evidenced in the discussion of homophobia in Chapter 6, discourses of rigor and science also permeate attitudes regarding tolerance of sexual diversity and anti-homophobia education manifesting in the production of scales that measure homophobia. Ideas and beliefs about the value of scientific rigor permeate many elements of progressive sexuality education.

SEXUALITY EDUCATION NEEDS TO PROMOTE SEXUAL AUTONOMY TO ENSURE THAT YOUNG PEOPLE ARE ABLE TO ACT AS AUTONOMOUS SEXUAL SUBJECTS

Wendy Brown, in an article titled "Civilizational Delusions: Secularism, Tolerance, Equality," challenges the idea that Western secularism generates gender freedom and equality. Brown breaks down the thinking that supports this understanding into several parts.

> Secularism is presumed to generate women's freedom and equality a) as part of its historical purpose and project; b) as a dimension of its universalization of justice; c) through its subordination of religious or cultural inequality to legal equality; d) through freedom formulated as individual choice; e) through the elimination of sex segregation in economic and public life; and f) through replacements of modesty with transparency, cover with exposure, replacements themselves presumed indexical of women's sexual autonomy.
>
> (Brown, 2012: n.p.)

Building on these ideas about gender and sexual autonomy identified by Brown, it is possible to begin to excavate some of the thinking that supports progressive sexuality educations' attachments to belief about young people and adults acting as autonomous sexual subjects. As I have argued in Chapter 2 and Chapter 5, I perceive ideas about the significance of sexual autonomy as intrinsic to progressive visions of sexuality education. Joan Scott maintains that thinking differently about autonomy is important because it can help progressives to better grasp "the sources of our own secular feminist desire to condemn [practices such as abstinence and ambivalence towards sexual and reproductive health service—see Chapter 3] as instances of forced subordination or false consciousness before we understand what they are about" (2009: 11). The young men I interviewed at Central High in Melbourne could construe abstinence-based education as something that you could only take seriously if you're on drugs. What is interesting to me about such observations is that liberal ideas about abstinence clearly have wide currency—these young people had never encountered an abstinence-based sexuality education in their formal schooling, but they already knew what a progressive response to such education might look like.

Participants in our study of sexuality education and cultural and religious difference, whether they were religious or nonreligious, also made clear distinctions about what types of sexuality education could enter into the domain of public education. Discussions of religious and cultural difference and their relationship to sexuality were generally seen as only appropriate outside school contexts. Introducing religion into public school contexts was perceived as potentially uncomfortable, educationally inappropriate, unreasonable, unscientific, and pedagogically unsound. These responses have to be apprehended in relation to broader understandings about freedom, sexuality, and gender that are part of Western secularism. Promoting the absence of religion in publically funded education is more broadly interpreted as a way of promoting sexual freedom and autonomy while simultaneously asserting the importance of legal equality in relation to religious equality (see discussion of GSAs and public funding of Catholic schools in Ontario in Chapter 8). In such debates "the neutrality of the state is presumed" (Scott, 2009: 11).

SEXUALITY EDUCATION IS RESPONSIBLE FOR THE CULTIVATION OF TOLERANCE OF SEXUAL AND GENDER DIVERSITY

> Increasingly, women and sexuality take center stage in invocations of the secular, which promises—or threatens—to liberate both from religion's tenacious hold.
>
> (Cady and Fessenden, 2013: 3)

Linell Cady and Tracy Fessenden look at numerous contexts, within and outside the US to make this argument and perceive their work as part of a burgeoning scholarly literature on secularism that has not given "sustained attention to discourses of gender and sexual emancipation" (2013: 6). In this detailed study of the relationships among secularism, discourses of gender and sexual emancipation, and sexuality education, I am also endeavoring to break new ground by thinking about how secularism in sexuality education situates itself as the guarantor of gender and sexual emancipation.

Joan Scott also troubles the belief that freedom related to sexuality and gender, including sexual and gender diversity, is related to secularism in her paper, *Sexularism*. She notes that "there is no necessary connection between secularism and gender equality, and the universality secularism promises was always and remains troubled by sexual difference" (2009: 29). Scott makes this argument to highlight different ways of thinking about the relationship between religiosity and agency, contending, "secularism is not the antithesis of religion but rather provides a different framework within which to address the problem that sexual difference seems to pose for us all" (2009: 12).

Different ways of configuring problems associated with sexual difference were apparent in Jesse Mills's (2012) analysis of the comprehensive sexuality education program, Project B.R.O, which catered to members of the Somali community in San Diego. Mills argues that this program was experienced by participants as too liberal on questions of homosexuality and sex before marriage. The program essentially affirmed participants' attachments to particular performances of religiosity that they perceived as providing distinctly different frameworks for apprehending sexual difference within their own Somali community.

Jasbir Puar's notions of queer secularism and sexual exceptionalism have also been important in challenging the idea that the task of progressive sexuality education is to cultivate tolerance of sexual and gender diversity. Wendy Brown argues, in her critique of tolerance, that

> [e]ven as certain contemporary conservatives identify tolerance as a codeword for endorsing homosexuality, tolerance knows no political party: it is what liberals and leftists reproach a religious, xenophobic, and homophobic right for lacking, but also what evangelical Christians claim that secular liberals refuse them. (2006: 2–3)

Brown and Puar illustrate different ways in which ideas related to tolerance can be mobilized by evangelical Christians and progressives. In researching progressive sexuality education, and in strongly identifying with this style of thought, I have not found it easy (or pressing) to imagine how tolerance is refused to evangelical Christians. However, Michael Warner's discussion of how sexual experts determine what ideas related to sex, sexuality, and gender become admissible in the public sphere is a useful provocation in thinking through how tolerance becomes a code word. What is admissible in sexuality education is, I have argued, increasingly tied to particularly secular notions of sexual progress. This is accompanied by campaigns, bringing together secularists and sexual and gender minorities that seek to exclude questions of faith and religion from the public sphere. The authority with which progressivism speaks also manifests in attempts to shape anti-homophobia education in ways that assume, in advance, general agreement about the ways in which students and teachers must think about sexual and gender diversity. Such habits of thought also extend to the belief that homophobia is primarily related to ignorance and thus can be effectively erased through the liberal application of appropriate educational initiatives. In short, liberal notions of tolerance in sexuality education may run the risk of reinforcing difference and sedimenting intolerance.

SEXUALITY EDUCATION IN PUBLIC EDUCATION PRECLUDES DISCUSSION OF THE INTERSECTIONS AMONG FAITH, RELIGION, AND MORALITY (SUCH CONVERSATIONS SHOULD HAPPEN IN PRIVATE SETTINGS, E.G., FAMILY, CHURCH, MOSQUE, OR TEMPLE)

In her discussion of Western LGBTQ activism on Iran, Mitra Rastegar (2013) points to the emergence of a defensive secularism. She chides secularists who perceive Islamic religious traditions as irrational, while they portray secularism as culturally neutral and universal (21). This idea that varieties of secularism are culturally neutral and universal is also persistent in the US context and in the other countries that I focus on in this research. This isn't to say that people who advance secular causes are not thoughtful about progressive politics but rather to observe that the impulse to attack religion in defense of secularism can be something of a reflexive response. This is partially why in Chapter 7 I focus on competing varieties of secularism in relation to the politics of choice. This discussion situates me, quite deliberately, as part of a progressive-secular imaginary but also illustrates some of the many fissures within secularism.

It is not surprising that in the US context, secularism is defensive about the role of religious groups in the promotion of abstinence-based sexuality education—many researchers perceive such programs as lacking an evidence base and argue they "rely on religion and fear as primary curriculum components in teaching about sexual health and sexuality to youth (Boonstra, 2009; Malone and Rodriguez, 2011; McKeon, 2006; Stanger-Hall and Hall, 2011)" (Elia and Tokunaga, 2015: 108). These programs have also had significant support in the form of funding from successive Democratic and Republican state and federal governments—(a stance undone, at least at the federal level, by the Obama administration's insistence that sexuality education be evidence based—see Williams, 2011). In the US context ". . . relations among religion, morality, and sex . . . time after time and issue after issue . . . become the measures of an individual's—and even a nation's—overall morality" (Jakobsen and Pellegrini, 2004: 5). The same could be said about the Irish context where one might argue advocates of progressive approaches to sexuality have experienced, and continue to experience, the dominance of Catholic perspectives in education provision. Particularly in the US and Ireland (among the countries in which I have studied in the preparation of this book) the religion, morality, and sex triumvirate has reflected religious stances that are particularly onerous for many individuals and groups of people who are constituted as failing to measure up to perceived standards.

Despite these histories, which I acknowledge and have also critiqued, I argue the value of thinking about religion in relation to sexuality education in ways that refuse the temptation to be immediately defensive about religion or that presume more secularism is emancipatory or a sign of progress. The idea that more secularism is emancipatory is often not explicit within research related to sexuality education. It is, however, implicit in the ways that proponents of a progressive approach depict and imagine progress and in the repeated absence of conversations about religion in relation to progressive sexuality education—unless religious ideas are being constituted as a problem in need of a secular solution. It is also implicit in research and practice that seek to privatize religion.

Researchers in sexuality education, such as Fine and McClelland (2006), have argued against the privatization of sexuality education, particularly when this means individual choices are pathologized as a means of absolution for bad public policy and poor sexual health outcomes (see Chapter 5). But the privatization of religion is also problematic when this is seen as axiomatic within a progressive approach. To my mind, sexuality education is impacted by race and ethnicity, class, sexual and gender identity, and religious and cultural identifications. And the relationship of any of these to sexuality and sexuality education is not straightforward, but nor can it be set aside. To my mind, sexuality education that is publically funded and that occurs in public schools and settings needs to better apprehend the significance of religious and cultural difference in people's imaginings of marriage, kinship, sexual pleasure, abstinence, gender and sexual identity, homophobia, masturbation, and consent. Such an expansion of sexuality education, within public schools, runs the risk of essentializing cultural and religious difference. Potentially for this reason, participants who identified as religious in our study of sexuality education and cultural religious difference in Australia and Aoteroa-New Zealand were reluctant to bring religion into the public school (see Chapter 3). I do not think such concerns mean that religious and cultural difference should continue to be privatized in sexuality education, but I do think that attempts to include these topics need to ensure that young people don't bear the burden of educating their peers about these matters.

Moving on from this discussion of some of the conceits of secularism in sexuality education, I now want to consider what Saba Mahmood refers to as the "feel-good part of the secular story" (Mahmood, 2008: 451):

> ... the feel-good part of the secular story cannot be belittled. It should in fact be studied in all seriousness so that we might apprehend the

visceral force that secular discourses and practices command today. While it is common to ascribe passion to religion, it would behoove us to pay attention to the thick texture of affinities, prejudices, and attachments that tie us (cosmopolitan intellectuals and critics) to what is loosely described as a secular worldview. (Mahmood, 2008: 451)

Inspired by Mahmood, in closing this book I now turn my attention to understanding the power of secularism manifest in strong affinities, prejudices, and attachments that shape progressive sexuality education. I do not understand progressive-secular imaginaries in sexuality education as in any way an organized project, nor are they spatially or temporally stable. Progressive-secular imaginaries of sexuality education have many offshoots flowing in multiple directions with often unpredictable or unknowable effects.

FEELING GOOD ABOUT SECULARISM AND SEXUALITY EDUCATION

In rethinking interrelations between secularism and sexuality, Oskar Verkaaik and Rachel Spronk argue that secularism moves beyond discourse and ideology and into the sphere of body politics—and is thus intrinsic to sexuality education. In this formulation, secular politics educates citizens in how they should think and feel about different sorts of sexual subjects and sexual practices—regulating tolerance. In this reading,

> [s]ecularism is no longer primarily about political arrangements, like the separation of religion from the state (Casanova, 1994; Habermas, 2008). Redefined as the sexular, secularism plays itself out in the intimate sphere of sexuality and religion . . . sexuality has replaced religion as the body-politics through which hegemonic ideology becomes internalized, naturalized, commodified, and authentic (Butler 1990; Foucault 1978; Weeks 1989).
> (Verkaaik & Spronk, 2011: 85)

Thinking about the Australian context, I would argue that secularism has replaced religion as a hegemonic ideology. In Chapter 2 I try to give a picture of one way in which secularism has infused the body politic and become hegemonic via an analysis of the humor of Tom Ballard, a popular gay comic. I see his stand-up as part of a politics of sexual exceptionalism that is sustained via queer secularism. The authentic White, gay subject, at the center of Ballard's performance, has been naturalized prior to this performance. We, the audience, are already intimate with this character and know what to expect. In fact, the success of the commodification of this particular type of performance rests on our strong identification with

Ballard—and a shared sense of the injustices that he has experienced due to religious intolerance. Together, we (the audience) are asked to take pleasure in Ballard's witty disparagement of religious intolerance toward homosexuality in Ireland, Iran, and Australia, and (at least on the night I attended) the audience appeared happy with the exchange. We got what we paid for, a jolly skewering of religious homophobes everywhere. In this exchange, religion is made to appear out of time, backward, and reactionary; it is not central to the body politic but rather represents a problematic throwback. Such performances help me grasp at secularism, which as Talal Asad notes, is so much a part of modern life that it is very difficult to pin down (2003: 16).

Ballard's shtick in some ways mimics progressive sexuality education. It echoes the faith and passion associated with ideas of freedom and autonomy that are intrinsic to progressive-secular imaginings. These notions of freedom and autonomy are informed, in part, by liberal political theory. A key figure in contemporary liberal thought is John Rawls. In a chapter evocatively titled "Saint John: The Miracle of Secular Reason," Matthew Scherer (2006) argues that it is important to study the relationship between readers of Rawls's oeuvre and his texts. Scherer goes on to argue "the faith Rawls seeks to inspire in his conception of liberalism" has resonances

> ... to modalities of religious faith, which Rawls has been taken to have escaped ... [I]t would appear that even an avowedly secular, liberal, democratic politics stands in need of its saints, and that this very need can serve as a vital source of moral and political instruction. (362)

Popular figures like Ballard resemble Rawls. Both are instructing audiences in the politics of secularism, with Ballard's focus squarely on sexuality and secularism. Rather than reading liberal ideas in progressive sexuality education (or performances such as Ballard's) in terms of the value of their arguments within the frame of liberalism, I now consider some liberal scholarship on sexuality education as part of the feel-good story of progressive sexuality education.

David Archard (1998), a philosopher from the UK, utilizes Rawls work in a paper "How Should We Teach Sex." Archard's focus is specifically on how public schools should engage the question of how to teach sex. He writes:

> A Christian or an Islamic education would surely comprise a religious approach to the teaching of sex. But that cannot, it will be said, be the case for a common curriculum within a liberal society ... If autonomy is the proper end of a liberal education [and we should assume it is] ... one should teach sex, as one should teach everything else, with a view to maximising the future citizen's autonomy.
>
> (Archard, 1998: 447)

186 *Conclusion*

Jan Steutel and Doret J. de Ruyter's discussion of the moral aims of sexuality education, which also draws on Rawls, echoes Archard. They argue:

> ... the state has the right to make sure that all schools offer a liberal sex education to all their students, whatever their comprehensive conception of the good or their moral-religious background.
> (Steutel and de Ruyter, 2011:76)

Archard, Steutel, and de Ruyter expertly execute precise arguments about the place of religion in sexuality education in public schools, steeped in the language of neutrality and strongly supported by clearly articulated understandings of the "good" life. This mode of argumentation, not to mention the arguments themselves, are part of the feel-good story of progressive sexuality education. Evoking deep attachments to Rawls, this story of the place of religion in the public square is one in which liberal ideals are situated above the fray, distributing a neutral vision for sexuality education on which we can all agree, regardless of one's "conception of the good or their moral-religious background" (Steutel and de Ruyter, 2011: 76).

Rather than endeavoring to unpack the logic of these arguments, I want to think about this scholarship as felt and thought—perceiving it instead as part of the feel-good story of secularism in sexuality education. Scherer observes that the language of Rawls structures feelings in particular ways:

> ... [A] reader may feel worthy only if he or she does not shirk the obligation to give and take reasons that all parties to the conversation could accept when these obligations have been so diligently, carefully, judiciously, sensibly, and painstakingly observed by Rawls himself [and his followers]—and this thought may be accompanied by a feeling of shame at perhaps not being worthy. (2006: 356, 357)

I have to confess that I have often felt unworthy in my engagements with liberal scholarship in sexuality education. I have attributed this unworthiness, in part, to my own lack of formal philosophical training and to a no-doubt related incapacity to engage in the painstaking discourse that structures liberal argumentation. Maybe this is why Scherer's characterization of Rawlsian liberalism appeals; it helps me rationalize my own feelings of unworthiness in the face of liberalism's rigor.

Another explanation for my reluctance to engage in with liberal discourse, which has been sustained through this study of secularism and sexuality education, comes from Talal Asad. In an article titled "Thinking About the Secular Body, Pain and Liberal Politics," Asad argues that within liberalism,

> ... political life is profane whereas belief about the sacred is located in a private self ... And even if that belief can be publicly acknowledged

> as a belief it cannot be publicly put into action because not everyone can be persuaded to accept it—and according to secularism as a political doctrine, beliefs may not (cannot) be imposed on others.
>
> (Asad, 2011: 661)

Intrinsic to liberal analyses of sexuality education are these distinctions regarding the public and the private, the sacred and the profane. Religion, in such a view, is necessarily privatized because it is constituted as embedded in belief rather than reason. The reasonably religious might be on firmer ground, Asad suggests, as long as their belief accords with secularism. Importantly, this liberal secularism does not "banish religion from the public domain but [seeks] to reshape the form it takes, the subjectivities it endorses, and the epistemological claims it can make" (Mahmood, 2006: 326).

In the field of progressive sexuality education, one place in which I have argued secularism is reshaping the epistemological claims that can be made about diverse sexualities is with regard to anti-homophobia education and its associations with imaginings of a post-homophobic time (Monk, 2011) (see Chapter 6). The possibilities for admitting different ways of thinking about tolerance and sexual identity that are embedded in belief and faith are increasingly constrained, and many would argue this is a desirable outcome—especially within public schools that are charged with the protection of always already at-risk LGBTI youth (for further discussion, see Harwood and Rasmussen, 2013). But characterizing religious objections to the development of organizations like GSAs as *necessarily* pathological, ignorant, or regressive depends on a way of seeing in which secularism has become its own political doctrine (see Chapter 8).

CONCLUSION

> No matter how we might differently resolve the issues for ourselves, living in pure immanence or orienting ourselves to some understanding of transcendent being, we still cannot escape the fact that we live with others who resolve it differently and this fact has significance for the quality of our own conviction . . . [M]ight this mutual fragilization . . . de-dramatize conflicts such as the culture wars?
>
> (Warner, VanAntwerpen, and Calhoun, 2010: 23)

In this citation, Michael Warner, Jonathan VanAntwerpen, and Craig Calhoun draw on the work of Charles Taylor to argue the importance of understanding different ways in which people resolve fundamental issues. This is recognition that these issues will continue to be resolved in different ways, by different people, because as Eve Sedgwick notes, "[P]eople are different from each other" (1990: 22).

The approach I have taken throughout this text might be read as having dual impulses. One is an attempt to de-dramatize the culture wars, as they pertain to sexuality education. Another is to consider the effects these culture wars have had, within the US and internationally, in shaping structures of feeling and thought in this field. This project of thinking critically about progressive sexuality educations' convictions and conceits is intended as a means to strengthen research and practice and to try and imagine different ways that this field might be fruitfully expanded.

In this research I have also tried to refuse the temptation to dismiss ideas and values that are located in faith and belief. As Ann Pellegrini, in her discussion of Hell Houses[1] in the southern US—haunted houses that are designed to "scare people to Jesus" (2007: 912)—argues:

> ... [B]y dismissing arguments that are not articulated in the terms with which we are familiar, we overlook the very places where politics comes to matter most: at the deepest levels of the unconscious, in our bodies, through faith, and in relation to the emotions. (Pellegrini, 2007: 932–933)

One of the unanticipated effects of preparing this manuscript has been the conversations it has opened up with people who do not identify with the progressive approach to sexuality education as well as encounters with people who identify as progressive and religious. These exchanges are not ones that I have encountered in previous research I have conducted in sexuality education, which I would characterize as being situated within the frame of the progressive-secular imaginary. Perhaps the absence of such exchanges—except maybe in oppositional terms—suggests this research has primarily been engaging with the converted, those who might also situate themselves within the progressive camp, recognizing that is a very big tent.

Taking account of faith, emotions, belief, and values doesn't mean my research and advocacy in sexuality education will suddenly evacuate all progressive political agendas. It does mean that I am more likely to elicit, and to be confronted by, perspectives that are informed by faith and belief in my future imaginings of sexuality education.

NOTE

1. "Hell Houses are evangelical riffs on the haunted houses that dot the landscape of secular culture each Halloween. Where haunted houses promise to scare the bejeezus out of you, Hell Houses aim to scare you to Jesus. In a typical Hell House, demon tour guides take the audience through a series of bloody staged tableaux depicting sinners whose bad behavior—homosexuality, abortion, suicide, and, above all, rejection of Christ's saving grace—leads them straight to hell." (Pellegrini, 2007: 912)

REFERENCES

Archard, D. (1998). How Should We Teach Sex? *Journal of Philosophy of Education*, 32(3): 437–450.

Asad, T. (2003). *Formations of the Secular: Christianity, Islam, Modernity.* Stanford, CA: Stanford University Press.

———. (2011). Thinking about the Secular Body, Pain, and Liberal Politics. *Cultural Anthropology*, 26(4): 657–675.

Baker, J. O., Smith, K. K., & Stoss, Y. A. (2015). Theism, Secularism, and Sexual Education in the United States. *Sexuality Research and Social Policy,* Springer. Available from http://link.springer.com/article/10.1007%2Fs13178-015-0187-8 (Last accessed May 14, 2015).

Brown, W. (2006). *Regulating Aversion: Tolerance in the Age of Identity and Empire.* Princeton, New Jersey: Princeton University Press.

———. (2012). Civilizational Delusions: Secularism, Tolerance, Equality. *Theory and Event*, 15(2). Available from https://muse.jhu.edu/ (Last accessed May 14, 2015).

Cady, L., & Fessenden, T. (Eds.). (2013). *Religion, the Secular, and the Politics of Sexual Difference.* New York: Columbia University Press.

Elia, J. P., & Tokunaga, J. (2015). Sexuality Education: Implications for Health, Equity, and Social Justice in the United States. *Health Education*, 115(1): 105–120.

Fine, M., & McClelland, D. (2006). Sexuality Education and Desire: Still Missing after All These Years. *Harvard Educational Review*, 76(3): 297–338.

Harwood, V., & Rasmussen, M. L. (2013). Practising Critique, Attending to Truth: The Pedagogy of Discriminatory Speech. *Educational Philosophy and Theory* [E], 45(8): 874–884.

Jakobsen, J. R. (2005). Sex + Freedom = Regulation: WHY? *Social Text*, 23(3–4): 84–85, 285–308.

Jakobsen, J.R., & Pellegrini, A. (2004). *Love the Sin: Sexual Regulation and the Limits of Religious Tolerance.* Boston, Mass.: Beacon Press.

Mahmood, S. (2006). Secularism, Hermeneutics, and Empire: The Politics of Islamic Reformation. *Public Culture*, 18(6): 323–347.

———. (2008). Is Critique Secular? A Symposium at UC Berkeley. *Public Culture*, Fall 20(3): 447–452.

Mills, J. (2012). I Should Get Married Early: Culturally Appropriate Comprehensive Sex Education and the Racialization of Somali Masculinity. *Spectrum: A Journal on Black Men*, 1(1): 5–30.

Monk, D. (2011). Challenging Homophobic Bullying in Schools: The Politics of Progress. *International Journal of Law in Context*, 7(2): 181–207.

Pellegrini, A. (2007). "Signalling through the Flames": Hell House Performance and Structures of Religious Feeling. *American Quarterly*, 59(3): 911–935.

Rastegar, M. (2013). Emotional Attachments and Secular Sympathies: Western LGBTQ Activism on Iran. *GLQ: Lesbian and Gay Studies Quarterly*, 19(1): 1–29.

Reiss, M. (2014). Sex Education and Science Education in Faith-based Schools. In J. Chapman, S. McNamara, M. Reiss, & Y. Waghid (Eds.), *International Handbook of Learning, Teaching and Leading in Faith-Based Schools* (pp. 261–276). Dordrecht, Netherlands: Springer.

Santelli, J. S. (2008). Medical Accuracy in Sexuality Education: Ideology and the Scientific Process. *American Journal of Public Health*, 98(10): 1786–1792.

Scherer, M. (2006). Saint John: The Miracle of Secular Reason. In H. de Vries & L. E. Sullivan (Eds.), *Political Theologies: Public Religions in a Post-Secular World* (pp. 341–62). New York: Fordham University Press.

Scott, J. W. (2009, April 23). *Sexularism*. Ursula Hirschman Annual Lecture on Gender and Europe, Florence, Italy.
Sedgwick, E. K. (1990). *Epistemology of the Closet*. Berkeley and Los Angeles, California: University of California Press.
Shipley, H. (2014). Religious and Sexual Orientation Intersections in Education and Media: A Canadian perspective. *Sexualities* (Special Journal Issue): Sexuality and Religion, co-edited by Ria Snowdon and Yvette Taylor, 17(5/6): 512–528.
Steutel, J., & De Ruyter, D. J. (2011). What Should Be the Moral Aims of Compulsory Sex Education? *British Journal of Educational Studies*, 59(1): 75–86.
Stranger-Hall, K. F., & Hall, D. W. (2011). Abstinence-Only Education and Teen Pregnancy Rates: Why We Need Comprehensive Sex Education in the U.S. *PLoS ONE*, 6(10): 1–11.
Svendsen, S. (2012). Elusive Sex Acts: Pleasure and Politics in Norwegian Sex Education. *Sex Education*, 12(4): 397–410.
UNESCO. (2009). *International Guidelines on Sexuality Education: An Evidence Informed Approach to Effective Sex, Relationships and HIV/STI Education*. Paris, France: UNESCO. Available from http://www.refworld.org/docid/4a69b8902.html (Last accessed November 5, 2014).
Verkaaik, O., & Spronk, R. (2011). Sexual Practice: Notes on an Ethnography of Secularism. *Focaal*, 59(Spring): 83–88.
Warner, M., VanAntwerpen, J., & Calhoun, C. J. (Eds.). (2010). *Varieties of Secularism in a Secular Age*. Cambridge, Mass.: Harvard University Press.
Williams, J. C. (2011). Battling a 'Sex-saturated Society': The Abstinence Movement and the Politics of Sex Education. *Sexualities*, 14(4): 416–443.

Index

A Secular Age (Taylor) 15, 24
Abolghasemi, N. 14–15
abstinence 36–38–39, 46, 50–52, 54,
    65–66, 75, 77, 88, 90–91, 94,
    105, 136–137, 152, 154, 167,
    178–180, 182–183
Abstinence Only Until Marriage
    Education (AOUME) 78, 79, 88,
    89, 92, 136
Accepting School Act (2012) 162
Addison, N. 98
Advocates for Youth 4
Age, The 69, 74, 76
Aggleton, P. 78
Alldred, P. xi, 145
Allen, L. xi–xii, 35
Aotearoa-New Zealand 48–70, 93, 94
Anti-Bullying Act (2012) 162
anti-homophobia 11, 22, 104–106,
    111–121, 160–162, 169,
    181, 187
Apatow, J. 130–133, 137, 141
Archard, D. 185
arranged marriage 52–53, 55, 58,
    61–62, 136
Australia 6, 10, 14, 18–19, 21, 23,
    41, 45, 48–70, 74–80, 85, 92,
    104, 106, 107–113, 144–145,
    148–155, 157, 172, 184
Australian Curriculum Assessment
    and Reporting Authority
    (ACARA) 152
Australian Medical Association
    (A.M.A) 74–77
Australian national curriculum (draft)
    152, 172
autonomy 1–2, 10, 12–13, 21–22, 37,
    43–45, 54, 60, 62, 88, 95–101,
    170, 177, 179, 180, 185

Baird, B. 23, 163–164
Ballard, T. 41–43, 184–185
Bederman, G. 81–84
Ben-Yehuda, N. 71, 74, 76, 84
Berzon, B. 111–112
Bijelic, N. 15
bogan 112, 122
Boonstra, H. 3–6, 15, 34
Brown, W. 133–134, 170, 179, 181
Buddhist 50, 68
Burgett, B. 2–73
Bush administration 7, 84
Butler, J. 3, 17, 118

Cady, L. 180
Calderone, M. 67
Calhoun, C. 15–16
Campbell, C. 148
Canada 9–10, 23, 95–96, 117, 120,
    144–155, 157, 160–172
Canadian Broadcasting
    Commission 167
Canadian Secular Alliance 9,
    147–148, 160
Casanova, J. 2
Catching on Later 150–151, 153, 172
Catholic Church 2–3, 6, 19, 116,
    145–146, 156, 158, 166
Catholic Education Office 154
Catholic Ethos 3, 146, 155–156,
    158–159
Catholic school 2, 9, 18–19, 144,
    147–148, 156–158, 160–167,
    172, 180
Cavazos-Rehg, P.A. 29–30
Central High 49, 50–53, 58,
    65–68, 180
Centre for Inquiry (CFI) 164–165
Chakraborty, K. 13–14

192 Index

"Challenging Homophobic Bullying in Schools: The Politics of Progress" (Monk) 105
Child fundamentalism 23, 162–166, 171
Christian conservatives 35–36
Christian right 8, 78
Clinton administration 7
Cody, D. 134–135
Cohen, S. 71–73
Comprehensive Sexuality Education (CSE) 6, 35–40, 66–67, 75–78, 90–94
Collins, A. 161–162, 169
Conchar, C. 62
Connoll, E. 95
Connolly, W. 17, 20
consent 6, 52, 62, 126, 150, 152
Corngold, J. 43
Croatia 12

Dawson, E. 166
Dawson, K. 167
democratic sexuality education 58–64, 68, 169, 170
Department of Education and Early Childhood Development (DEECD) 13, 153, 172
Desai, P. 40–41
Deutscher, P. 22,-23, 126–129
Devondale High 50, 55, 68
Doyle, J. 129, 141
During, S. 130, 131, 168

Edmonton 23, 166–169
Edmonton Public School Board 168
Elliot, D. 163–164
Elliot, K. 93–94
emotional publics 79–81
Employment Equity Act 156
Enlightenment 13, 20–21, 23, 49, 54, 58–64, 66–67, 83, 113

faith-based organizations 5, 34
fallen woman 63–64, 69
Fessenden, T. 180
Fields, J. xii, 7, 28–29, 35
Fine, M. 14, 22, 87–94, 96, 102, 158, 183
Finer, L. 35
Formations of the Secular (Asad) 24, 93

4 months, 3 Weeks and 2 Days 125–130
Freeman, H. 126–132, 141

Gahan, L. 157
Gaydos, L. 30
Gay and Lesbian Mardi Gras (Sydney) 149
Gay-Straight Alliance (GSA) 162–166, 171, 187
gay youth 22, 121, 165,
Gemell, A. 35
Gibson, S. 79–80
Gilbert, J. xi, xii, 154, 171
Goldstein, T. 161–162, 169
good aborter, the 126–130, 134
Gray, B. 146
Griffith, M. 83
Guardian, The 126, 138
Guttmacher Institute 3, 6–7, 23, 34

Haffner, D. 4–6
Halder, M. 161–162, 169
Hall, D. 30–31
Halstead, M. 52
Harrison, L 107–108
health versus morality 92–95
Hell houses 188
Hicks, M. 5–6
Hillier, L. 154
HIV/AIDS 155
HIV/AIDS strategy 155
Holzner, B. 13
homophobia 104–121, 144, 150–159; post-homophobic time 22, 106, 119–121, 187; provocations 121
Hooghe, M. 117–118, 120
Hornaday, A. 136–137
Huffington Post, The 5, 127

"I Should Get Married Early: Culturally Appropriate Comprehensive Sex Education and the Racialization of Somali Masculinity" (Mills) 32–34
Indonesia 13
International Sexuality and HIV Curriculum Working Group 153
Iran 14–15
Ireland 41, 145–147, 149–155–156, 158–159, 171, 182
Irish curriculum 149–153

Irvine, J. 3, 7–8, 21, 35, 71–74, 76–85
Islam 10, 15, 33, 38–39, 50, 63, 76–77, 83, 92, 98, 105, 117, 120, 182, 185
It Gets Better 164

Jagose, A. 45
Jakobsen, J. 8, 11–12, 39, 42
Johnson, B. 79
Jones, P. 72
Jones, T. 10, 154–155, 158
Juno 40–41, 125–139

Kendall, N. 7, 59, 67, 78, 81, 169–170
Kiely, E. 158
Kippax, S. 14
Kitching, K. 151
Knocked Up 125–139
Knox, S. 127–128
Korducki, K. 160

Lamb, S. 87, 91, 96, 99–100
Landry, D. 35
Latimer, H. 137–138
Lesko, N. xi, 29, 36–39, 43, 136
LGB teachers' group 156
LGBTI students/youth 9, 23, 162, 164, 165, 171, 187
LGBTI teachers 159
liberalism 40, 43,-44, 60, 81, 170, 185, -186186–187; and feminism 44, 125, 130–136; Rawlsian, 60, 185; secularism 125
Linberg, L. 35
Lodge, A. 158
Lottes, I. 35
Love the Sin: Sexual Regulation and the Limits of Religious Tolerance (Jakobsen and Pellegrini) 11, 24, 42
Luker, K. 7
Luttrell, W. 125

McAlister, M. 3
McClelland, S. 14, 88–94, 102, 183
McKay, A. 59–61, 68–69, 168–170
Maddox, M. 6, 147–148
Maharaj, C. 107–108
Mahmood, S. 10, 20, 43–45, 59, 146, 183–184, 187
marriage equality 42, 61, 116, 145
Martinez, A. 156–157

Martino, W. xi, 171
Mayock, P. 151
McLure, D. 76–77
Merghati-Khoei, E. 14–15
Miller, A. 9
Mills, J. 32–34, 38, 91, 181
Mitchell, A. 155, 157
Modood, T. 84
Monk, D. 22, 105–106, 118–121, 187
moral panic 21, 71–85
Moran, J. 35, 36, 66–67
Morgan, M. 151
Morgan, S. 95
Mullally, S. 146
Murray, D. 118–119

National Council for Curriculum and Assessment 153
natural cultural authority 91, 92
Neary, A. xi, 145, 156, 158–159
neoliberalism 2, 90–91
No Apologies 65–67
Northern Territory Emergency Response 85

Obama administration 7, 182
Obvious Child 138–139
O'Donovan, D. 146
Oetomo, D. 13
Ollis, D. 106–111, 113
Ontario Catholic English Teachers' Association (OECTA) 166
Ontario sexuality education curriculum (revised) 149–153, 172

Pacific High 50, 54–55, 61, 68
Page, E. 135, 138
Pellegrini, A. 8, 11–12, 39, 42
Peppard, J. 79
Perz, J. 62–64
Phillips, K. 156–157
Pinar, W. xi, 18, 171
pleasure/desire 96–97
Politics of Piety: The Islamic Revival and the Feminist Subject (Mahmood) 10, 24
Pope Benedict XVI 5–6
Precious 125, 131
Pregnancy Care Centre (PCC) 167–168, 169
"process known as secularization" 21, 49

Proctor, H. 148
Progressive Conservative Party (PCP) 54
progressive-secular imaginary 10, 11, 20, 44, 59, 168–170, 182, 188
progressive sexuality education 20–22, 28, 31, 37–38, 40, 42–45, 66, 79, 92, 98, 125; and feel-good story 185
public pedagogies 21, 22 85; of pregnancy and choice 22–23, 125–141; Northern Territory Emergency Response 23
Puar, J. 3, 21, 29, 37–42, 96, 120–121, 164, 181
public schools; religion 147–149; sexuality education; 6, 18, 20–21, 30, 48–68, 75, 78, 80, 88, 93, 115, 149, 161, 167–170, 178, 183, 185–187

queer secularism 8–9, 21, 29, 37–42, 45, 181, 184
Quinlivan, K. xi-xii, 57

Rastegar, M. 182
Rawls, J. 185–186
Rayside, D. 145, 155, 171
reason 2, 21, 136–139, 187; critical thinking 97; curriculum 150; distinct from religion 66; faith 66; feminism 139; free pursuit of 59; freedom 60; instrumental 16; mistake in 84; moral panics 84; progressive sexuality education 92; religious 58, 68, 118; scientific 100; secular 58, 68, 118, 185; sexuality education 66; transcends religion 66; universally valid 66; versus faith 93
reasonable person 10
reasonably religious 187
Reiss, M. 52
Reitman, J. 130, 133, 135, 137
Religion in Public Schools (Pew Research) 37
religious exemptions 156, 159, 164, 172
Religious Institute on Sexual Morality, Justice, and Healing 4
Riddle, D. 108
right reason 5

rights: equal 82; human 52, 67, 83, 89, 92–93, 94, 134, 147, 166; individual 59, 170; Lesbian, Gay, Bisexual, Transgeder and Intersex (LGBTI) 23, 91, 110, 117, 160–164; liberal 17; of the Child 13, 53; religious 83, 93; sexual and reproductive 23–24, 35, 46, 79, 80, 83
Risoy, S. 126
Rubin, G. 1
Ruyter, D. J. de 186

Sands, K. 100–101
Santelli, J. 178
Scherer, M. 185–186
Schwartz, E. 116
Sciortino, K. 138
Scott, J. 43, 88, 90, 95, 100–101, 179–181
Secular Heretic, The 77
Secular Party of Australia 172
Sedgwick, E. 187
Seitz, D. 56
Sex Education Debates, The (Kendall) 59, 67, 78
Sex Information and Education Council of Canada (SIECC) 168
sex panic 79–85
sexual ethics curriculum 91
sexual exceptionalism 21, 29, 37–42, 45, 181, 184
sexuality education curriculum; anti-homophobia 114; constraints 157–158; critical thinking 97; Health and Physical Education (HPE), 149–151; Healthy Active Living Education (HALE) 149; personal development, health, and physical education (PDHPE) 149–152; Relationships and Sexuality Education (RSE) 149–151. See also Catching on Later; and Catholic ethos 158; common 185; and fear 182; happy clashes 48; *No Apologies*; politics 9
"Sexuality Education and Desire: Still Missing After All These Years" (Fine and McClelland) 88–89
sexual freedom 17, 22–23, 43–45, 60, 64, 68, 88, 139, 147, 162–166

Sexuality Information and Education
    Council of the United States
    (SIECUS) 4, 24, 35–36, 67
"Sexuality, Schooling, and Adolescent
    Females: The Missing Discourse
    of Desire" (Fine) 22, 88, 96
sexularism 1, 90, 95, 101, 181
Shah, S. 62
Sherlock, L. 147, 156
Shipley, H. 177
Sirnes, T. 126
Smith, G. 14
Smith, T. 14–15
Spring, L 9–10
Spronk, R. 184
Stark, J. 74–75
states of exception 22,-23, 126–130, 139
Steutel, J. 186
Stranger-Hall, K. 30–31
Svendsen, S. 177
subtraction stories 15–18
Sullivan-Blum, C. 19–120

Taking God to School (Maddox) 6
Taxis, Rainbows and Hatred 41
Taylor, C. 15, 16, 24, 36, 58, 60, 68
teachers 22, 28, 31, 48–49, 61–62, 76,
    104–121, 151–162, 166, 169, 171
*Terrorist Assemblages:
    Homonationalism in Queer
    Times* (Puar) 3
theory of secularization 2
thick desire 88–92, 9
Thoma, P. 134
Thompson, K. 71
Tillman, L. 151
tolerance 1, 2, 11, 41, 82, 110–111, 133,
    170, 177, 179–182, 184, 187

Tonti-Filippini, N. 75–77
Toronto 2, 9, 23, 144, 160–166
transnational progressivism 1, 7, 1–15,
    147,
Trottier, J. 165

United Kingdom (UK) 62, 98, 185
United Nations Educational, Scientific,
    and Cultural Organization
    (UNESCO) 11–12, 15, 48, 178
Ussher, J. 62–64

Van Antwerpen, J. 15–16
Vance, C. 72–73
Verkaaik, O. 184
Victoria, Australia Curriculum 152. See
    also Catching on Later

Waitress 125–126, 134, 136, 138–139
Waidzunas, T. 165
Walcott, R. 104
Warner, M. 15–16, 51–52, 81, 181,
    187
Washington Post 136
Washington Times, The 5
Weaver, H. 14
Weigman, R. 87, 101
Whitehead, D. 96–97, 178
Wilcox, C. 145
Withers, K. 129, 132
Witthaus, D. 106, 111–113, 119
Woodhead, L. 83
Wray, A. 62–64

Yang, Z. 30
Young, P. 84

Zack, J. 113–116